GNP 12

Tarnished Brass

ALSO BY BRIAN NOLAN

Hero: The Buzz Beurling Story

King's War: Mackenzie King and the Politics of War, 1939–1940

Champagne Navy: Canada's Small Boat Raiders of the Second World War
(with Brian Jeffrey Street)

Airborne: The Heroic Story of the 1st Canadian Parachute
Battalion in the Second World War

Tarnished Brass

CRIME AND CORRUPTION IN
THE CANADIAN MILITARY

Scott Taylor
and
Brian Nolan

Canadian Cataloguing in Publication Data

Taylor, Scott, 1960-
Tarnished brass : crime and corruption in the Canadian military

ISBN 1-895555-93-0

1. Canada. Canadian Armed Forces – Corrupt practices
I. Nolan, Brian.   II. Title.

FC603.T3   1996   971.064'8   C96-930990-2
F1028.T3   1996

The publisher gratefully acknowledges the assistance of
the Canada Council and the Ontario Arts Council.

Lester Publishing Limited
70 The Esplanade
Toronto, Ontario
Canada M5E 1R2

Printed and bound in Canada

96 97 98 99 6 5 4

Contents

Acknowledgments

The authors wish to acknowledge the contributions of the dedicated individuals who assisted in the production of *Tarnished Brass*: James G. Scott, the editor emeritus of *Esprit de Corps*, was an invaluable asset as a researcher on this project; it was a pleasure having him back in the ranks.

Most of the information in this book was released under the Access to Information Act and came as the result of persistent digging by Novatip Consulting. It should be noted that Novatip provided expertise in this unique field on a pro-bono basis.

Laurie Coulter's editing work on this book was exceptional, and it should not go unmentioned.

Recognition is also due to Katherine Taylor, Cathy Hingley and Julie Simoneau, who helped with the research, and provided administrative and moral support throughout this seven-year project.

Peter Worthington, the editor emeritus of the *Toronto Sun*, must be credited with the role of mentor. Without his belief and guidance, *Esprit de Corps* would have foundered in its infancy, and this book would never have been possible.

Finally, the generous financial assistance provided by F.M., H.M. and H.J. cannot be overlooked.

Dedication

I first met Jim DeCoste in the autumn of 1984, while we were both candidates on the French army's commando course. He was twenty-nine years old at the time and already a senior non-commissioned officer (NCO). Having joined the Canadian military at the impressionable age of seventeen, DeCoste was warily regarded by recruits as a "lifer" or career soldier.

I was just a young private, halfway through my "short term" three-year stint in the infantry. Although I had already completed basic training, graduated from battle school and served as a rifleman for over a year, everything I learned about what it means to be a soldier I learned from Jim DeCoste.

As platoon warrant officer and disciplinarian, he drove his men to hate him and respect him alternately during that punishing three-week course. His expectations seemingly defied the limits of human endurance, yet his force of will ensured that our contingent consistently topped the daily standings.

I'll never forget our initial test, first morning, day one; it was a ten-kilometre *marche commando* run in full thirty-kilogram field packs. To pass this gruelling trial, forty members of a platoon must cross the finish line, with all of their equipment intact, in less than sixty minutes.

Although we had pretrained and conditioned for weeks prior to the commencement of the commando course, our platoon, excited by this multinational competition, set off at an ill-disciplined, too-fast pace.

By the eight-kilometre mark, the strain had taken its toll on weaker members of our unit. Even after their weapons and gear were grudgingly redistributed to those still fit, our pace dropped to a crawl. As his platoon faltered, DeCoste was seemingly everywhere, shouting obscenities, offering encouragement and tirelessly attempting to maintain some semblance of a formation. By the time we limped across the finish line, our contingent looked more like a defeated guerrilla band than a group of professional soldiers.

DeCoste reassembled us in three ranks and then launched into a furious tirade. His anger was focused on the fact that, once the going got rough, we had forgotten the importance of teamwork and acted as individuals. To demonstrate how "unworthy" we were, he instructed us to remove the regimental cap badges from our berets and to strip the epaulettes from our uniforms. To add to our ordeal, French, British and American soldiers from the other commando platoons had gathered around in amusement to watch our public humiliation at the hands of this tough little NCO.

Later, when it was announced that our platoon not only had won the international competition, but, with a time of fifty-one minutes, had also set a commando school record, DeCoste never softened his position. The objective had been to demonstrate teamwork, and in that capacity we had failed. "The mission is paramount" was the simple statement DeCoste used to sum up what soldiering was all about, and it was how he lived his life.

After the commando course, I was fortunate enough to serve closely with him in our battalion's intelligence section and, during this two-year period, he became something of a mentor to me. As a result, even after I had left the service, I maintained a close relationship with him up until his tragic death.

He was a soldier's soldier in every sense, a hard man who led by example and scorned those who coveted a softer life. When he detected any "weakness" in his own psyche, he would meet his fears head-on. Despite a fear of heights, or because of it, Jim took up mountain-climbing as a hobby. Though not a strong swimmer, he would spend his leave ocean kayaking. He habitually took calculated risks, but always with the strict goal in mind that they would improve his ability to soldier.

In 1988, DeCoste made it his "mission" to command and enrolled in the officer training program. Despite his "advanced" age of thirty-two, and lack of formal education (he had to study in his off-duty hours to complete high school), DeCoste graduated as the top candidate on his course.

There are three distinct social classes in a military society: the junior ranks, senior NCOs and commissioned officers, and by having worked his way successfully through all of them, DeCoste was known and respected by every rank of his regiment.

He believed in the military system because it was all he had ever known and, with his firm adherence to a martial ethos, he thrived within its defined structure. For soldiers such as myself, DeCoste's professional bearing was at a level that could only be envied and rarely duplicated.

Jim DeCoste was a soldier among actors.

At age thirty-seven, he was killed while on operational UN peacekeeping duty in the former Yugoslavia. A Serbian army truck had attempted to pass a slower-moving farm tractor on a blind curve. The driver of DeCoste's jeep, a young female militia corporal, never had a chance to react. In the ensuing head-on collision, the lightweight Canadian Forces jeep was crushed on impact. DeCoste was killed instantly, his driver and a fellow officer badly injured.

What happened next was never publicly reported by Canadian military authorities for fear that it would give Canadian citizens the "wrong" impression about the political necessity of having our troops "keep peace" in the Balkans.

The Serb soldiers, unhurt in the accident, rushed to the Canadian jeep. Unfortunately for our personnel, their intent was not to provide medical aid, but to loot the wreckage and the victims. Stacey Bouck, the twenty-one-year-old driver, had both her legs broken, and the steering-wheel had punctured her lung. Despite her critical condition, the Serb soldiers pulled her from the jeep, manhandled her, stole her money and removed various items of her clothing for "souvenirs." After DeCoste's body had been similarly searched for valuables, Captain Rick Turner, the other injured passenger, was hauled from the wreckage, robbed and left in the roadway. It was later discovered that three rifles and ammunition had also been looted from the Canadian vehicle.

Incredibly, not only was no action taken by the United Nations against the Serb soldiers involved, but the Canadian government actually paid to repair the damage done to their army truck! Since both of the Canadian survivors were unconscious when UN police arrived, the only statements taken were those of the Serbian "witnesses." Consequently, by the time Corporal Bouck regained consciousness in hospital, the investigators had already concluded the accident was her fault. Even when the other side of the story had been told, and the thefts confirmed, Canadian military offi-cers found it easier to accept the blame, pay restitution and let the whole affair drop.

Jim DeCoste lived his life devoted to upholding the four virtues that he believed a soldier must keep sacred: loyalty, integrity, truth and courage. Sadly, in their handling of events surrounding his death, the Canadian military failed to adhere to *any* of these principles, thereby breaking faith with a man who embodied them.

This book is written in memory of a fallen comrade, and dedicated to the preservation of his ideals.

Scott Taylor
Ottawa, Canada
Summer 1996

CHAPTER ONE

Fall from Grace

They appeared that summer and autumn of 1945 like a human tidal wave sweeping the land from coast to coast. The first of the 630,000 men and women who made up the active Canadian Army were coming home. "The train windows are crowded with their sunburned excited faces," wrote Charles Ritchie, the diplomat and diarist who was aboard one train as it thundered west from Nova Scotia. "They lean out in their shirt sleeves whistling at the girls on station platforms, making unflattering remarks about Mackenzie King." Newspapers and radio had alerted the population when the troop trains were expected, so the returning heroes were greeted everywhere by farmers waving from hayricks; knots of young women, with Andrews Sisters' hairdos, blowing kisses; and singing schoolchildren in their Sunday best waiting at level crossings. Everyone gave them Winnie Churchill's famous V-for-victory salute, and everyone blamed the cinders in the billowing clouds of steam that washed over them for making their eyes water. After six grim years of war, peace had finally broken out, so suddenly that it left all Canadians delirious with joy.

As journalist June Callwood wrote of the peace of 1945: "The young country was radiant with hope and confidence. We believed we were invincible. We thought Canadians could do anything. We had just spent six years proving it."

Our battle-hardened young men came back with their proud battle colours that spoke of Dieppe, Ortona and the Hochwald; they had travelled many roads in the long campaign after leaving home, roads that led to Falaise, Ravenna and Apeldoorn. They had crossed many rivers, too: the Orne, the Seine, the Po, the Meuse, the Scheldt and the last river of all, the Rhine. Their victories and defeats would win for Canada, although they didn't know it then, a place in the councils of the world in the postwar peace that followed the largest, deadliest and costliest conflict in history.

So, they came home, the glory of their times; "every man his own Hotspur," mused Ritchie, "impetuous to get on with living."

Most of them had seen enough blood and death and were eager to begin rebuilding their lives. With the nightmare of war behind, now was the time to savour the dreamy peace. Most couldn't wait to be "demobbed," demobilized.

A few of their fellows, however, chose to make the military their career. In the transition from war to peace, they became the cadre that built one of the finest professional armies in the world. Although other Allied nations had to invoke national service because there were not enough volunteers to serve in response to the many crises in the fifties and sixties— Cyprus and Suez for Britain, Algeria and Vietnam for France, Korea and Vietnam for the United States—Canada continued to attract more than enough volunteers to serve in its ranks and officer corps. Never was there a lack of young Canadian men and women to pledge duty and service in the same spirit as had their wartime predecessors.

True enough until the night of March 16, 1993, in the desert wastelands of Somalia. That ghastly night, Canadian paratroopers from the elite Canadian Airborne Regiment tortured to death Shidane Arone, a sixteen-year-old Somalian youth suspected of pilfering army stores. The horrific testimony that emerged from the numerous courts martial of those accused of murdering the boy, and later testimony before the commission of inquiry into the army's conduct in Somalia, stunned the nation. In the wake of the trials, two home-made videos also came to light, the first containing racial slurs, and the second showing disgusting hazing rituals carried out by the paratroopers. The combination of the murder and the tapes was enough for the government to disband the Canadian Airborne Regiment, the first time a military unit was so dishonoured and disgraced in Canada.

At this writing, the Commission of Inquiry into the Deployment of Canadian Forces to Somalia continues to sit and gather evidence as shocking as the murder itself, testimony that clearly shows professional incompetence, ineptness, corruption and an orchestrated attempt by the high command to cover up criminal activity, an indictment that has shaken and discredited the Canadian military establishment. While most of the blame can be traced to National Defence Headquarters (NDHQ), the scandals have unfairly besmirched the good character of the rank and file, plunging morale to unfathomable depths. The underground or "jungle" telegraph in the services is as swift as any computer-driven communications system.

The soldiers, sailors and airmen know what happens long before the craven deals of the high command become national headlines.

In the Forces-wide Phillips Employee Feedback Survey conducted in the summer of 1995, it was found that a staggering 83 per cent of military personnel had lost confidence in their senior leaders. Not surprisingly, the most common complaint voiced by service members was that top officers were seen as "self-interested careerists and empire-builders." The "mishandling of the Somalia affair" was a key concern for many, but once again their anger was directed towards the top brass for their failure to accept any responsibility whatsoever for the scandal.

While the words "loyalty," "integrity," "truth" and "courage" are still boldly emblazoned on every officer's commission scroll, it has largely been self-preservation and personal aggrandizement that senior military commanders have come to exemplify in exposé after exposé by the media. Unfortunately for Canadian taxpayers, these recently uncovered events are not "isolated incidents," as the military contends, and as testimony has shown during the Somalia courts martial, nor are they the handiwork of just a "few bad apples."

To understand the enormity of the betrayal of trust by the brass and the widening gulf it has created between themselves and their troops is to know why the morale of the thousands of conscientious men and women who follow the honourable profession of arms has fallen so low. They have been cheated by the generals. An officer's first duty is to his troops, a duty that is in fact a sacred obligation. George S. Patton, the brilliant and flamboyant U.S. general of the Second World War, was haunted by the fear that he would fail his soldiers, says his biographer Carlo D'Este. Moreover, Patton believed that true leadership was achieved only by example. If this axiom is true, and it is, then Canadian soldiers have been doubly wronged by the contemptible actions and example of senior officers and bureaucrats in the Canadian military who have put self-interest and gain before duty and commitment to the troops they are supposed to lead.

So what went wrong with one of the most respected institutions in Canadian society? How did this descent into chaos happen? There are as many theories as there are theorists. Some say the decline began back in 1968, when Liberal defence minister Paul Hellyer demanded the three services be integrated. His original blueprint for military restructuring was put forward under the working title "integration," but by the time the scheme was foisted upon our three armed services, the name had been changed to "unification." Whatever the name, many critics saw the move as the "disintegration" of a once-proud military tradition.

In theory, the idea of breaking up the existing army, navy and air force empires to create one "common purpose" all-arms force made good sense, especially for a national defence force the size and scale of Canada's. Undeniably, it was mutually beneficial for the three services to have one central procurement policy supported by common logistic facilities. The driving force behind this bold experiment was the elimination of costly redundancy within the Forces.

Hellyer, however, wanted to go even further with the idea. In addition to a central headquarters and a common budget, he wanted the three-way marriage of the services to include training, rank structure and uniforms. At the time, many senior officers strongly objected to Hellyer's radical concepts on the grounds that traditions are meant to be upheld. Several top naval commanders resigned in public protest, the most notable being Admiral William Landymore—but it was all for naught. Canadian soldiers, sailors and airmen quickly found themselves bedecked in the nondescript green "bus-driver" uniforms that amused their international counterparts and dampened their collective morale for the better part of two decades.

The real threat unification posed to the Forces was not even entirely foreseen at this juncture—the erosion of basic leadership principles through the forced merger of three diverse doctrines. First to go was the old army practice that permitted constructive criticism of senior army officers by subordinates. This internal criticism was discouraged by the new establishment during the troubled implementation phase of unification. Presumably, it was felt that the practice could subvert the military reorganizational process. Sadly, what should have been a temporary measure became popular with the high command and has now become a fixture.

There was one more significant change. The previous distinct division between the Armed Forces and the Department of National Defence (DND) started to become blurred. In 1972, the Canadian Forces headquarters was merged with the Defence Research Board and the civilian component of DND into a single entity called the National Defence Headquarters. It was during this period that career civil servants began to be parachuted into positions of real influence within NDHQ to oversee military compliance with often unpalatable political decisions. General officers who had spent their entire careers studying the profession of arms were often relegated to positions of impotent subservience. Increasingly, the criteria for promotion to general rank depended on candidates' political correctness rather than their military competency. In order to be able to work "with" their newly acquired civil servant counterparts, top officers had to learn the unique traits and qualities of career bureaucrats.

The language barrier posed a problem at first, but this was not a rift between francophones and anglophones: it was a more difficult gap to bridge between military directness and political bafflegab. Characteristically, the mandarins held their ground and the generals quickly adopted the newly learned non-language as their own. One of the first words discarded by the brass from their old army vocabulary was "leadership," which was soon replaced with the less specific term "managerial principle."

So it was that in short order Canadian officers were converted to "managers" instead of "leaders." Instructors at the officer cadet school began teaching about Maslow's hierarchy of needs, while making only passing reference to such things as duty, discipline and honour. Although experienced officers and non-commissioned personnel at the school understood that what they were teaching recruits was "crap," the young officer students were wrongly trained to believe they could simply apply a theoretical formula to achieve positive leadership results.

It was at this crucial juncture that the "career management system" and Personnel Evaluation Reports became geared to promoting cautious managers rather than troop-oriented officers. Decisiveness, which was formerly seen as a prerequisite quality for promoting military commanders, was now regarded as an eccentric career-inhibiting handicap. Startling testimony before the commission of inquiry into the Somalia disaster revealed just how debilitating a policy the career management system had become.

After listening to hours and hours of testimony detailing the character flaws and professional shortcomings of a military officer, the commissioner interrupted the inquiry proceedings to ask his witness: "Just how was it possible that such an 'incompetent' officer could have been selected to take command of the Airborne Regiment in the first place?"

The witness calmly replied, "Because on paper he was a perfect candidate." Visibly bewildered by this comment, the commissioner pressed his point: "But why wouldn't annual evaluation reports have revealed this alleged lack of leadership?"

Unflustered, the staff officer in the witness box answered, "Because commanding officers are reluctant to make a written record of a subordinate's faults for fear that it may one day adversely affect [his or her] promotion or career advancement."

Sadly for the Canadian Armed Forces, the irony of such a surprising admission had long since been lost on the officer corps. Nevertheless, in that brief, largely unreported testimony, the public inquiry stumbled upon the root of the problem it had been created to identify: the breakdown of discipline which had occurred in East Africa was not an isolated incident perpetrated by a rogue regiment but rather the *product* of a system that disguised the incompetence of an officer so as not to affect his career.

With high-ranking civil servants controlling the policy agenda, and politically astute generals managing such vital functions as personnel, the trickle-down of the bureaucratic ethos soon became a flood.

Ambitious young officers whose career aspirations outweighed their talent and dedication to their chosen profession quickly found themselves a seat on this cushy bandwagon. Commanding a unit or a ship had previously been seen as the highlight of any officer's career, a rarely attained responsibility and personal challenge. It soon became viewed as a stepping-stone to promotion, a necessary evil to be tolerated rather than enjoyed. For some officers, it was much easier to be "noticed" while toiling obediently for a general at headquarters than to tackle the potentially career-damaging task of commanding a unit. It was not always this way. Twenty years ago, any officer who turned down a command would have simultaneously submitted his resignation. Now such a practice is not only condoned, but encouraged and rewarded.

In 1978, Major William Leach took a finance position in headquarters rather than assume command of a Germany-based service battalion. Leach was given the desk job he requested and continued to move up the corporate ladder. By 1995, despite never having held a command position, Major-General Leach was appointed deputy-commander of the Army. In this role, *he* was now responsible for all personnel and promotions.

More to the point, Leach's executive successes were swiftly achieved by the opportunity created by unification. Overnight, the Canadian Armed Forces became the single largest corporation in the land. To succeed in the new forces required the same instincts of survival that prevailed in any large Canadian corporation—the need for acumen and caution.

It was in this atmosphere that dramatic changes began to take place in the daily conduct of military affairs. The system became so convoluted that new arrivals posted to Headquarters were left confounded by the complex structure of cliques, cabals and opposing factions. It is a story of such complexity that readers would be wise to absorb the facts in stages; otherwise, they too might become confounded by the machinations of the numerous individuals portrayed here.

Two of the most prominent figures in this tale were a civilian and a soldier.

The civilian was a brilliant and ambitious Ottawa mandarin named Robert Ramsay Fowler, who joined the Defence Department in June 1986 as assistant deputy minister (policy). By May 1989, Fowler was appointed deputy minister (DM). As elusive as the Scarlet Pimpernel, Fowler ordered his minions that he was never to be photographed in public.

The soldier in this drama was a man with the aristocratic name John de Chastelain, a suave technocrat with the aloof air of a Count Palatine. De Chastelain's appointment as Canada's top soldier—the chief of the defence staff (CDS)—was announced in July 1989. Taking over the position as a newly minted full general, he served until January 1993, when he was posted to Washington as Canadian ambassador to the United States. He held this position until January 1994, when he was resurrected for an unprecedented second term as CDS, serving until his retirement in January 1996.

Together, de Chastelain and Fowler presided over Canada's military, their presence pervasive and, in time, both legendary and notorious, for it was under their stewardship that greed and corruption flourished in the high command.

CHAPTER TWO

"Just a Simple Civil Servant"

The rise to power of Robert Ramsay Fowler was as measured as his tailored suits. He had put his career together piece by piece, never with a false step. In just twenty years he had waltzed his way to the top of Ottawa's bureaucratic heap. Muhammad Ali's motto, "Float like a butterfly, sting like a bee," could have been Fowler's own. Neat and bespectacled, Fowler was in appearance a cross between the owlish Knowlton Nash and the Man from Glad. His hirelings nicknamed him "Teflon Bob" because he saw to it no scandal would ever stick to him. But by the early 1990s, for the first time in his impeccably managed career, he came under public scrutiny for his questionable behaviour at the Department of National Defence and the excessive use of public money.

By January 1995, he was removed from DND under a cloud. There had been several damaging media reports about his wasteful use of DND funds, and the Reform Party had demanded (although to no avail) a full inquiry into his management of National Defence. Even though the Liberal government recognized the political liability Fowler had come to represent, he was still protected as part of the establishment and appointed Canada's ambassador to the United Nations.

Reform Party Foreign Affairs critic Bob Mills invoked a rarely used parliamentary process to challenge Fowler's UN appointment. The media and spectators who attended the House of Commons Committee on Foreign Affairs hearing were witness to such a spectacle of Liberal solidarity that one could only speculate whether Fowler's past political connections were now paying him dividends. Twice previously the chairman of the committee, John Graham, had pressured Mills to drop the whole affair, presumably to avoid any further media revelations. However, when the novice Reform MP stood his ground, the eight Liberal members changed their tactics.

Throughout the two-hour, fixed-time hearing (which was suspiciously interrupted by a fire alarm following Fowler's opening address), the Liberals counter-attacked Mills's questions on the grounds of relevancy—

without Fowler even having to put forth his own defence. Eventually, out of frustration at the procedural debate, Mills posed the unanswerable question to Chairman Graham: "If Mr. Fowler is really such a capable individual, then why has the Liberal government demoted him three rungs with this UN ambassadorship?"

The Liberals thumped the table in unison and Graham angrily ruled Mills out of line with his question. Mills had seen through the government's duplicitous façade. For six years, Fowler had managed the largest and most complex department in government, and he had directly controlled the largest discretionary federal budget. He had reached the salary cap for civil servants as a level-three deputy minister ($170,000). And for six years, he had had a Headquarters staff of 12,500 personnel at his virtual beck and call.

In 1994, Fowler had boasted to close associates that the only promotion left open to him was to chief clerk of the Privy Council, and he fully expected to be named to that position within a year.

Unfortunately for Fowler's aspirations, by the autumn of 1994 he had been publicly linked to the Somalia scandal, the $387,000 renovations of his office suite had been questioned in Parliament, and the suspicious 1992 suicide case of Denys Henrie (a senior defence executive) had been reopened by the Gloucester, Ontario, police. In a suicide note, Henrie had named Fowler and others as "responsible" for his death, but there had never been an inquest.

By January 1995, the overqualified Fowler found himself New York bound to occupy a position that is rated as only an executive level-five post in Ottawa's bureaucratic hierarchy. When he ruled DND, he had often had business lunches with his counterpart, the deputy minister at Foreign Affairs. Now, as a UN ambassador, Fowler found himself answering to this same gentleman—*through* an assistant deputy minister. The total staff at the permanent mission in New York is a scant seventeen workers, and thanks to continued media scrutiny of his lavish expense accounts, he is forced to write explanatory covering notes to accompany his hospitality claims.

While many would argue that an ambassadorship could hardly be construed as a fall from grace, to comprehend Fowler's unique persona it is imperative to understand the man's motivation and to study his rise through the power corridors of the civil service.

Robert Ramsay Fowler was born with the proverbial silver spoon in his mouth on August 18, 1944, and drew his first breaths in a white mansion in Ottawa's wealthy Rockcliffe Park. His father, Robert MacLaren Fowler, was a highly connected Liberal party grandee who counted among his friends C.D. Howe, the so-called minister of everything in Prime Minister Mackenzie King's wartime cabinet. Howe had convinced Fowler to take a dollar-a-year posting as a general counsel and secretary on the Wartime Prices and Trade Board. A decade later he headed the Royal Commission on Broadcasting in 1956, giving one of the most memorable quotes in Canadian public life: "in broadcasting all that matters is program content; all the rest is housekeeping." Young Fowler grew up surrounded by politics and Liberal politicians. The presence of power was a fact of life.

After the wartime assignment, Fowler senior moved the family back to Montreal, where he was president of the influential Pulp and Paper Association. The Fowlers lived at 36 Summit Circle, a fashionable address on an exclusive street in the then almost totally anglo Westmount. The street was so exclusive it had only eleven houses. One neighbour was no less than Colonel Gerald W. Birks, a son of Henry Birks, jeweller to the Canadian establishment.

Not surprisingly, Fowler opted to attend Queen's University in Kingston, Ontario, taking political science in a department that boasted a long-standing connection with political Ottawa, especially with what was known then as the Department of External Affairs. Of five professors canvassed to comment on Fowler's academic skills, only one remembered teaching him. John Miesel, the former head of the department, remembered Fowler as only a "good student," hardly a ringing endorsement for someone who possessed a mind like a steel trap. Curiously, one of the professors canvassed declined to be interviewed until he received written permission to do so from Robert Fowler himself.

Doubtless, his family connections helped Fowler win his first job in the federal public service after graduating from Queen's in 1968 with a bachelor of arts degree. First step up the ladder was an entry-level job with the Canadian International Development Agency (CIDA). Since Lester Pearson and Pierre Trudeau held foreign aid in high esteem, CIDA was a valuable addition to his résumé. Fowler, however, was smart enough to know that the agency was a dead end. "It was so overcentralized that the field agents only had a few hundred dollars in spending authority and getting anything out of Ottawa was nearly impossible," said Bill Twatio, a former CIDA employee. Besides, there was a vast middle management, and the likelihood of quick promotion was remote. "Their toenails were grown into the carpets in most offices, and they were indestructible. The only way to advance was with transfers," Twatio added.

Advance Fowler did—after one year at CIDA he was transferred to External Affairs. It was here that Fowler first made the acquaintance of a young Jean Chrétien and other prominent Liberals. He obviously made a good impression on the right people because, within the remarkably short span of two years, the now twenty-seven-year-old Fowler was off on his first international posting—to the Canadian embassy in Paris.

In January 1974, he returned to Ottawa to tackle his first management role, running the trade desk at the Commercial Policy Division. Once again, it didn't take Fowler long to impress his bosses with his work ethic, and by 1976 he was on the upward move again. This time he was assigned to Canada's permanent mission to the UN as first secretary, and within mere months he was promoted to counsellor. By December 1978, he was back from New York to take on new duties as the executive assistant to Undersecretary of State for External Affairs Allan Gottlieb. It was in this capacity that Fowler's skills came to the attention of none other than Trudeau himself. By March 1980, at just thirty-five years of age, Fowler was seconded to the Privy Council Office (PCO) as assistant secretary to the cabinet (foreign and defence).

Fowler's first chance to shine for his newly found mentor was during Trudeau's famous peace initiative of 1983–84 in which he visited world leaders to persuade them to negotiate the reduction of nuclear weapons. External Affairs didn't think much of the idea and tried spiking the exercise, but Trudeau wouldn't hear of it. Two of the key players on the working group were Fowler and the group's leader, the elegant and perceptive Louis Delvoie, then the director general of the International Security and Arms Control Bureau in External Affairs. The working group met for the first time on September 23, 1983. As Trudeau's PCO adviser on foreign and defence policy, Fowler was front and centre in challenging External Affairs.

"Both he and Trudeau were insistent that ideas come forward in raw form, not blended out of existence by the bureaucracy. Fowler, in other words, was the man to whom the officials were responsible, not the Department of External Affairs, which was bypassed yet again," wrote historian J.L. Granatstein and Robert Bothwell in *Pirouette: Pierre Trudeau and Canadian Foreign Policy*.

World leaders paid Trudeau little more than lip-service at best, and the peace initiative was best remembered for Trudeau's witty riposte about "Pentagon pipsqueaks." While the exercise was more or less a flop, Robert Fowler was recognized by many as being Trudeau's most trusted adviser.

In 1984, Fowler faced one of his greatest challenges when Brian Mulroney's Tories bulldozed their way to power. During the election campaign, Mulroney had vowed to excise every living Grit who had come to power under previous Liberal regimes. With Fowler's having been a devout Liberal both in ideology and in party politics since his days at Queen's, many thought that the Conservative election victory would cap his upward momentum through the public service. However, as many novice politicians quickly learn, the true power rests with the top bureaucrats. It would take Mulroney's fledgling government several years to remove prominent Liberal mandarins and replace them with loyal Tories.

In the meantime, Fowler was rapidly changing his outward image to suit his new political masters. On June 2, 1986, Fowler, having proven his competency, was promoted from the Privy Council Office to become the assistant deputy minister (policy) at National Defence Headquarters. In the following months, he and an old associate on the peace initiative, Dr. Ken Calder, worked directly with Defence Minister Perrin Beatty on the 1987 White Paper on Defence.

Trudeau's successive governments had continuously eroded the Canadian military's efficiency through the demoralizing effects of unification, budget cuts leading to equipment rust-out and a growing reliance on our NATO allies to shoulder the burden of collective defence. Fowler was well aware of Trudeau's contempt for Defence, and during his years at Privy Council, he had been an ardent supporter of the Prime Minister's emasculation of the military in favour of increased domestic social programs. Now that he was at National Defence, and the Progressive Conservative policy was aimed at paralleling Ronald Reagan's Cold War strategies of military preparedness, Fowler quickly remoulded his ideals to suit the circumstances. Because it was politically expedient, overnight Fowler went from dove to hawk.

The White Paper recommendations put forward by Fowler and Calder would have effectively reshaped the Canadian military into a modern and capable force. The single-force uniform was to be replaced with three distinct branch uniforms. The total number of Regular Force personnel was to increase by 10 per cent, to 90,000 troops. Our long-neglected Reserves were to be boosted to a strength of 40,000 soldiers (from a nominal total of approximately 24,000) and they were to become amalgamated with Regular units. Ageing Leopard and main battle tanks already considered obsolete for the modern battlefield were to be replaced with a new generation of 400 fighting vehicles. For the Navy, it was proposed that they acquire twelve modern nuclear submarines, at a total cost of $8 billion. The number of troops committed to the North Atlantic Treaty Organization (NATO) and stationed in West Germany was to be increased to the pre–Trudeau era strength of a full mechanized brigade and a modern air division.

To finance such a massive restructuring, the Conservative government set aside enormous budgets, which included real growth and projected inflation over the next decade. Within DND, scores of project management offices were established to accommodate the procurement of the new equipment. Usually these offices were directed by a full colonel and staffed by a dozen officers and civilians. However, in the case of major capital acquisitions, such as the nuclear subs, the senior manager was a rear-admiral, and the number of administrators topped one hundred.

By 1988, the new uniforms were making their debut, reinforcements were arriving in Europe, recruiting was up across the country and construction was taking place on virtually all of the major bases. The submarine purchase was controversial, but when Mulroney's Conservatives won a second straight majority, international arms dealers thought the 1987 White Paper was destined to become a reality.

The first indication that things were not running as smoothly as hoped was when Mulroney shuffled the charismatic Perrin Beatty out of the defence portfolio and replaced him with the little-known and ineffectual Bill McKnight. There were rumblings in the defence community that Finance Minister Michael Wilson was going to make drastic cuts to DND in his upcoming budget. Removing Beatty ahead of the crunch would spare him the ignominy of having to implement the scrapping of his own blueprint.

In April 1989, the budget axe fell as predicted and the 1987 White Paper was history. The nuclear submarines were cancelled immediately, as were the main battle tanks, while other capital acquisitions were delayed, and then scrapped in future federal budgets.

Ironically, just six weeks after the first devastating blow was dealt to the military's restructuring plan, its author, Robert Ramsay Fowler, was promoted to the position of deputy minister at National Defence. From May 19, 1989, until January 13, 1995, Fowler was to oversee and direct the re-emasculation of the Canadian Forces.

All those who worked closely with Fowler admit that he possessed a rare intellect and a superbly analytical and incisive mind. He radiated an aloof confidence and was noted for his eloquence in both official languages. What set him apart from other senior bureaucrats was his nerves of steel and a rare ability to summarize large amounts of disjointed information and draw appropriate conclusions from it.

He became known to those on the thirteenth floor of NDHQ as the "Volvo Man" after a character in a popular TV commercial. In the ad, the driver of a Volvo rockets towards a brick wall at full speed on wet pavement. When the brakes are finally applied, the automobile stops just inches shy of destruction. The driver displays no emotional reaction to the danger; in fact, he doesn't even blink.

Even in the latter days of his reign, when he himself was personally under attack both in the media and in the House of Commons, Fowler still displayed this rare talent. Allegations of his excesses and abuses would be chronicled in pages of press clippings, yet he would conduct the daily executive meeting as if nothing was amiss. He'd never blink.

During Fowler's regime at National Defence, he demonstrated the ability to manage a complex organization, but it was his imperious style of management that eventually invited public criticism and ultimately led to his removal. Due to his personal ambition, his well-placed political connections and the absence of an effective senior command, Fowler was able to extend his influence into the management of military affairs. Once he was able to exert his influence over the careers and senior promotions of general officers, he held immeasurable power.

The case of Vice-Admiral Larry Murray illustrates Fowler's penchant for advancing his protégés.

As a relatively junior-grade flag officer (a one-star commodore), Murray caught the eye of Fowler during the Gulf War. Fowler was fascinated with the media, and Murray's ability to deal with them convincingly during the daily televised press conferences was seen as a valuable asset. With Fowler's support, Murray was promoted, ahead of more experienced peers, to the rank of rear-admiral in the summer of 1991. Just two years later, when the deputy chief of the defence staff was being reinstated as a three-star position, Murray was promoted to vice-admiral and selected for the job. At forty-five years of age, he was the youngest peacetime sailor to hold the rank.

As the deputy chief, effective January 1993, Vice-Admiral Murray found himself flung into the vortex of the Somalia deployment just as things began to fall apart. Throughout the brewing scandal, he was in the chain of command responsible for the deployment of the Canadian Airborne Regiment, its day-to-day operations in Somalia, the Significant Incident Reports and the subsequent police investigations. Despite Murray's deep involvement in the whole affair, or perhaps because of it, he was shuffled again eighteen months later to take command of the Navy in Halifax. In January 1995, Murray was designated to return to Ottawa as the youngest vice-chief the defence staff had ever had, the heir apparent to de Chastelain.

Unfortunately for Murray, the reality of the Somalia inquiry and a wave of damaging revelations put an end to the planned succession. Pending the findings of the public commission, Murray remains in the relatively powerless office of vice-chief of the defence staff. However, he has kept both a strong social and business link to his mentor since Fowler's demotion to UN ambassador. The two gentlemen spent a summer holiday (August 1995) and New Year's Eve 1995 on the Fowler farm, and frequently exchange official letters.

Senior generals were also aware that the government's selection for CDS after de Chastelain's retirement would be based on Fowler's recommendation. This knowledge was supported by the unprecedented resurrection of John de Chastelain following his short-lived stint as ambassador to the United States.

Once the generals realized who was calling the shots, it served to reinforce their careerist tendencies and affected their submissive behaviour accordingly.

The flip side of Fowler's displays of favouritism, or his dangling-carrot approach to management, was his notorious vindictiveness towards those who dared to question his vision, wisdom or authority. Fowler didn't need to ascend to the top job in DND before he started to flex his corporate muscles and demonstrate his powerful connections outside the department.

During the nuclear submarine program, a former senior naval officer had been seconded to Treasury Board to assist them in the assessment of this major capital acquisition program. In the autumn of 1988, the ex-officer forwarded a paper to Privy Council stating several of his concerns. Essentially, he believed the French consortium's bid was being favoured over the British bid, for reasons that had nothing to do with the actual merit of the proposal. Shortly thereafter, the ex-officer's secondment was terminated at Treasury Board. The old sailor said he would fight dismissal in the courts and the whole story would eventually come out.

Following the navy man's departure, Fowler summoned his aide, a young man named Denys Henrie, and several other executives into his office. According to the entry in Henrie's notebook, Fowler instructed one of the group to look into the whistle blower's background so as to exploit any weak points and give him a thorough insight into the ex-serviceman's personal situation. When the submarine program was killed just a few months later, the issue became a moot point. The ex-officer took a cash settlement from the department for his wrongful dismissal.

By that time, Fowler had been promoted to deputy minister and was already exerting his control over the entire department. It didn't take him long to demonstrate his lust for power, contempt for military traditions and disregard for fiscal responsibility. One of his first actions upon assuming office was to demand that he be provided with a personal driver. His argument was that, since he was equal to the CDS, who was authorized to use a military car and driver, then as Mr. Deputy Minister he should be entitled to a civilian chauffeur. It didn't matter to Fowler that a senior officer, by reason of military etiquette, must exit a car through a door opened by the driver and return salutes (hence the need for a military driver), or that prior to Bob Nixon, his predecessor, deputy ministers were not even entitled to a government car. With the entire department's future on hold due to fiscal restraint, its new senior manager made it his first task to grant himself a chauffeured Crown Victoria.

The decision turned out to be a costly one for the Canadian taxpayer. The civilian chauffeur was the equivalent of a military corporal, but unlike soldiers, civilians are entitled to overtime pay. Since much of Fowler's driving requirements occurred before and after regular working hours (Fowler usually put in twelve-hour days at the office), his driver, Gerry Hébert, ended up costing the department an estimated $60,000 in salary alone. During the daytime, when Fowler was engaged in running the department, Hébert would spend some of his time performing personal chores for the Deputy Minister. Many insiders felt that the employment of a government driver as a manservant was an excessive abuse of authority, but no one dared to report the situation for fear of retribution.

One staff member, who since 1973 had worked directly for three previous deputy ministers, quit her job shortly after Fowler assumed control. It had been Barbara Shore's job to process petty cash payments, and there were several questionable practices authorized by Fowler which she could not in good conscience be a party to.

She was instructed, for example, to submit claims for the preponderance of traffic tickets which Hébert would accumulate. Apparently, due to his boss's authority within the federal government, the chauffeur felt he did not have to abide by Ottawa's parking regulations or speed limits. When convictions were issued, Shore had to find a plausible finance code for what she knew to be a questionable claim.

Fowler's hospitality expenses were another source of contention among the staff members in the Deputy Minister's suite. Denys Henrie, Fowler's former executive aide when he was assistant deputy minister (policy), now ran the Executive Secretariat. As such, he was still very much Fowler's right-hand man, and he ensured that what Fowler desired he produced. Henrie always managed to find the money to finance the Deputy Minister's imperial tastes.

Fowler's first marriage had ended in divorce in 1977. He had remarried shortly afterwards, and Mary, his second wife, proved to be a valuable asset in her husband's social networking. They purchased a home in the well-to-do Glebe district of Ottawa, but they would entertain select guests on their nearby farm, located north of Buckingham, Quebec, about an hour's drive east of the capital. The house is a square-cut log cabin with dovetailed corners. A visitor said it was tastefully furnished with rustic pine and offered guests a wonderful view of rolling hills. To be invited was to be recognized as "in." The well-catered summer barbecues at the Fowler retreat were regarded as "social happenings" among the civil service and political elite.

No one who attended these cookouts could have had any idea that Fowler was actually billing the taxpayer for these functions. The tab for lunches at expensive downtown Ottawa restaurants was also billed to the Defence Department budget as working lunches. Fowler would regularly take senior generals or other government officials out for a midday meal, on average twice a week. In 1993 alone, the Deputy Minister filed claims for such meals totalling $3,250. Of course, top defence officials followed the example set by their senior mandarin, and they would repay his generosity by taking him out to lunch—again at the taxpayer's expense.

When Fowler was promoted to deputy minister, there were 87,000 troops in the Forces and the defence budget stood at $12.7 billion. By the time he was replaced, the manning level of soldiers had dropped by 25 per cent, to a mere 68,000, and roughly $2 billion had been trimmed from the annual budget. Yet throughout this massive downsizing, Fowler's own empire had dramatically expanded and his own remuneration was increased to the maximum possible salary.

Bob Nixon, Fowler's predecessor, had been a deputy minister level two; however, on assumption of his duties, Fowler was promoted to level one. The two in-grade promotions Fowler received during his tenure at DND were inexplicable in light of the shrinking scale of his department. The over-ranking merely allowed Fowler to receive substantial pay increases while the public service (and the military) were experiencing a morale-dampening pay freeze.

Fowler's grandiose extravagances extended not only to the size and rank of his immediate staff, but also to the actual square-footage his "office suite" occupied. Between May 1989 and April 1994, the size of the DM's entourage, in direct defiance of what was happening in the rest of the department, had increased 200 per cent, from five assistants to an unwieldy ten aides and clerks. In November 1989, after having barely moved into the new office, Fowler ordered renovations done to the entire suite. These modifications saw his inner chamber increase from 1,800 square feet to an enormous 3,410 square feet.

The cost of the physical renovations was budgeted at $160,000, but within days the project manager at the Directorate of Facilities Management had been advised of an "expected" increase. Rick Williams refused to sign the work order. Williams's boss, A.J.K. McKinnon, approved invoicing to a separate construction project in order to cover Fowler's excessive cost overruns, but even the $327,000 in total construction costs was not the entire extent of the project. An additional $50,000 was spent on furnishings from 1989 to 1992, a whopping $5,000 worth of desks and chairs for each of Fowler's ten assistants. Also purchased during this period were computers and audio-visual equipment, the exact value of which has never been released by the department.

One of the "necessities" Fowler ordered for his office boardroom was a full-functioning kitchen, designed for the preparation of "working lunches." Unfortunately for taxpayers, once the kitchen was built at public expense, the facility was rarely, if ever, used. Apparently it proved less stressful for Fowler to take his business discussions down to the ritzy National Arts Centre café and submit the claims to Denys Henrie.

The other "critical" changes Fowler insisted upon, regardless of the cost, provide further insight into his character and obsession with control. He had a new visitor waiting area built sufficiently separate from his and his assistant's work area to be out of earshot. The entire organization of the office dividers had to be altered to allow Fowler and his administrative assistant to "be able to see visitors entering the DM's inner office complex." As for personal ablutions, Fowler had the door changed on the washroom to allow him sole access to the facility, and complete privacy.

When junior officers reported accounting irregularities and unusually excessive expenditures involving the renovation to the RCMP, as a matter of course the case was handed back to the Defence Department to investigate. Doug Lindley, the associate assistant deputy minister (personnel), whose responsibilities included picking suitable candidates for inquiries, selected a junior-level executive, Pierre Lagueux, to conduct the delicate and potentially damaging investigation. Fowler had already recognized Lagueux's talent in managing "difficult" procurement issues. Ten months later, Lagueux submitted a 200-page report. It was immediately classified as "Protected C," making it virtually a national secret and unavailable for scrutiny. Following the submission of the report, Lagueux's career really took off. In three years, he moved up three rungs to become chief of supply and, when Lagueux ran out of climbing room, Fowler upgraded his position to that of an assistant deputy minister.

Even such minute details as the interior decorating did not escape scrutiny by the fastidious DM, and his taste did not come cheap to the public purse.

Famous war art had traditionally hung in the Deputy Minister's suite at Headquarters. The Canadian War Museum had a long-standing casual lending arrangement with DND whereby the artwork was provided free of charge. The senior mandarin at National Defence would be required to entertain foreign military emissaries and foreign heads of state, so where better to display some of our country's masterpieces depicting past military glory? However, Bob Fowler immediately ordered the war art removed from "his" suite and instructed that it be returned to the war museum's already overcrowded storage facilities.

Packaging, insuring and shipping the priceless works cost DND thousands of dollars, but Fowler was not done adding his personal touch. He had his aide Denys Henrie find a budget for the rental of modern artwork from the Art Bank of the Canada Council. At a cost of between $2,500 and $3,000 annually, Fowler leased various abstract works, which he would personally replace on a yearly basis. Staff members described the modern canvasses as "porridge flung in a frame." Following the redecoration, senior officers at NDHQ quickly realized that their new boss disliked martial images.

Once the military hierarchy had been brought under his control, only his bosses, the various defence ministers, could have curbed Fowler's style. On the surface, Fowler would make a great show of being helpful and responsive to his ministers. If they made a request, streams of colonels and generals would appear, bulging briefcases dutifully tucked under their arms. In next to no time, the overwhelmed politician would have presentations, viewgraphs, neatly tabbed study papers and briefing books coming out of his or her ears. Fowler's slick salesmanship was consistent, well packaged and utterly impenetrable. Ministers never had a chance to implement their will or initiate their own agenda. By the time they had learned to be wary of Mr. Fowler, most were already *en route* to a new portfolio.

"Fowler is an extremely capable, extremely intelligent individual," said retired Colonel Brian Reid, armoured officer of thirty-two years. "He really did his homework and often knew more than the officer briefing him. When the officers around the table would hesitate or prevaricate, he would jump in decisively and decisions are made this way. His special talent, though, was to influence rather than make decisions for people. He simply had to make it known what he thought was to be done, and it often was."

Another observer, Sean Maloney, reserve armoured officer and historian, thought that Fowler's close connections to the Department of Foreign Affairs gave him more pull than he deserved. "He's an elected civil servant dictating policy and that's not his job. His job is supposed to be administrative and housekeeping."

But Colonel Reid said there was another side to Fowler, especially when he turned his charm afterburners on. "Fowler could talk to the troops. He made them feel his interest in what they were doing. He was actually fascinated by military minutiae."

When Fowler was sent to New York in January 1995, his demotion of three rungs seemingly failed to change his disregard for the public purse. His first claim submitted to External Affairs in April 1995 amounted to thousands of dollars for meals, wine and clothing. However, the ultimate statement on his elitist bearing was the submission of a $70 claim for the "framing of [the] ambassadorial appointment scroll."

It would be far too simplistic to lay all of the present problems of our demoralized military on the doorstep of one individual. It takes more than the personal will of even a determined bureaucrat to bring an entire national institution to its knees. When Robert Ramsay Fowler ascended to the top bureaucratic post within the Defence Department, twenty-five years of bureaucratic decay had left the senior command impotent and inefficient—in other words, ripe for the picking. To a man of Fowler's capabilities and driving ambition, the circumstances proved too tempting, the power available too seductive, for him not to seize the initiative.

Curiously, though, for a man with such influence, Robert Fowler remained essentially anonymous to the troops, as the following exchange— which took place at a Canadian Forces post in Germany—illustrates.

The young militia lieutenant had been drinking alone in the Schwarzwald officers' mess when a tall, bespectacled civilian entered the lounge. Although he was stationed at CFB Lahr on only a temporary posting, the subaltern felt obliged to offer a greeting to the stranger and welcome him to the club. Despite the reservist's cordiality, the civilian was aloof in his manner, and he introduced himself by using his full name, "Robert Ramsay Fowler."

"And what brings you to Germany?" asked the lieutenant.

"Official business. I work for DND," replied Fowler.

"Oh, in what capacity would that be?" inquired the junior officer. "You see I'm researching a book on the Canadian military's role in postwar Germany, and I want to cover the political and bureaucratic angles as well."

"Oh, I'm afraid I'd be of little help to you. I'm just the deputy minister and, as such, I have a very limited role in key decisions made within the department," replied Fowler, adding, "Despite the fancy title, I'm just a simple civil servant."

Fowler then excused himself from the conversation to read a newspaper.

The militia lieutenant later discovered just who this Robert Ramsay Fowler really was, and how instrumental he had been, not only in overseeing Canada's role in NATO, but also in running all aspects of the Canadian Forces. In retrospect, the young officer analysed Fowler's odd, self-deprecating comment: "He was an intelligent, complex character—far from 'simple.' There was nothing 'civil' about his disposition, and he was definitely nobody's 'servant' when he ran DND, least of all John de Chastelain's."

CHAPTER THREE

"*Thank God That's Over!*"

Lieutenant Colonel John de Chastelain, PPCLI

It was a summer day in Winnipeg. The year was 1972. Six hundred soldiers of the Second Battalion, Princess Patricia's Canadian Light Infantry (PPCLI), were drawn up in disciplined ranks on the scorching parade square. The occasion was a change of command—outgoing Lieutenant-Colonel John de Chastelain was handing over the battalion to his successor, James Allan. As per tradition, the parade lasted several hours before the command was given to "March off the colours" and "Fall out the officers."

With the conclusion of the formal ceremonies, the two commanding officers were casually strolling towards the officers' mess for refreshments when, unexpectedly, de Chastelain turned to Allan and said, "Well, thank God that's over with." Thinking he was referring to the gruelling parade conditions, Allan quickly agreed with the statement.

"No, I meant, thank God my command is over with. This battalion is your headache now," said de Chastelain.

Allan was astounded by this comment. He always believed that commanding an infantry battalion would be the crown jewel in any officer's career. On paper, the Second Battalion, Princess Pats, had looked to be an exemplary unit. Their discipline reports indicated that they were a virtually trouble-free formation. Unfortunately for the fledgling commander, reality proved to be a different case altogether. All too soon, Allan discovered the reason for de Chastelain's relief.

The regiment he took over had a serious problem with insubordination and drug use. Within weeks of assuming command, Allan had called in the Special Investigations Unit to root out his drug problems, and he soon began laying criminal charges. Even though the problems had been inherited, and Allan had chosen to deal with them rather than continue to ignore them, to the Army high command it appeared as though 2 PPCLI ceased to be a cohesive unit immediately following de Chastelain's departure.

The situation left Allan critical of John de Chastelain: "He knew he was going on to bigger and better things." De Chastelain, in fact, was going to a plum assignment, a one-year French course in Quebec City, to which he was allowed to bring his wife. Most officers went on a six-week crash course without their wives.

Jim Allan retired from the Forces as a respected colonel, and John de Chastelain went on to become the chief of defence staff. Allan still views his two-year command of 2 PPCLI as the highlight of his professional military career. To de Chastelain, it was a worrisome stepping-stone.

Anyone glancing at General de Chastelain's impressive résumé would think he was a remarkable soldier who had enjoyed a stellar career. To see him in person—handsome, fit and seemingly self-confident—only completes the façade which this officer perfected during his service.

John de Chastelain was born in Bucharest, Romania, on July 30, 1937, the son of an English Army colonel. He was considered a British subject because his father was attached to the embassy as an attaché. Once the Second World War erupted, the de Chastelain family was repatriated to England. John went through the English school system and later transferred to Fettes College in Scotland.

Sometimes called the "Eton of Scotland," Fettes College is situated in Edinburgh in a bucolic setting of woods and playing fields. Joe Hill, the secretary of the Old Fettesian Association, remembered that John was on the swim team and was a house prefect, one of five for about fifty junior classmen. While Hill called Fettes non-denominational, it possessed all the trappings of muscular Christianity. In promoting itself in a brochure to attract students, "the school aims to make full use of its proximity to the sea, the Dry Ski-Slope and the mountains of Scotland. Outdoor activities are encouraged for the enjoyment that they give and the valuable personal qualities which they help to develop." De Chastelain "passed through the Sixth Forme (English 'A' levels) at age 18," said Hill.

After graduating from Fettes, de Chastelain emigrated to Canada, where he soon joined the militia as a private soldier in the Calgary Highlanders. While much public relations mileage was gained later in his career for having "served in the ranks," even de Chastelain himself acknowledges that such a statement is misleading. During his brief few months with the Highlanders, he was a novice piper in their band. As such, he gained little practical military experience.

By the autumn of 1956, de Chastelain was a member of the Regular Force and was enrolled at the Royal Military College in Kingston. In 1960, he completed his studies with a Bachelor of Arts degree in History and was commissioned as a second lieutenant in the Princess Patricia's Canadian Light Infantry. In part because of his clipped British accent and in part due to his aloof, regal bearing, de Chastelain was nicknamed "Prince John," and the moniker stuck with him throughout his career.

Jim Stanton, a fellow officer in 2 PPCLI, recalled that, "regardless of how a situation actually developed, somehow de Chastelain had a knack for positioning himself where he stood to benefit from the outcome."

In the first five years of his active military service, de Chastelain was promoted a remarkable three times. He was a company commander at the tender age of twenty-seven. He saw duty in West Germany and Cyprus with the First Battalion, PPCLI, before taking command of the Winnipeg-based Second Battalion, PPCLI, in 1970. Subsequently, he commanded Canadian Forces Base Montreal during the 1976 Olympics, and that same year he returned for a second tour in Cyprus as the Canadian contingent commander.

After being promoted to the rank of brigadier-general, de Chastelain became the commandant of his old school, the Royal Military College in Kingston. From 1979 to 1981, Prince John was given command of Canada's high-profile NATO Brigade, which was known to be a mandatory career requirement on the ladder to high command. True to tradition, de Chastelain was promoted to major-general upon his return to Canada, and his last direct affiliation with Land Forces (Army) was served in the capacity of deputy commander, mobile command.

By 1982, he was posted to National Defence Headquarters, where he quickly worked his way through a variety of doctrine and policy positions. After being promoted to lieutenant-general, he was finally admitted to the thirteenth-floor power corridor with his appointment as assistant deputy minister (personnel). In 1987, he moved up the ladder again when he became the vice-chief of the defence staff.

Even among the Defence Department's powerful elite, where arrogance is often displayed, de Chastelain made a name for himself as a callous micro-manager whose fingers were in everyone's pie. He prided himself on his mastery of the English language and would often refuse to read reports if the grammar was not impeccable—regardless of the content or the urgency of the issue.

In one instance, a colonel employed as an aide to de Chastelain had worked through an entire night to meet a morning deadline for a vital fourteen-page document. Later the next afternoon, well after the appointed time for delivery, de Chastelain summoned the colonel into his office to show him a neatly drawn pencil line, one-third of the way down the first page of the draft report.

"Here," said de Chastelain "is where I stopped reading, and I had already come across three mistakes in your punctuation. Don't submit this again until it's perfect." The colonel was furious.

Other documents released following access-to-information requests show that de Chastelain's obsession with grammar was almost pathological. A December 1992 letter to him from Lieutenant-General Paul Addy defined the Canadian Airborne Regiment's strict Rules of Engagement (ROEs) for the Somalia mission in painful detail. It was the first peace-making role assigned to Canadian ground troops since the Korean War. Because of the mission's high profile and unique role, these rules were con-sidered to be a crucial element of the planning phase. De Chastelain approved Addy's suggested regulations with the single notation "O.K." along with his initials in the margin. Following this curt approval of such a complex proposal, de Chastelain added a comment: "But I *hate* split infinitives!!"

Somali civilians were shot, paratroopers jailed, colonels court-martialled, a regiment disbanded and a public inquiry commenced as a result of the Airborne violating those ROEs, but at the time they were drafted General de Chastelain seemed more preoccupied with sentence structure than substance.

In September 1989, just three months after Bob Fowler became deputy minister, John de Chastelain replaced Paul Manson as the chief of the defence staff. During his tenure as vice-chief of the defence staff, de Chastelain had observed General Manson's close association with various defence industry "contacts." Upon retirement from the military, Manson had been immediately hired by Unisys as a senior executive. Manson's close friend Admiral Ed Healey retired as assistant deputy minister (materiel) the same summer and established himself as a top defence lobbyist.

Up until this juncture, de Chastelain had never really been involved in any of the temptations offered by the world of defence procurement. But now that he was CDS, he began to receive tentative invitations from industry representatives for him to follow in Paul Manson's footsteps. In the case of Baxter Publications, de Chastelain jumped a little too quickly at their offer of personal favours in exchange for a government contract—and it almost cost him his job.

Bill Baxter had a long-time arrangement with the Department of National Defence to publish a journal entitled *Canadian Defence Quarterly*. In theory, this magazine was an independent publication, but DND purchased 90 per cent of the press run as a bulk subscription. Top generals and bureaucrats would be invited to write essays for *CDQ*, and they would receive an honorarium from Baxter for their efforts. Since the Defence Department spent $80,000 more annually buying an independent magazine than it would have cost them to print their own, the lure of these tax-free honorariums went a long way towards explaining this unique arrangement.

When de Chastelain took over the top rank, he not only agreed to continue the arrangement, but also made the mistake of accepting two free trips from Baxter. One month after assuming overall command of the Canadian Forces, de Chastelain and his wife, MaryAnn, flew to Nassau, Bahamas, for an "editorial board" meeting of *CDQ* courtesy of Baxter Publishing. The next year's "meeting" was held in New Orleans, and once again the de Chastelains junketed on the Baxter tab. Inside the department, this appearance of conflict of interest was clear, and de Chastelain's acceptance of free travel was the source of much high-level gossip.

Like much of Ottawa's public service water-cooler chit-chat, the smoke indicated fire, but the paper trail to prove such allegations was non-existent. Nevertheless, a disgruntled aide working in de Chastelain's office forwarded the details of the New Orleans junket to *Frank*, a political satire and gossip magazine. The *Frank* article, which appeared in November 1991, contained enough quickly referenced facts that both the Privy Council and the Registrar General began asking General de Chastelain for clarification.

On November 23, 1991, a flurry of telephone calls were exchanged between de Chastelain and Bill Baxter to try to find a solution to the embarrassing dilemma. A total amount of $1,531 was agreed upon as the cost for both trips, and de Chastelain sent a personal cheque for that amount. In his covering letter to Baxter, de Chastelain states that he would appreciate receiving two separate invoices for the trips.

On November 28, de Chastelain forwarded the two invoices and his cancelled cheque to George Tsai, the assistant deputy registrar. In the covering note, the CDS asked for confirmation that the matter "may now be considered closed." He also advised the Privy Council that his name and that of his director general for public affairs would no longer appear on *CDQ*'s masthead.

Throughout his entire career, prior to being posted to National Defence Headquarters, John de Chastelain had lived in government-leased married quarters or residences. Upon arrival in Ottawa, the de Chastelains had purchased a small ($145,000) bungalow on Noel Street in one of the oldest neighbourhoods in Ottawa, New Edinburgh, called the "Burgh" by its inhabitants. These included Margaret Trudeau, who lived a few blocks away, and the Governor General of Canada, whose sprawling residence was just a block from Noel Street. Once he was promoted to chief of the defence staff, both John and MaryAnn felt that their diminutive house was inappropriate for such a high-profile job. Moreover, de Chastelain thought it was the taxpayers who should pay for an upgrade to his lodgings.

Through his wife's social contacts at the prestigious Maycourt Club, de Chastelain had learned that the National Capital Commission had taken possession of Maple Lawn. This $500,000 heritage home in the west end had been donated by the Rochester family, and the NCC were looking to sell the property to a government agency. Vice-Admiral Chuck Thomas, the vice-chief, was put in charge of reviewing the feasibility of such an acquisition. Having no love for de Chastelain, he in turn committed himself to derailing the whole scheme. Somehow, the story was leaked to *Maclean's* magazine, and when contacted by the press, Thomas confirmed the essence of the story.

Deputy Minister Fowler had originally concurred with the idea of a CDS residence, but once the concept was being pilloried in print and attracting unwanted political heat, he pulled the rug on the deal. DND's offer to the NCC was repealed and de Chastelain was apparently furious. But there were more than enough crises to take his mind off house-hunting.

⌐

The Oka crisis and the Persian Gulf war were fittingly the high-water mark in de Chastelain's military career. Both of these confrontations, from the Canadian military perspective, amounted to more show than substance. In both cases, while our soldiers and airmen demonstrated discipline and professionalism, it was the total absence of Canadian casualties that made these two military operations so politically saleable to the Canadian public.

Prime Minister Brian Mulroney was a shrewd enough politician to see an opportunity to increase his government's popularity in the polls. With the yellow ribbon campaign at a fever pitch across the country, Mulroney's advisers thought that he should be seen in closer contact with military authorities. De Chastelain and Fowler arranged for Mulroney to enter the inner sanctum to attend a daily executive meeting. It was to be the first and last time that the media were allowed onto the thirteenth floor at NDHQ.

Unfortunately for Mulroney and all in attendance that day, once the cameras were ordered out of the boardroom and the briefings began, it quickly became apparent that the Prime Minister was well out of his element. Although he listened intensely throughout the lectures, he made no comments and asked no questions about the complex situation developing in the Middle East. The Prime Minister did not make a repeat appearance for the duration of his tenure.

Both de Chastelain and Fowler had actually been dealing closely and informally with Brian Mulroney since 1989. It was that year that Karl-Heinz Schreiber was in Ottawa allegedly orchestrating million-dollar kickbacks to secure Air Canada's purchase of Airbus Industrie's A310 airbuses. Also on Schreiber's client list was the German defence consortium of Thyssen-Henschel, represented in Canada by Bear Head Industries, which was actively lobbying the Conservative government for a major armoured vehicle contract. At that juncture, General Motors Diesel Division in London, Ontario, was (and is) the only industrial plant in Canada capable of producing armoured cars, making GM the unchallenged recipient of any major vehicle purchase order.

Thyssen-Henschel proposed to change all that by establishing an assembly line in Cape Breton. Canada's thirty-year-old M113 Armoured Personnel Carriers were overdue to be replaced, and Thyssen was developing a new generation of fighting vehicle, the TH 495. Their proposal involved the Canadian government investing millions of dollars in seed money, along with a contract for the M113 replacement (valued at approximately $1 billion). In exchange, Canada would receive the updated technology, jobs in a depressed area and industry benefits resulting from the world-wide sale of the TH 495s. Even in theory, this scheme failed to recognize the limited scale and scope of Canada's defence industry's requirements: the capability of the single GM Diesel plant already exceeds our domestic demand for military vehicle production.

By the end of de Chastelain's first term as CDS, in the spring of 1992, it was Mulroney himself who announced a one-year extension to the CDS's contract rather than naming a successor, as was expected.

That summer, despite our military forces already being overcommitted on peacekeeping missions in Yugoslavia, Cambodia and Cyprus, Mulroney still wanted to assist the United States with their upcoming operation in Somalia. When the Privy Council and Ken Calder, at DND Policy, downscaled Canada's commitment to that of an airlift and observers, de Chastelain was furious. He wrote a note to Calder saying, "I thought we told External Affairs that we were sending [a battalion-sized battle group]." Calder rewrote the directives, and the Airborne Regiment was subsequently assigned to deploy to the Somalian port of Boosaaso.

By early December 1992, when the advance reconnaissance team from the Airborne Regiment reported that Boosaaso was a peaceful zone and the United States had upgraded their role to that of an intervention force, de Chastelain again became directly involved. Following a phone call with General Colin Powell, the U.S. joint chief of staff, de Chastelain had the impression that Canadian troops were not even being considered for a pivotal role in the coalition force. At this point, he summoned Bob Fowler to his office, where they discussed the political implications of Canada seeming to be a bit player in the mission. The Gulf War had generated a positive public response, and this operation promised to be just as crucial a victory.

Fowler and de Chastelain agreed that Vice-Admiral Larry Murray and Ken Calder would fly down to the United States immediately to make their intention of full-scale participation known to the U.S. strategic planners. Murray was to represent himself as de Chastelain's personal envoy. The delegation succeeded in their mission; the Airborne Regiment was deployed to the more volatile region around Bele Doggle. To understand the extent to which public relations played a part in General de Chastelain's eagerness to participate in the operation, it is worth noting that he made the announcement of Canada's increasing role on CTV's *Canada AM*—before he advised the Privy Council or the Airborne Regimental Operations staff.

Unbeknownst to all but Bob Fowler, de Chastelain had already had private discussions with Brian Mulroney about his appointment as Canada's ambassador to the United States. When the *official* announcement was made later that month declaring that General de Chastelain would be leaving the Forces early, the entire military community was shocked: the Forces were at a crucial juncture, yet their CDS was accepting an unprecedented patronage post.

Both de Chastelain and Defence Minister Marcel Masse had just made a presentation to the parliamentary defence committee in November stating that at the present level of commitment, the Canadian Army would be "burnt out" by November 1993 (in one year's time). That presentation was *before* the Somalian mission had been doubled in its scale to a full battle group.

At a hastily arranged operations briefing, Colonel Mike O'Brien presented the statistics on the Canadian Army's diminutive order of battle, a list of operational units and their groupings, along with a chain of command. He showed its state of overcommitment and the future implications of this. The main conclusion was that the Canadian Army could not afford to deploy a second contingent to Somalia—even if it became required.

"Well," said the newly appointed ambassador, "that's something I'm afraid my successor will have to deal with." And with that he excused himself from the briefing.

Despite his obvious disdain for the future welfare of the rank and file, de Chastelain still felt that his retirement should be fêted in grand style. On February 22, 1993, the Armed Forces spent $40,000 in travel costs and accommodations flying in representatives from each command and Europe to attend a farewell luncheon for de Chastelain. In the official message sent out to the regional commanders, it was noted that "the CDS [de Chastelain] sees this as a unique opportunity . . . to recognize deserving service members." (By having them honour *him* and present him with a gift!) The note regretted that "due to the economic realities of today a wider representation [more guests] is not practicable."

⌐

Once de Chastelain left the Forces the first time, he really developed a taste for the high life, at taxpayer's expense. Upon retirement, de Chastelain had received a cash severance package valued at $150,000, and he began collecting his annual military annuity of some $84,000. Added to this was his ambassadorial salary of $129,000 to $140,000, along with an enormous tax-free hospitality allowance. The Canadian government charges ambassadors a flat yearly fee of $10,000 (Canadian) for room and board at the palatial Washington embassy, so, all in all, the de Chastelains were well remunerated, to say the least.

A forensic audit of the "hospitality" and "representative" claims submitted by the de Chastelains during their twelve-month ambassadorial tour illustrates their taste for the good life.

In their first two months abroad, MaryAnn de Chastelain submitted no receipts for hairdressing. In March 1993, she submitted but one modest claim for a haircut. However, by December 1993, she was spending $45 (U.S.) every three days at the hair salon and billing it to the Canadian taxpayers (a total of ninety-one visits in ten short months). In one shopping trip, MaryAnn paid more than $1,000 (U.S.) for a pair of shoes and a handbag. The bill was submitted as a representational clothing expense.

His excellency, the ambassador, discovered a taste for $2,000 custom-designed suits and a thirst for imported wine at $286 a bottle (stocked at the embassy courtesy of the Canadian public). Even John's socks, handkerchiefs and underwear were charged to the federal government as representational clothing items.

Despite living high off the hog, the de Chastelains were not seen to be effective in their new role. The social circuit in Washington is a unique and cliquish world into which the ex-soldier was not welcomed. John and MaryAnn invited many former military acquaintances to visit the embassy and attend various functions, and the two cultures did not blend well.

When the Tories were eliminated in the October '93 election, and Jean Chrétien's Liberals flooded back into power, de Chastelain's days as ambassador were numbered. The Washington posting is considered to be the crown jewel of foreign affairs assignments. It is a high-profile and important office, and the incumbent must, at the very least, be seen to be effective. In being parachuted directly into this post by his friend Mulroney, de Chastelain had invoked the ire of many senior foreign affairs officials who felt he'd jumped to the head of a long queue. Jean Chrétien's nephew Raymond, a career diplomat, was one of those who had been in line for the job, but under the Tories had been shuffled off to the less glamorous embassy in Belgium instead. In order to send his nephew to Washington, first Prime Minister Chrétien had to make the position vacant.

In November 1994, John de Chastelain flew to Ottawa and had lunch at the Ichos Restaurant with his former boss, Robert Ramsay Fowler. At this meeting, Fowler informed de Chastelain of the government's intention to remove Admiral John Anderson, the new CDS, because of his inability to manage the mounting Somalia affair. De Chastelain knew about the need to remove him gracefully from Washington, so he negotiated his terms with Fowler from a relative position of strength. This was despite the fact that such a resurrection was unprecedented; de Chastelain, at fifty-seven, was beyond mandatory retirement age; and there was bound to be a wave of resentment throughout the high command. The deal was closed following that luncheon, and it was agreed that de Chastelain would be "reactivated" from the supplementary reserve (rather than having to re-enrol), and his salary would be increased to $170,000.

Former Liberal defence minister Jean-Jacques Blais learned of this development from Fowler's office, and he indirectly contacted *Frank* with the startling news. When the story appeared in their November 21 issue, Admiral Anderson questioned the allegations. Bob Fowler quickly reassured him. Several days later, Anderson was told the truth, and the media were informed that he was simply being "reassigned" to a job at NATO headquarters, not terminated to make room for de Chastelain's return.

Although Anderson did in fact move to Belgium, he went there as a civilian, not a soldier.

The start of General de Chastelain's second incarnation as CDS began in a remarkably similar way to that of the first tour, only this time around he showed a blatant contempt for public service regulations. His old friend Bill Baxter was still publishing *Canadian Defence Quarterly*, but during de Chastelain's absence, the magazine's twenty-year contract with DND had been terminated. There was another scheme afoot, however, and this time they had the unwitting assistance of none other than Jean Chrétien's office. During the 1993 elections, the Liberals had made a campaign promise in Nova Scotia that, if elected, they would reverse the Tory government's decision to close the Canadian Forces Recruit School at Canadian Forces Base Cornwallis in Deep Brook.

After the Liberal candidate won the riding and the party was in power, the reality of implementing their election promise took on a whole new perspective. With a drastically downsizing military, there was no substantive reason to keep CFB Cornwallis functioning as a recruit school: the modern facility at CFB St. Jean, Quebec, was more than capable of handling the present workload.

For two years, Alex Morrison, the executive director of the Canadian Institute of Strategic Studies, had been trying to sell the idea of establishing a "peacekeepers college" in his home town of Sydney, Nova Scotia. Following the election, Bill Baxter, a long-standing Liberal "friend," approached his old associate Alex Morrison with a proposal. (Morrison was a former editor of *CDQ*.) The plan was for Baxter Publishing to become a "founding member" of the peacekeeping college and for the proposed venue to change to Cornwallis.

To Chrétien's advisers, it mattered little that no one inside DND could define a logical need or role for such a privately run peacekeeping college. The existence of Morrison and Baxter's proposal offered what they required: a political solution.

In February 1994, John de Chastelain's twenty-seven-year-old son, Duncan, was named by Morrison to sit on the peacekeeping college's board of directors. Board members do not receive a salary but are paid a per-diem allowance. Duncan had spent a summer in the militia and had just been called to the bar by the Law Society of Upper Canada two weeks earlier. Although Jean-Jacques Blais, now a senior partner in a law firm, was chairman of the new board, Duncan de Chastelain was apparently chosen to provide the college with legal expertise.

Four days after Duncan was named a director, the fledgling peacekeeping college received a huge financial shot in the arm. In the 1994 budget, the Liberal government announced they would provide this "independent" venture with $10 million in start-up money, CFB Cornwallis would be leased to Morrison for a dollar a year and the college would continue to receive $1 million annually in perpetuity.

One of the first things established at the Lester B. Pearson Canadian International Peacekeeping Training Centre was a publishing arm called the Canadian Peacekeeping Press. In addition to other titles, this new enterprise took over the publishing of *CDQ*, and within one year Alex Morrison was the editor again.

In October that year, following the college's first board meeting in Nova Scotia, young Duncan used his "legal skills" by enlisting the aid of his father to invite Defence Minister David Collenette to the college's November opening ceremonies. The Baxter–de Chastelain loop was complete.

This time when de Chastelain moved to Ottawa, he knew that the little bungalow on Noel Street no longer suited his lifestyle needs. While he had retained possession of the property throughout his posting to Washington, he had no intention of ever moving back into the New Edinburgh district.

Although his situation was unique in that he was being repatriated from an External Affairs overseas tour and simultaneously reactivated as a full-time reservist, under neither department's regulations did he qualify for a house-hunting trip or a hotel stay during the transfer. Because the de Chastelains already owned a house in the capital, the taxpayers were responsible only for moving them from Washington to Ottawa. Even if the de Chastelains had qualified for an "interim lodging allowance," the maximum allowable hotel stay would have been twenty-one days at a maximum cost of $75 per night. These moving rates and regulations are standard throughout the public service, regardless of rank or executive privilege. Nevertheless, de Chastelain used his authority to submit a claim for thirty-eight days' worth of commercial lodging at $145.60 a day. During this period, the de Chastelains purchased a ritzy home in the prestigious Rockcliffe Park district for the sum of $450,000.

While living in the hotel and arranging their upcoming move to Rockcliffe, the de Chastelains spent three weekends with MaryAnn's parents in Kingston, Ontario. Although de Chastelain was already claiming for lodging in Ottawa, he submitted additional claims for these weekend junkets. When they stayed overnight at his in-laws' home, de Chastelain still filed a claim for the lower government rate of $12 a night, plus his meal allowances and the $6-a-day incidentals. The major who processed these claims never questioned how even a general could stay in two hotels at once, or eat two sets of meals in the same day (after all, the government was paying the tab).

Once the de Chastelains were established in their new home, they continued to submit allegedly improper claims for unauthorized personal services. As an ambassador's wife, Mrs. de Chastelain had been provided with a full-time domestic helper and cook. Making the adjustment back to military life included cleaning her own house again, but the transition was apparently not that easy to make.

From February to November 1994, the de Chastelains were in possession of both the Noel Street bungalow, which was up for sale, and their new spread on Acacia Boulevard.

During that period, every seven days, General de Chastelain submitted a claim for domestic cleaning services, the amounts ranging between $50 and $150. The only time that the CDS could claim for such a service was for clean-up related to an official function which he had hosted in his home. The records show that not only did the de Chastelains *not* host weekly authorized functions, but on many of the dates for which cleaning was claimed, both John and MaryAnn were out of the country.

The maid, Judy Gnam, admitted that, during this ten-month period, she cleaned both of their properties on a weekly basis. On November 26, 1994, as a result of the Noel Street house being sold, de Chastelain's mortgage burden was reduced and the cleaning claims ceased.

In February, when they purchased the Rockcliffe residence, the de Chastelains had taken out a $201,000 mortgage on the Noel Street house to place a $201,000 down-payment on their new home. So, for the duration of his ten-month dual ownership, John de Chastelain was carrying a mortgage of $400,000 on an (after taxes) income of $175,000. Throughout this period, the CDS travelled frequently, often accompanied by his spouse. Their submission of petty, incidental claims indicate just how tight things were at the de Chastelain household while they carried the massive overhead of the two mortgages.

On four separate occasions, John de Chastelain indented for $4 per diems after completing expenses-paid government trips to Winnipeg, Montreal, Halifax and Washington. In June 1994, he was picked up at NDHQ at 10:00 a.m. by his driver to catch a 10:30 flight from the Ottawa airport. He flew on a commercial flight to Toronto, where he was met by a staff car and driver from the Land Forces Central Area Headquarters. From Toronto airport, he was driven to the officers' mess at CFB Downsview for a luncheon. He was the guest of honour at this function and was given a token gift in honour of his visit. By 2:00 p.m. he was back at Toronto airport, and by 3:15 p.m. he was back behind his desk at NDHQ in Ottawa, writing up a claim to the Crown for a $4 incidental per diem. (The administration cost alone to process a claim is budgeted at $18.50 per submission.)

During a three-day stay in London, England, de Chastelain submitted a hotel bill for $2,700, or $900 a night. He claimed his and his wife's meal allowances, and even the $4 incidental per diems for the trip. John also submitted an additional $0.40 receipt for a newspaper he bought at Heathrow airport.

On the outside, John de Chastelain always tried to portray himself as a traditionalist, and he was relatively convincing in this role. He carried himself with a soldierly bearing, he still played the bagpipes, he performed Scottish folk dancing and he steeped himself in regimental folklore. The façade which he displayed belied the reality of what he had come to represent: he was the embodiment of the new "me first" generation of officers.

As a student of military history, de Chastelain would have been familiar with the folklore surrounding his own regiment's founder, Hamilton Gault. At the outbreak of the First World War, Gault had used $100,000 of his own family's money to help raise and equip the Princess Patricia's Canadian Light Infantry. Although he himself was wounded three times, including losing a leg, Gault repeatedly returned to "his" regiment, eventually being given command. Even throughout the war, it had been Gault's personal money that kept his PPCLI outfitted with buttons and cap badges. Needless to say, the men of the regiment loved Gault and would have followed him through the gates of hell if that had been his wish.

By the time de Chastelain hung up his holster for good in December 1995, 83 per cent of his soldiers polled in the 1995 Phillips Study had admitted they "no longer had faith in the senior command of the Canadian Armed Forces." In response to the results, de Chastelain stole a line from the Hollywood movie *Crimson Tide*; he flippantly told a colleague, "We're here to defend democracy, not to practise it."

On his second departure, de Chastelain tried to project an image of frugality by forgoing two lavish farewell banquets. Instead, he quietly exited NDHQ, following a lone piper. At the time he was under military police investigation for improperly claiming his maid service in 1994; in

November he had been the subject of ridicule in the press for his expenses while ambassador to the United States; and he had yet to appear before the Somalia inquiry for his planning role in that operation. In the summer of 1996, de Chastelain made partial restitution for claiming his maid service.

Despite the image-damaging cloud under which he departed, de Chastelain had made sure that he would be well provided for upon retirement. When he had been recalled from Washington, Bob Fowler had negotiated the order-in-council terms of his reinstatement. Although on the surface de Chastelain received only a $30,000 a year raise to $170,000, the real benefit was the provision of *two* additional pensions. De Chastelain had already qualified for a full military pension, which totalled a respectable $84,000 (fully indexed). With the addition of his second "special" pension, and by his qualifying for the unpublicized "deputy minister's annuity," de Chastelain's retirement pay was increased by $46,000, to a staggering $140,000 annually (all fully indexed).

Plus, in seven years, when John de Chastelain actually reaches the national retirement age of sixty-five, he will add his Canadian Pension Plan benefits to this total.

Prior to terminating his duties as CDS, General de Chastelain had already been appointed as Canada's representative on the Irish peace initiative. As a member of this committee, he receives a federal per diem, and all travel and other expenses are publicly reimbursed. This remuneration is in addition to his three government pension cheques.

So, John de Chastelain took his leave. Prince John's two tours of duty were turbulent and controversial. By personal example, he had altered the public's perception of the Canadian military high command from one of dutiful service to one of career opportunities where greed, pettiness, self-promotion and self-preservation flourished.

Yet, as late as May 1995, the former chief of the defence staff denied any command crisis existed. Instead, he blamed the media for having strung together "a series of unrelated problems," thereby creating the "false" impression of confusion, corruption and careerism in the Forces.

The facts, however, do not bear him out.

CHAPTER FOUR

The Generals:
There's No Life Like It

In a military society, more so than any other subculture, a leader is judged by the example he sets, and it is his professional standard that establishes the mark to which his followers must aspire. Most Canadian military bases, and the communities surrounding them, are rather small and isolated. Their "fishbowl" environment, where co-workers are also neighbours and social companions, makes incredible demands upon the life of commanders. Unlike most civilian executives, they are unable to escape their work façade and relax into a separate private life. Commanders' residences are located right in the middle of the personnel married quarters, and it is a safe assumption that all activity at these homes is the subject of speculation and gossip throughout the community. Everything from viewing new furniture purchases to overhearing domestic disputes is enough to spark rumours of "kickbacks" and "divorce."

Unfortunately, in such a strict hierarchical society, the role model for personal conduct is one rung above you on the rank ladder. So, if the top-ranking soldier shows not only a blatant disregard for obeying regulations, but also a flagrant contempt for the negative impact such actions will have on his troops' morale, then the standard has been set for a moral melt-down. While it would be wrong to claim that *all* Canadian generals who served in this era were cast in the same mould, the majority could easily be labelled as self-serving careerists.

The "privileges of rank" which exist in any military have been expanding in Canada for decades, and the abuse of federal assets for personal pleasure had become so institutionalized that it was considered a tradition. Newly promoted generals were made to feel that they were now a breed apart, even from the other officers, and they were certainly on a different social plane. There is actually a distinctly separate commission that generals receive upon attaining their rank, as they pledge a second allegiance to the chief of the defence staff. (An officer cadet or an enlisted recruit swears loyalty to the Queen.)

In Ottawa, where the majority of Canada's one hundred plus serving generals are stationed, they have a separate social mess. Although this is physically located inside the army officers' mess, the distinction is clearly made between the ranks, and all functions are held separately. The only exceptions are occasions where a general is hosted as a guest of honour by his branch or corps, in which case it would be a tremendous *faux pas* for his hosts to pose potentially embarrassing questions, or even engage in small talk.

Traditionally, all military messes provide the opportunity for commanders to hear the concerns of their charges and assess their morale through relatively informal functions. Alcohol is the great equalizer when it comes to a young subaltern summoning up the courage to let off some steam with his company commander. These often heated exchanges are known as "chest-poking sessions" and inevitably the higher-ranking individual wins the debate. However, in the cold-sober light of day, the issue will normally be reviewed by a good commander and positive reforms may result.

By removing themselves from even the possibility of having to be confronted with honest, informal (possibly insubordinate) criticism, the general officer corps collectively lost touch with their rank and file.

Given that the military system has very few official means of self-correction or restraining authority, the creation of a separate and unassailable social class made a significant contribution to the onset of ethical decay.

One of the most illuminating examples of how total authority, without any inherent checks and balances, invited abuse is the self-controlled commander's grants. These tax-free, receipt-free stipends were issued on an annual basis from the Canadian Forces Central Fund, a non-public fund created from the profits of the CANEX (the military's exchange stores, which have a monopoly on all Canadian Forces bases). Since the Central Fund's revenue comes from soldiers' purchases (groceries, gas, etc.), the idea was to redirect the money back into the military communities in the form of such things as recreational facilities.

In 1995, the fund reported cash assets of $96 million, so the scale of this virtually unaudited fund was not inconsiderable. The "board of directors," who determine how to spend this money in the best interests of Canadian military personnel, consists of the vice-chief of the defence staff (chairman), the assistant deputy minister (personnel) and the three commanders of the service branches (air, maritime and land forces). In recognition of their own "representational expenses," the board authorized that an annual $60,000 be distributed as what they called "commander's grants." The amounts differed according to theoretical obligations, and other individuals, such as the CDS, were included in the handouts to keep everyone of import onside and in agreement with the scheme.

Although all of these officers could claim a virtually unlimited amount of official entertainment funds from the public purse, such reimbursements required authorization and the submission of receipts. The commander's grants were issued by the same individuals who received them and the recipients were accountable only to themselves. Army commander Lieutenant-General Gordon Reay received two such allowances while he was the commander of the army in St. Hubert, Quebec. The total amount of the money he received was $25,200, but after six months of delays following an access-to-information request, General Reay could only account for having hosted *two* social functions during his twenty-four-month command. One was a Christmas cocktail party in his residence (three guests present) and the other was a midsummer barbecue (a total of six friends in attendance).

General John de Chastelain was granted $7,000 in each of the five years he served as CDS, and for the $35,000 he received in money taken from his soldiers, no records released under access-to-information requests indicate any related expenditures.

In 1994, the generals were informed by Revenue Canada that, from then onwards, government staff cars and military drivers were to be considered a taxable benefit. The commander's grants, as non-public funds issued on an honorarium basis for work-related activities, were still tax exempt. While soldiers and public servants at DND had their pay frozen from 1992 to 1996, the commander's grants were fully indexed at 2.6 per cent growth (to cover the cost of inflation).

In his 1994 report on the state of military morale, Colonel Robert Meating made the suggestion that the $96 million in the Central Fund should be reduced substantially by issuing cash-strapped soldiers with small "grants" to offset their frozen pay and increased housing costs. He also suggested that many of the fund's existing service member loans be converted to grants and written off.

Under the existing system, hard-pressed soldiers can plead their case with their commanding officer. If it is felt circumstances warrant it, the service member can qualify for a low-interest (once-in-a-career) *loan* of up to $5,000.

Needless to say, Meating's report went up the chain of command, but at the 1995 Central Fund board of directors meeting, it was unanimously decided to reject grants. However, the directors did approve an increase in the representational allowance granted to the Canadian military's NATO representative in Belgium.

This "Elite Club" mentality of the general officer corps did not spring up overnight but grew over a period of thirty years. In the early sixties, Canadian Air Force generals began a tradition of hosting several of their American counterparts on summer fishing trips in Labrador. By the time these excursions were cancelled (due to media awareness) in 1994, they had ballooned into a massive annual operation.

The "camps" catered to six guests at a time, three Canadian and three American, and they were attended to by a service support staff of thirty-six military personnel (not including the air crew). Each summer, from June through August, a total of ten weekend camps would be held under the code name "Eagle River."

The hard costs of these junkets had escalated by 1992 to a mind-numbing $960,000 and involved fixed-wing aircraft, helicopters and river boats. The American generals would fly to Ottawa on a Friday afternoon, where they would be wined and dined at the officers' mess and would meet their Canadian "fishing buddies." After dinner, the six Eagle River guests would board a Cosmopolitan jet and be flown directly to CFB Goose Bay. From there, Labrador or Twin Huey helicopters transported them into the wilderness camp on the Labrador coast. Awaiting the weary travellers would be cocktails served by the six camp stewards and snacks prepared by the three chefs. Once the fishing got under way, any catches would be immediately rushed back upstream by motor launch and flown by helicopter back to Goose Bay. There the fish would be flash frozen and boxed in a wooden case complete with an engraved plaque bearing the fisherman's name. Back at the camp, the generals dined in style, with white tablecloths and an array of china and crystal, and made their dinner selections from daily *printed* menus.

It was a northern safari that no one could have afforded without having access to the unlimited Defence Department resources. The per-capita cost to entertain each American general on a three-day fishing trip amounts to $32,000, or $10,700 per man, per day.

Deputy Minister Robert Fowler was often a guest at Eagle River, and each year he took a personal interest in the planning stages. It was Fowler who would decide which Canadian general hosted which American guest at each of the camps.

The existence of an extravagant fishing lodge was a well-circulated rumour among the Forces for the thirty years of its existence, but very few people, outside of guests and hosts, had any real proof of Eagle River's scope.

In the early 1970s, a new Labrador helicopter crashed into a tree stump while ferrying fresh fish from the camp. There was little media interest at the time because the multimillion-dollar accident hadn't claimed any lives and was reported as a routine training flight.

In 1992, the *Globe and Mail* published an exposé on Eagle River, but the article was conservative in its cost estimates, and the most damaging information was not released following the access-to-information request. Nevertheless, Bob Fowler knew that any additional media coverage could be potentially damaging politically, so he ordered the 1993 camp aborted.

When de Chastelain returned as CDS in 1994, it was felt that the media interest had waned sufficiently that Eagle River could safely be resurrected. The warning orders went out in January for various units to provide the required support staff (cooks, boatmen, stewards), but by February, Eagle River was history.

What happened? The media had gotten hold of the planning papers for "Operation Palm Tree." This was a golf junket held every year in Florida by the U.S. Air Force in reciprocation for the Canadian Eagle River camps.

Like the fishing expeditions, Operation Palm Tree had developed into an ever-escalating "tradition" over the span of four decades. The documents obtained by the media under access-to-information legislation showed that, in 1992 and 1993, Canadian taxpayers spent a total of $68,000 in commercial airfare to send nineteen of our air force generals to Florida. The destination was Eglin Air Force Base, located on Florida's northern panhandle, an area known as the "Redneck Riviera." The planning agendas for Palm Tree outlined a single two-and-a-half-hour training seminar as justification for the three-day outing. The rest of the schedule was booked with golf tournaments, deep-sea fishing, free time and a gala awards-night banquet to honour the top golfer.

When the story first broke, DND spokesmen tried to play up the importance of air force generals from different countries knowing their counterparts on a social basis. However, an unrelated report of navy sailors in Victoria having to live on welfare and use food banks hit papers the next day. Editors were quick to make the linkage. General John de Chastelain himself made a quick announcement that the upcoming Palm Tree would be cancelled, and Defence Minister David Collenette reversed his earlier position and denounced the golf trips as "not in keeping with the department's policy of fiscal restraint."

As with so many other Defence Department press announcements, the hard line taken by de Chastelain was strictly posturing for the cameras. He had certainly known about Palm Tree since his arrival in Ottawa in 1982, and as CDS from 1989 to 1993, he had four opportunities to shut down these tax-funded soirées. Instead, they had increased in both attendance and cost as a direct result of de Chastelain making commercial air travel restrictions more lenient for senior commanders on January 2, 1990. In an official directive, he had even given his top brass (including himself) the heretofore unauthorized privilege of booking their spouses on commercial air flights, at federal expense.

De Chastelain's contradictory public statements on Palm Tree were noted by his commanders as another example of their CDS's political skills, but in a world where leadership is by example, the abuse of travel benefits was destined to persist.

In May 1995, a Defence Department insider tipped off the media that an air force airbus was scheduled to fly to Australia for the ostensible purpose of appearing as a static display in the Sydney Airshow. The *Toronto Sun* and Global Television had confirmed the rumour through the Australian High Commission without alerting DND to the fact that they were onto the story.

The 150 passengers on the aircraft manifest for the seven-day trip included generals, senior bureaucrats and their spouses. Even Reform Party Defence critic Jim Hart had been briefed on the imminent junket, and he was prepared to raise the issue in Question Period immediately after the air-bus left CFB Trenton.

Unfortunately for the generals and bureaucrats who had their bags packed and visas stamped, the flight was cancelled four hours before its take-off time. Editors at the *Toronto Sun* had wanted to scoop Global TV, and since the airbus was due to leave on a Saturday, they had their reporter contact DND Public Affairs on Friday afternoon.

No official comment was made at that time, but within NDHQ the wheels began to spin. By 10:00 a.m. Saturday, it was announced that the flight had been cancelled due to a "shortage of collateral airlift." In other words, its cargo could not be justified against the expenditure of nearly $500,000 in flight costs and crew expenses. Robert Benzie, the *Sun* reporter who had made the original request to DND, essentially saved taxpayers $500,000 with a $0.25 phone call. But, because there was no media cover-age, nobody was reprimanded for "attempting to abuse" federal resources.

Such a flight would have been approved by no less than the commander of Air Command, and it would have been scheduled at least three months earlier at the Quarterly Airlift Planning Session.

Undaunted by this near-scandal, senior commanders booked a similar airbus flight in the Air Force Airlift Plan for the next quarter. In mid-August, a Canadian Forces flight left Winnipeg for New Zealand with 160 passengers and crew on board. The airbus touched down in Honolulu to deplane 150 officers and bureaucrats, and then it proceeded on to New Zealand. The justification given for this half-a-million-dollar flight was the repatriation of three Canadian exchange officers along with their families, and the opportunity for the airbus aircrew to gain "experience in long over-ocean flights."

Air Force personnel in Winnipeg leaked the details of this flight, includ-ing the names of the senior officers who were to spend a week in Honolulu, to the *Winnipeg Free Press* newspaper. The story soon got picked up nation-ally and received fairly broad coverage, especially once it became known that the Air Force had cancelled a similar flight in May due to media scrutiny.

This time the Air Force was forced to take action, but not by holding responsible the commander of Air Command, Lieutenant-General Al DeQuetteville; instead, it was *his* decision to cancel all future "priority five" bookings for service personnel. Priority-five travel has been used by junior-ranking soldiers for decades as a means of travelling home when on leave. This arrangement allowed scheduled military flights that were not fully booked with "duty" passengers to offer the remaining seats on a last-minute, stand-by basis to passengers preregistered as priority fives. Soldiers on leave who used this risky system had to be prepared to pay full-fare, one-way commercial rates if no seats were available for them to return to their units on time.

The punishment was aimed at the junior ranks and the message was clear: if you blow the whistle to the media about high-level perks, we will strip *you* of whatever privileges you might have available to you.

General DeQuetteville and the rest of the general officer corps were, of course, entirely unaffected by the priority-five cancellation, because they were still fully empowered by John de Chastelain to fly on commercial air-lines (and to bring their spouses if authorized).

In April 1996, Al DeQuetteville demonstrated this double standard when he spent more than $300,000 on a weekend jaunt to Goose Bay, Newfoundland. Documents released under access-to-information requests reveal that the commander of Air Command sent a three-hundred-seat Canadian Forces airbus en route to the Labrador base, a cross-country tour to pick up sixty-five honorary guests, mostly retired Air Force generals, at various ports of call. To make their own way to Goose Bay, DeQuetteville's three-man entourage commandeered a Dash-8 passenger plane at an addi-tional cost of approximately $76,000. In addition, their tab for a single dinner at the exclusive Goose Bay officers' mess totalled more than $5,000.

This three-day junket was officially described by DND public relations officers as "a good opportunity for Airborne generals to get direct input from the Canadian public." However, this explanation defied logic, given that more than half of the invited guests were either serving or retired gen-erals, and the venue was an isolated air base.

One of the Canadian Forces' most prolific travellers was Army Commander Gordon Reay. Naturally, one would expect a general to visit his troops in the field, and during Reay's tenure as top soldier from January 1993 to August 1995, Canadian soldiers were deployed on a vast array of operational missions. Although Reay did make two trips to visit the troops in Yugoslavia and a single junket to the contingent in Rwanda, a review of his travel claims illustrates a very unsoldierly taste for "diplomatic" excur-sions. Often accompanied by his wife, Lesley, Lieutenant-General Reay made dozens of exotic trips, which could, at best, be described as marginal in their justification of public expenditures.

Just weeks after assuming command of the Army in mid-February 1993, Reay accompanied Deputy Minister Bob Fowler, Brigadier-General Ernest Beno and Admiral Peter Cairns to Belet Uen, Somalia. During their ten-day visit, only three days were spent in East Africa; the remaining seven days were put to good use in Kenya and Amsterdam, well away from the troops. Even so, this power quartet of senior managers failed to observe any signs of the Airborne Regiment's impending troubles, just days before the first murder of Somalia looters.

In fact, by the time NDHQ got word of the first shootings (March 5), General Reay was in Atlanta, Georgia, for a week attending a "conference" with his American colleagues. That May, despite the mounting crisis surrounding the Airborne in Somalia, Reay and his wife spent a week in Germany at taxpayers' expense. While Gordon took in the scheduled lectures, Lesley entertained the wives of various other military officials. In September, the Reays enjoyed a week in London. By October, Reay was back in Germany for another week of "conferences"—this time without his spouse. The list of travel claims submitted by the Army Commander show that he would "jet set" to Europe every couple of months, but more curious were the annual two-week trips to South America "on military business."

After the December 1991 budget cuts, it was announced that Canadian troops would no longer be stationed in Germany; yet along with the downsizing of our NATO commitment had come a concurrent increase in the need for UN peacekeepers, and Canadian politicians heeded the call. In November 1992, Defence Minister Marcel Masse and John de Chastelain had gone to the House of Commons Committee on Defence to report that our tiny army was overstretched on international deployments and would suffer a complete collapse within a year. The last thing it could contemplate at that juncture was new alliances or military commitments. However, in mid-November 1993, at the precise moment that Masse was claiming the Army would be "spent" through overtasking, General Reay was departing for Brazil. The justification was a "conference" with his South American counterparts, which included a weekend in Rio de Janeiro before flying home to a wintry Canada.

From a military perspective, there was no rationale for Reay's Brazilian visit, as even our country's membership in the Organization of American States is strictly for diplomatic purposes. (Canada was the only member state that did not take part militarily in the 1983 invasion of Grenada.)

While the taxpayers were footing the bills for airfare, meals, hotels and incidentals, the Army Commander decided to use $4,239 of non-public money from the Central Fund to buy gifts for his new South American contacts. Captain D.A. Neill, Reay's executive assistant, soon found himself browsing the expensive "Canadiana" tourist boutiques on Ottawa's Sparks Street Mall with his wallet full of money—money collected from service members for use in the military community. It is safe to presume that the General received reciprocal "tokens" of goodwill in exchange. These South American souvenirs would have become Reay's "personal" property.

One year later, the Somalia scandal had erupted, resulting in a public inquiry, and the government had announced additional budget cuts, including the cancellation of the EH-101 helicopters. Despite the domestic crises, plummeting troop morale and the downsizing of our army's peacekeeping contribution to Yugoslavia, General Reay headed back down to South America. This time it was to be an eleven-day, four-country affair during which Reay was to meet with the various Canadian ambassadors and his Latin American counterparts. Mrs. Reay did not accompany her husband on this trip, but Captain Neill did go along to assist with the bags.

In isolation, this exotic junket would only be a flagrant abuse of public funds and a serious misapplication of the privileges afforded to the General's rank. However, given what was happening in Canada at that time, it would also be viewed by the troops as neglect of his duty on the part of Reay.

Following the Liberal government's November 1994 announcement that a public inquiry would be held into the Airborne Regiment's ill-fated deployment to Somalia, General Reay had immediately flown by helicopter to CFB Petawawa. There he assembled the demoralized paratroopers and told them to maintain their discipline throughout the inquiry, and not to fear its outcome. In true Hollywood fashion, the diminutive Reay boldly told the grim soldiers, "If anybody wants to get at you [the Regiment], they'll have to go through me first."

But in January 1995, when the "Somalia" video showing Canadian paratroopers vowing "to kill niggers" was aired on national television, followed three days later by a second video showing disgusting hazing rituals of troopers eating faeces, the Army Commander was not available to the public. He didn't defend the men he had promised he would put his career on the line for. He was busy planning his next trip to South America for the ostensible purpose of wining and dining with ambassadors.

General Reay was certainly not the only senior officer to take advantage of his position at Defence Department (taxpayer) expense.

Documents show that in June 1994 Vice-Admiral Larry Murray visited our peacekeepers in Rwanda. Out of a six-day trip, he spent four days at the plush Safari Club Hotel in Nairobi, Kenya. Murray's actual visit to the "front lines" was a mere twenty-three-hour snapshot. The cost of this whirlwind morale-boosting, fact-finding mission was more than $5,500, including airfare, meals and lodging at the Safari Club.

The previous spring, Admiral Murray had toured Southeast Asia on a similar foray. That time the justification was to inspect the Canadian troops on UN duties in Cambodia. One of seven days was spent talking to the peacekeepers, but the remainder of Murray's itinerary had him visiting Kuala Lumpur, Tokyo and Bangkok. Again, the cost, including business-class air travel, would have exceeded $5,000.

In September 1992, Rear-Admiral Bruce Johnston and his wife flew to Mexico City. The justification for this naval officer to fly to the landlocked mountain capital of Mexico was to celebrate the 82nd anniversary of Mexican independence. Not including airfare, the meals and lodgings for the Johnstons' sojourn cost taxpayers $2,785.38.

In December of the same year, Vice-Admiral Peter Cairns was also junketing abroad. One would have to question the rationale for the commander of Canada's Navy making a week-long trip to Riyadh, Saudi Arabia— especially when the official purpose was for "liaison." The Gulf War had been over for nearly two years, and all Canadian service members had long since left the region, including the crew of Canada's single frigate contribution to the coalition forces' extended naval embargo against Iraq. However, Cairns's trip to Saudi Arabia did coincide with the attempt by Saint John Shipbuilding, the Canadian yard that is building our new patrol frigates, to sell their design to the expanding postwar Saudi Arabian navy.

In February 1993, Cairns was once again a sailor out in the desert, this time visiting the Airborne soldiers patrolling the dusty, hot streets of Belet Uen. (He accompanied Deputy Minister Fowler, General Reay and Brigadier Beno.)

Two and a half months later, this vitally important senior naval commander took his wife on a three-week tour of Russia and England to commemorate the "Fiftieth Anniversary of the Battle of the Atlantic." The Cairnses' meal-and-lodging claim for this twenty-day social outing came to $4,278, which, when totalled with the airfare (approximately $3,500) and the salaried time for the Admiral ($7,500), brings the tax-funded total to well over $15,000.

Barely four months later, the Admiral and his spouse spent two weeks "visiting Swedish naval facilities." The trip, according to DND policy, must have been approved by Chief of the Defence Staff (and long-time colleague) Admiral John Anderson, despite the fact that Sweden is not a member of NATO, and thus Cairns had no operational rationale for the trip.

Seemingly collectively spoiled by their unlimited (or unchecked) access to travel funds, the senior command of the Defence Department has become seduced by the lure of no-cost high living, and it has entered their operational doctrine.

Several times each year they conduct what are known as "senior management symposiums" at exclusive hotels in the Ottawa area. The attendees at these mini-conferences are the entire twenty appointees who comprise the upper tier of the Defence Department's power pyramid. The defence minister usually puts in a brief appearance, and then the deputy minister and his top military and civilian managers discuss the details. Canadian citizens would probably be shocked to realize that the implementation of the 1994 White Paper on Defence was actually orchestrated at the Sam Jakes Inn in Merrickville, Ontario—not in the secure conference rooms (specially built for that purpose) at National Defence Headquarters.

Although Merrickville is barely a forty-minute drive from the nation's capital, the top managers in DND decided to spend $7,635 to rent a block of nineteen $160-per-night rooms at the cosy inn. In addition to the accommodations, they paid $130 for newspapers to be delivered to their retreat, and each "manager" filed an independent $42.50 per-diem meal claim along with associated travel costs. General John de Chastelain also submitted an entertainment claim of $546, indicating that he generously ran a bar tab for his well-remunerated colleagues during the two-day "conference."

Uniforms are not worn at senior management symposiums for "security reasons," and the other guests at the Sam Jakes Inn would have been completely unaware that these were military officers in their midst, or that they were discussing a $10.8-billion defence budget. They met in a second-storey room usually reserved for wedding receptions.

The rationale given to the media for these quarterly outings is that the top managers need to meet "informally," escape the phone-call interruptions and be able to "burn the midnight oil discussing complex issues."

Unfortunately, most media outlets accepted the cover story, but when Charlie Greenwell, a reporter with CJOH TV in Ottawa, showed up to film the proceedings on December 8, 1994, the military's Special Investigations Unit threw a blanket of security on the conference. Defence Minister Collenette was whisked out a back door into a staff car, while Deputy Minister Fowler and General de Chastelain retreated behind closed hotel doors. As a result of this "security breach," the location of the next symposium was changed to the even more prestigious Château Montebello, again just outside Ottawa (a one-hour drive).

While the generals' abuse of travel privileges may be regarded as an additional factor in the breakdown of the Canadian Forces' senior leadership, what is less publicized and more illustrative of the prevalent greed is the abundance of generals who are living abroad on foreign postings. Theoretically, the huge expense of maintaining these highly ranked officers at embassies negates the necessity of top commanders having to travel the "social circuit." For instance, the Canadian embassy in Moscow has a full-time military attaché, and the High Commission in London has no less than a brigadier-general. Given our Defence Department's limited resources, couldn't these officers have handled the Battle of the Atlantic fiftieth-anniversary celebrations without having to send Admiral Cairns and his wife?

In total, Canada pays twenty senior officers to live overseas on operational and attaché duties. This represents 20 per cent of our general officer corps, and by their accumulated rank authority, they misrepresent our total military strength by some 200 per cent. That is not to say that ten generals of all ranks could effectively command the Canadian Forces, but in terms of actual army brigades, naval flotillas and air divisions, we have twice as many generals posted in foreign countries than we require to command our entire field force.

The number and grade of generals assigned to these positions with the North American Aerospace Defence Command (NORAD), NATO and various embassies was established at the post–Second World War zenith of our armed forces. Even in the mid-fifties, when the Army alone numbered 120,000 and our NORAD commitment entailed scores of aircraft and a fully manned Distant Early Warning (DEW) line, having twenty generals serving abroad was an excessive luxury. Now that our total armed forces consist of 68,000 personnel (and dropping), such a bloated brass-hatted façade is insupportable. Very few soldiers are even aware of how many generals we still have in foreign lands, especially since all our combat troops were pulled out of Europe in 1992. However, no one has targeted these positions for either downscaling or elimination for the simple reason that they've become far too personally lucrative for the incumbents.

Even two-star generals, with the right posting, can make more money in salary and tax-free allowances than the four-star chief of defence staff makes. They're rarely in the public spotlight and they have no troops to command, so there's little chance that they'd have had to exercise all of their leadership skills. Their lives are filled with social functions, and the taxpayer foots the bill. All in all, there's no life like it.

For instance, the position of deputy commander-in-chief at NORAD has been held by a Canadian lieutenant-general since the organization's inception. Canada, as of the 1995 budget, operates a total of only sixty CF-18 fighter aircraft. This means that, even if we were to commit our entire air force to the defence of North America, it could easily be commanded in battle by just a colonel. Nevertheless, we foot the bill for a three-star general to represent our resources to our U.S. allies. Not only do we pay this officer $128,900 a year in salary, but he lives *rent-free* in a Canadian government (5,300-square-foot) residence in Colorado Springs, Colorado. On top of that, he receives $10,716 in foreign allowances, a sizeable clothing stipend and a $20,305 entertainment allowance.

The 1996 incumbent, Lieutenant-General Lou Cuppens, is not bilingual, so he also receives a $9,139.20 "education" allowance for private French tutoring. A car and driver are also provided at public expense. Despite the overwhelming abundance of tax-funded perks already at his disposal, the board of directors at the Canadian Forces Central Fund still feel he should be entitled to a "small" commander's grant. Every year an additional $5,000 of non-public, tax-free, receipt-free money is directed to this appointment.

Also stationed at this same headquarters are a major-general and a brigadier-general. Both of them receive the same foreign allowance, free accommodation, staff car and French-tutoring subsidy as the lieutenant-general. Their government-provided entertainment allowance is substantially reduced, however, as each receives only a meagre $1,425 for his annual hospitality.

Yet another Canadian Air Force general performs his duties in the harsher climes of Alaska. To offset any hardship he might endure, his (free) accommodation entitlement is a sizeable 4,000 square feet.

A fifth Canadian senior officer resides in Florida and operates as the NORAD deputy regional commander. He is entitled to $4,000 a year in entertainment, a staff car, foreign allowance ($12,000), free rent and French tutoring.

The entire Canadian Navy consists of sixteen fighting ships and three obsolete submarines. While the destroyers are divided into two squadrons, one for each coast, by international standards both of these flotillas are somewhat understrength. Notwithstanding our lack of combat capabilities, Canada foots the bill for a commodore (one star), a rear-admiral (two star), and even a vice-admiral (three star), just to *represent* our limited naval assets to allied nations.

To put this in the proper perspective, during the Gulf War, the U.S. 7th Fleet was commanded by only a vice-admiral (three star). The naval combat capability directly under his control amounted to 108 ships, including 5 aircraft-carrier battle groups, 2 battleships and 13 submarines.

The same sort of deceptive over-representation exists for our diminutive and thinly stretched ground forces. In total, the Canadian Army has three undersized brigades on its order of battle. However, even the 1994 defence budget review noted that Canada, given its present resources, could maintain a maximum operational deployment of only some two thousand troops. In the U.S. Army, this size of unit would be a regimental battle group and would be commanded by no higher rank than a colonel. Yet, working with the UN, NATO and various embassies, the Canadian Army has a lieutenant-general, three major-generals and five brigadiers.

All of these foreign postings entitle the incumbents to live in grandiose residences, free of charge or for a token charge, and normally provide them with unseemly public "expense" accounts.

The military attaché to Great Britain resides rent free in a Canadian government four-bedroom house valued at $1 million in 1970. His hospitality allowance, the largest of those for generals posted abroad, is $63,000 annually.

The brigadier-general posted to Paris lives without charge in a 2,700-square-foot downtown apartment, with a market value of $2.1 million (Canadian). He receives $43,800 every year in entertainment funds (but he must share this sum with three other officers).

At the NATO Defence College in Rome, the Canadian lieutenant-general is provided with a free apartment—$4,000 Canadian a month—a tax-free foreign service allowance of $37,332, a $20,000 "expense account," and a personal driver (salary $43,200). When you add a lieutenant-general's $129,000 paycheque to the list, the total cost to Canadian taxpayers for this *single* officer amounts to $280,500.

Yet our country has not even fielded an army formation commensurate with this rank since the Second World War.

Unfortunately for taxpayers, the military brass have used their unchecked authority over the years to improve their personal circumstances, regardless of where they are stationed. The most publicized case of this sort of systemic abuse would have to be that of Rear-Admiral Barry Keeler.

This officer is the chief of financial services within the Department of National Defence and, as such, could be regarded as the man responsible for the fiscal integrity of the military. In 1990, Keeler was posted to Ottawa to take over this job, but because his family was already well established in Halifax, he asked to be granted an "imposed restriction posting."

Ordinarily, under the terms of a restricted posting, the military provides rations and quarters to the service member (i.e., a barrack room and mess hall), and a small allowance of $4 a day is issued to cover the cost of additional "incidentals." From the time Keeler arrived in Ottawa in 1990, he took up lodging in the comfortable Les Suites Hotel and, as of April 1996, he was still residing there at taxpayers' expense. In six straight years, Admiral Keeler has collected more than $113,000 in tax-free "temporary" lodging benefits. (The average length of a standard military tour is four years, and even the CDS appointment is only a three-year term.)

DND regulations explicitly state that any member granted such a posting must make every possible effort to seek a solution to his "compassionate" restriction. It also stipulates that each case must be reviewed every six months by the granting authority to determine the validity of continuation.

Les Suites Hotel, conveniently located one city block from National Defence Headquarters, is among the three most expensive rental properties in the city. Even a long-term extended one-bedroom lease at this hotel is quoted at $2,200 a month. Keeler was so confident of his impending permanence that he began establishing solid roots at the hotel. Just weeks after taking up residency, he made arrangements with the hotel and Bell Canada to have a private phone line installed in his suite. For the next five years, B. Keeler was actually listed in the Ottawa telephone book as living at 130 Besserer Street (the street address of Les Suites Hotel).

The national media obtained details of Keeler's excessive "separation expenses" and his luxury hotel accommodations in December 1994. At that juncture, there was a fair bit of embarrassing press coverage and the Reform Party's Defence critic, Jack Frazier, raised the issue of Keeler's scandalous circumstances in Parliament.

Defence Minister David Collenette chose to defend the whole affair by deliberately clouding the issue. Instead of addressing the specific case of Admiral Keeler, Collenette simply stood up in the House of Commons and rationalized the existence of all service members' "imposed restriction postings" by saying that the system was established to save the department money. Nearly a year later, in November 1995, when it was discovered that Admiral Keeler still resided at Les Suites (and at public expense), the matter was raised again by a Reform MP. Collenette artfully dodged the question by saying the issue had "already been addressed" (although it was never dealt with).

When the 1996 National Capital phone book appeared with Keeler's number still listed at Les Suites Hotel, the message sent to the NDHQ rank and file was loud and clear: the senior brass would openly defy their own strict regulations with impunity.

In February 1995, yet another mini-scandal involving top generals' lifestyles came to the fore. This time it was the revelation that senior commanders were living in palatial-sized residences and paying virtually no rent. Comparably, the men under their command were being charged more per month for 1,200-square-foot "ghetto" housing.

Access-to-information documents revealed that Navy Commander Vice-Admiral Larry Murray was living in a 5,387-square-foot mansion in a posh Halifax neighbourhood. His monthly deduction for this official lodging was a meagre $619 from his $129,000 annual salary. At the same time, young sailors making just $22,000 a year were reimbursing the government $569 per month to live in their tiny 1950s-vintage quarters.

Documents showed that the top air force general was living in a massive 6,713-square-foot residence and was being charged only $581 in rent. The public affairs officials tried to dampen the media coverage of the rent disparity by describing these official residences as "draughty old buildings." However, few editors were fooled by the ruse, as it was obviously another case of putting self-interest ahead of even the appearance of self-restraint. When a general is paid a salary six times greater than a private receives, and he lives in a government-provided house six times larger than those of his soldiers, it defies reason that he would pay only the same amount for his rent.

In the case of Army Commander Lieutenant-General Gordon Reay, the situation was even more extreme. Although it was noted that the official residence he occupied was only a 3,600-square-foot house and his rent was listed as a modest $959.18, the facts given to the media were misleading. Lieutenant-General Reay actually lived there "rent free" because he had managed to convince CDS John de Chastelain to approve an imposed restricted posting for him. Reay's wife, Lesley, had a career in Ottawa, and they had just purchased a large home in the suburb of Orleans. Rather than quit her job, rent their house and relocate to Montreal, the Reays decided it was better for Gordon to live alone in Montreal and make the two-hour commute home to Ottawa on weekends.

This should have been a personal choice—weighing the value of two incomes against the cost of maintaining two residences. However, thanks to the power of his rank, Reay was granted free room and board plus an incidental allowance for the duration of his tenure. The annual cost to taxpayers for Lieutenant-General Reay's domestic circumstances was approximately $20,000, even at the subsidized rate for the commander's lodgings.

Once again, leadership by example can be applied to the case of Major-General Armand Roy. As the commander of Land Forces, Quebec Area, he answered directly to Lieutenant-General Reay. As discussed earlier, the military world is one without many internal secrets. As such, Roy was well aware that his boss was bending the imposed restriction posting rules and was, therefore, in no moral position to deny others the same privilege. Although Roy's family lived in a village less than a one-hour drive from his downtown Montreal headquarters, he decided he would rather not commute. He applied to Reay for an imposed restriction, and it was approved. At taxpayer's expense, Roy rented an apartment on Sherbrooke Street for $3,000 a month. During his tenure as Quebec's army commander, the total cost to the public coffers exceeded $54,000.

When insiders at Roy's office alerted the auditor general to this situation in June 1995, it was agreed Roy's circumstances were not in accordance with Treasury Board guidelines. A letter to that effect was sent from the auditor general to the military's chief of review services. At this point, Armand Roy was promoted to lieutenant-general and appointed as the deputy chief of the defence staff. (As DCDS, Roy also assumed control of all military police operations.)

As of April 1996, Roy still insisted that all of his dual residency costs were allowable and "above board." He also stated that his accommodation claims had never been investigated, yet the letter from the auditor general would indicate otherwise.

A natural progression from using your authority to avoid having to pay for your own accommodations would be having someone else pick up the cost of your home furnishings.

Once again, Lieutenant-General Gordon Reay set the moral standard for the officers under his command. Because Gordon and his wife, Lesley, already had their home established in Ottawa, the idea of purchasing another full complement of furniture for just a two-year tour would have been unappealing. So to outfit his 3,100-square-foot commander's residence, Reay turned to his base finance officer for some non-public support.

Admittedly, Reay procured only the barest minimum in terms of brand-new living-room and dining-room sets (he utilized two standard-issue barrack bunks for his bed). The fact is, he spent his soldiers' money to obtain these items. Although he was earning in excess of $125,000 a year and living room-and-board free, Gordon Reay dipped into his soldiers' non-public kitty to buy himself a television set and a VCR ($612.47).

With such a role model to follow, it should not have been surprising that similar excesses would occur when Brian Vernon, Reay's deputy commander, was promoted to major-general and sent to take command of Land Forces, Central Area, in Toronto. There was a fair bit of media controversy in December 1994 concerning Vernon's indiscretions involving a $500,000 furniture purchase for his new headquarters. The luxurious officer tower was dubbed "Fort Finch" in the papers, due to its location at Finch and Yonge streets, and the expenditure of such large sums of public money was much decried in editorials at the time.

Major-General Brian Vernon was not entirely blameless in the affair— his wife had been part of the committee assigned to decorate the executive suites—but the media were wrong to latch on to him as the sole culprit. In fact, the Defence Department was probably relieved that the Fort Finch "scandal" was wrongly reported as an isolated incident. Editors failed to compare the cost of outfitting Vernon's four entire office floors with furniture and computers to the similar sum spent by Deputy Minister Robert Fowler in renovating a single office suite at NDHQ.

When the cost of Fowler's office had been raised in the House of Commons, Defence Minister David Collenette had defended the expense as "part of the cost of running a government." Major-General Brian Vernon was not so fortunate. Ironically, it was Lieutenant-General Reay himself who told the press that there was to be a full inquiry launched into the Fort Finch purchases. The implication was that Vernon had exceeded his authority and had done so without higher approval.

Major Ray Deygood had originally been responsible for the overall move of the Land Forces Headquarters from their old location at CFB Downsview to the office complex known as Fort Finch. According to him, 85 per cent of the furniture and office equipment that were purchased were well within the original budget. However, once Vernon's staff became involved in the procurement of the executive furniture, that's when the costs began to escalate.

Lieutenant-Colonel Walter Simianow was Vernon's operations officer, and it was he who took over the moving project from Major Deygood. Subsequent to that, furniture invoices for some "opulent" items turned up at the base finance office. At that juncture, Base Commander Colonel Ed Nurse put a stop order on the payments. He notified not only General Vernon, but also Lieutenant-General Reay and NDHQ, of his actions.

Once the furniture store got wind of the cancelled order, they threatened to sue DND for breach of contract. At this point the brass panicked, fearing the public relations impact of a lawsuit for unpaid (expensive) furnishings, and the vice-chief of the defence staff, Lieutenant-General "Paddy" O'Donnell, ordered Colonel Nurse to pay the bills.

After the story was leaked to military reporter Dale Grant and published in the *Toronto Star*, the brass resorted to their typical tactic of distancing themselves from the issue and ordering one of their own colleagues to conduct an "inquiry."

In this case, the individual chosen to preside over the board of inquiry was none other than Major-General D.R. Williams. The irony of this officer passing judgement on a fellow major-general accused by his own junior officers of financially abusing his authority was that Williams himself had recently been investigated under similar circumstances.

In January 1994, fighter pilots at CFB North Bay had sent Defence Minister David Collenette a registered letter outlining how their commander, Major-General Williams, was using a CF-18 as his personal air taxi. The cost per hour to operate a CF-18 is roughly $7,000, and in the previous twelve months Williams had logged 160 hours "behind the stick." Fighter command headquarters is located in North Bay, but there were no operational CF-18s stationed there. In order to accumulate his flying time, Williams would have a pilot from Bagotville, Quebec, or Cold Lake, Alberta, ferry a plane to him. This officer would then stay in a hotel (at public expense) awaiting Williams's return.

The pilots who wrote to Collenette noted that previous commanders had logged, on average, fifteen to twenty hours of flying in fighters. But these were for training purposes. In Williams's case, the majority of his air time was racked up merely transporting himself to U.S. air bases, air shows and conferences. He could have, and should have, flown by commercial jet.

The estimated cost of Williams's CF-18 sorties was worked out to be approximately $750,000. In order to estimate this figure, the pilots who blew the whistle were still respectful enough of his rank to allow for the twenty hours he should have flown, and they subtracted the maximum commercial airfares from the total for each of his trips. The costs of ferrying the planes to North Bay and the temporary-duty costs of these shuttle pilots were also not included.

Investigators did fly from Ottawa to check out Williams's flying log, and shortly thereafter, he was grounded and replaced as commander of fighter group. There were, however, no charges laid or administrative action taken against him. Instead, he soon found himself making a ruling on the activities of Major-General Vernon. His final report, not surprisingly, noted no action should be taken against any of the officers involved.

Subsequent to conducting the board of inquiry, General D.R. Williams was assigned as Canada's military attaché to the United States. One of Williams's recent predecessors in this embassy job was Brigadier-General Ian Douglas. He, too, had been sent abroad (to represent the Canadian military to our most powerful ally) following a damaging personal scandal. Douglas had been the commander of the Special Service Force at CFB Petawawa from September 1987 to August 1989. During his tenure there, it was alleged that troops, including Douglas himself, were hunting wild game on military lands, not just illegally but in a manner that gave environmentalists nightmares. The Brigadier was hunting moose from a helicopter. Brigadier Douglas was found guilty, lightly fined and then sent to the United States to finish out his career in a subsidized mansion and with a sizeable expense account.

One of the most visible status symbols enjoyed by generals is the provision of luxurious staff cars, complete with flags and military drivers. In 1995, documents obtained under the Access to Information Act showed that the top commanders' chauffeured cars cost taxpayers just over $1 million. Prior to the release of this figure, DND public affairs officials effectively headed off any negative press by announcing that these "perks" were being revoked immediately, as a cost-saving measure.

Most mainstream media outlets gave the story very little play, and those that did picked up the editorial tone of the press release—the upper echelon of DND was showing an example of self-discipline and restraint. Unfortunately, the fine print of the press release showed that "cost-cutting" was not the issue, but rather, once again, this announced cut was actually in the generals' own best interests.

In essence, what DND had done was to simply make an administrative change so that cars and drivers would be assigned to a general's headquarters rather than to him personally. A car and driver would still be available to these commanders on a full-time basis, because no other officer would have the required authority to requisition the vehicles. The change came about as a result of Treasury Board's amendment of the Taxation Act in 1994. Under the new rules, a general had to report personal use of government vehicles (not their drivers) as a taxable benefit. Since the amendment was declared retroactive, going back two years, those military commanders with staff cars were faced with having to reimburse the Crown substantial sums.

One general who owed Revenue Canada a sizeable cheque for these unpaid taxes was none other than Lieutenant-General Gordon Reay. As the occupant of the Army commander's residence in Montreal, and the owner of a new home in Ottawa, Reay frequently used his staff car and driver to make the two-hour commute to work.

DND documents show that General Reay's driver would, on average, log more than 5,000 kilometres of travel per month, and he often submitted travel claims (authorized by Reay) for overnight hotel stays in Ottawa. However, due to the fact that the personal usage of a government vehicle is assessed by the commander himself, the taxable benefit claimed by General Reay amounted to less than 1,000 kilometres per year. At a cost of $0.22 per kilometre added to his income, with roughly half that being taxable, Gordon Reay's annual cost to commute 200 kilometres a week in a chauffeured Crown Victoria staff car came to less than that of a single return train ticket.

In other cases of Army generals misusing their resources, all too often that "federal asset" has in fact been their own personnel. For years at CFB Valcartier, young soldiers were provided by their unit commanders to groom the officers' golf course. Such chores should be paid for from the base's non-public funds or the golf club's operating budget. However, if soldiers, trained as infantrymen, could be utilized, the green fees could be reduced and the Central Fund (profits from the CANEX) would not be required.

Another scam would have been worthy of an episode in the old *Sergeant Bilko* television series. Up until 1993, the officers at Valcartier actually operated an autoshop, where military vehicle mechanics would be ordered—salary paid by DND—to perform maintenance and repairs on officers' cars. The only cost involved for the commanders would be the purchase of parts. The low-ranking mechanics, who had had their pay frozen, threatened to report the "auto club" to higher headquarters, and reluctantly it was shut down. However, CFB Valcartier's curling club, skating arena and golf course are still maintained by twenty-two fully trained combat soldiers.

A more personal example of misemployment of human resources would be the extravagant 1995 change of command parade organized by Major-General Archibald MacInnis. Before turning over responsibility for Land Forces Atlantic Area (LFAA) to his successor Major-General Ray Crabbe, MacInnis went to great public expense to make the routine ceremony an extravaganza.

A finance clerk at LFAA estimated that the cost of the two-hour parade was more than $250,000. Armoured vehicles were brought in all the way from Gagetown, New Brunswick, to Halifax, Nova Scotia; reservists' training sessions were extended by two weeks just to ensure their drill was up to par; special uniforms had to be custom tailored, etc., etc. Many of the same reservists who stood on guard for MacInnis that day would soon be without a parent regiment as a result of the restructuring of the militia. The troops were all told that fiscal restraint was the reason for the drastic cuts. The soldiers of the Atlantic region were getting a mixed message: a militia regiment payroll is just $300,000 for an entire year, yet the commander preaching fiscal restraint had just spent nearly that amount in a 120-minute tribute to his own passing.

As the ethos of the general officer corps deteriorated, the self-interest of some individuals was expanded to include their immediate family members as well. Along with unchecked greed and power comes a natural tendency to use one's authority to provide the same special benefits to one's family members.

Setting the pace for the wave of nepotism that has infected the senior echelon of the military was none other than John de Chastelain himself.

John's son Duncan, as has already been mentioned, had secured himself a directorship at the DND-subsidized peacekeeping college, no doubt through General de Chastelain's close contacts with Bill Baxter and Alex Morrison. As a young lawyer, recently called to the bar, Duncan could offer little to the college's board of high-profile and distinguished directors. By comparison, Duncan stood to gain acceptance into society's elite, by rubbing shoulders with such high-powered individuals as former Liberal defence minister Jean-Jacques Blais, former Tory cabinet minister Barbara

McDougall, plus a host of university presidents, influential editors and retired bureaucrats.

General de Chastelain's daughter, Amanda, was also a recipient of favouritism. As a student at Queen's University in Kingston, Ontario, Amanda received a personal services contract from the Department of National Defence. The monetary value of the agreement was a dollar per year, but this figure is misleading.

As a student of sports medicine, Amanda required on-the-job experience with athletes to make herself saleable in a competitive job market. The arrangement with DND was for young Ms. de Chastelain to provide medical services to the Royal Military College's hockey team. As she was an employee, technically, of the government, potential malpractice suits resulting from her treatments would be the responsibility of the Crown. Free travel was also part of the deal, and claims submitted show that Amanda made DND-funded trips to Victoria and Washington in addition to accompanying the RMC hockey team on numerous other occasions.

Once the example was set from the top, many other military commanders realized that discretion no longer needed to be maintained to avoid the "perception" of abusing their rank privileges. Major-General John Adams went one step beyond his military authority to secure a career in the Forces for his daughter Erin. And he paid an embarrassing price as a result.

Erin Adams as a young teen had been a very competitive swimmer with the Kingfish Swim Club in Ottawa. It had been hoped that her physical talent would enable her to attend university on a sports scholarship. However, as Erin matured, her interest in swimming waned. According to coach Edward Levitas, the Kingfish Swim Club had nothing but trouble trying to chaperone Erin during out-of-town competitions.

Once it became obvious that a sports scholarship was out of reach, Major-General Adams wanted Erin to attend the Collège Militaire Royale as an officer cadet (free tuition and a guaranteed job upon completion). Although Erin's academic grades would not qualify her for enrolment, General Adams met with the commandant to discuss the situation. It was determined that a letter of reference from the Kingfish Swim Club as to Erin's discipline and character would tip the balance in her favour.

When John Adams approached Ed Levitas for the required recommendation, the coach turned him down flat. By this point, Erin had pierced her nose and her tongue and was considered to be "virtually out of control" by Levitas. Adams was a vice-president of the Kingfish Club and he pulled rank on Levitas, threatening to fire him if he wouldn't sign the bogus letter of reference. Once he had coerced compliance and a signature from Levitas, John Adams went back to his colleagues and successfully placed his daughter on the CMR entry roll for the following semester.

Unfortunately, the 1994 budget ended the free educational opportunity for the Adamses. It was announced that CMR would be closed and even fewer candidates would be enrolled at the Royal Military College. In the tougher competition, Erin's submission did not make the grade.

Although Ed Levitas had caved in after Adams threatened to fire him, the whole affair was later leaked to the satire magazine *Frank*, complete with details of Erin's curious behaviour.

In the end, Major-General Adams's attempt to abuse both his civilian and military powers netted him nothing in return and resulted in a public embarrassment for his entire family.

With more and more examples of generals and senior DND officials' heretofore unquestioned privileges being leaked by whistle blowers to the media, the resultant public pressure has forced some errant individuals to better monitor their claims.

In several cases, an access-to-information request, submitted with a detailed account of the alleged misdeed, has been enough of a warning to force the generals named to make full restitution. By the time DND releases the file to the requesting media outlet, included in the folder is a cancelled cheque indicating full reimbursement to the Crown. Although such action more or less certifies the guilt of the general in question, no charges are laid and no police investigations are conducted. The paper trail is minimal and no administrative action is taken against the perpetrator.

In March 1995, *Esprit de Corps* magazine learned through a finance clerk at Land Forces headquarters that two generals had been bilking the system. Based on the detailed information provided (the file numbers and finance codes which were used), access-to-information requests were drafted and submitted to DND.

In one instance, Brigadier-General Jean Laliberté decided to send his daughter to a private school in Quebec after being posted to CFB Trenton in August 1986, where there were no French schools. Laliberté thought that the taxpayers should reimburse him for his daughter's French education. Two years later, the general was posted to Ottawa, where there were any number of top French schools. Still, he left his daughter at the private school in Quebec and claimed expenses. When an access-to-information request was submitted, DND finance clerks discovered that he did not have any entitlement claim and Laliberté was ordered to reimburse the department to the tune of more than $5,000. The paperwork was tidied up and the file was released to the media. For Laliberté?

No charges were laid, no administrative action was taken, no reprimand was issued.

Major-General Romeo Dallaire, best known to Canadians as the hero of Rwanda, was also caught out by the same whistle blower and access-to-information process. In Dallaire's case, the finance clerk had questioned why DND was paying to fly Mrs. Dallaire, on her own, to Niagara Falls, Ontario.

Obviously, the informant had recognized the abuse of privilege for what it was (i.e., there was no official rationale) before the travel claim was processed for the media. General Dallaire had to cough up $958 out of his own pocket to repay the Crown. Once again, there was no investigation and no repercussions. In fact, Romeo Dallaire was promoted shortly thereafter.

General John de Chastelain, upon returning for his second tenure as CDS, had certainly planned ahead for his golden years as a pensioner. Most of his general officer corps were following in his footsteps and making the most of their powers to provide for a cosy retirement.

Lieutenant-General Gordon Reay is a classic example of this forward thinking. In November 1995, Reay announced that he was retiring from the Armed Forces and, as is often the case, he would be taking his accumulated vacation time before turning in his uniform. However, it wasn't until a finance clerk advised the media that Reay would not officially retire until July 1997 that the whole story started to come out. Apparently this ambitious officer had saved up nineteen months' worth of holiday time, a full seventeen years' worth over a twenty-two-year period of eligibility.

By not taking leave when he was still a poorly paid captain, or even a major, the general was able to "retire" on a full salary of $129,000. Those two additional years would then be averaged as part of his best six years of remuneration to determine his pension. With a full 70 per cent annuity, even after

Reay officially retires in 1997, he will collect an (indexed) $91,000 annually.

Many of Reay's own staff officers pointed out his abuse of travel privileges to illustrate the compounding nature of the situation. By taking all-expense-paid junkets to South America and Europe, the General had no need to take an official holiday. Because Reay did not use up his leave days, the taxpayers get stuck again when he retires, in this case for $225,000 up front plus an additional $6,000 a year for as long as the General (or his widow) remains alive.

Two generals who did not plan so far in advance still wanted to cash in on their careers before they retired. In 1994, Brigadier-General Claude Archambault and Major-General Pierre Lalonde received full benefit packages in accordance with the downsizing Canadian Forces Force Reduction Program (FRP). Unfortunately for all those involved, general officers were not entitled to receive these cash incentives.

In fact, the whole concept behind the FRP was to encourage soldiers who were in mid-career to leave the Forces with a bit of a financial bridge. Those who were near retirement (i.e., with over thirty years' service) were naturally not included in the offer as they could be terminated at any point by the Forces without penalty, on thirty days' notice. Of course, those discharged in such a manner would still be entitled to a pension of 2 per cent per year of service and 240 days' severance pay.

Between the two officers' settlements, the amount issued would have amounted to approximately $220,000.

When Lieutenant-General Jean Boyle took over the position of assistant deputy minister (personnel) from Lieutenant-General Paul Addy in August 1995, the Archambault and Lalonde files were a matter of great concern. The correspondence trail shows that General Addy passed the buck to P.A. Reny, the director of senior appointments. In turn, Reny wrote to General John de Chastelain asking that he submit a backdated "note to file" approving the two generals' FRPs in order to establish an auditable trail. De Chastelain complied, but he was careful to share the blame if the situation should ever come to light. In his note, de Chastelain admitted to directing Reny verbally, but only after "consultation" with Deputy Minister Robert Fowler.

Although Jean Boyle had appeared reluctant to take over the file without protecting himself from future incrimination, once he was established as associate deputy minister (personnel), his first task was to rewrite the FRP policy.

Under the new terms, the 1996 FRP will be made available to general officers. With an announced downsizing of six general appointments from
DND's roster in 1996, subtracted from the twenty-two promotions to general rank in that same year, it means sixteen of these top officers will now be
entitled to collect these massive severance benefits. With an average severance
of $170,000 per general, the taxpayers will be on the hook for an additional
$2.72 million. Of course, this money will be drawn from an ever-decreasing
defence budget, but as soldiers tighten their belts yet another notch, they will
be blissfully unaware of this top-level, self-serving expenditure.

Boyle knew that if the troops learned of this substantial change to the
FRP policy, it could dampen morale. Because of that, the guidelines for
general officers are submitted on a separate correspondence, available only
to the addressee (i.e., the general who is eligible). John de Chastelain not
only approved Boyle's changes to the policy, but also supported the idea of
keeping the details from reaching the rank and file.

Shortly thereafter, de Chastelain recommended to the Prime Minister
that Jean Boyle should be the one to replace him as chief of the defence staff.

When John de Chastelain gave up his command of the Canadian Forces
on December 28, 1995, he left behind a powerful legacy embodied in the
general officer corps: self-interest, careerism, greed, nepotism, a disregard
for the public trust and a disdain for the soldiers they command.

If there's no life like it as regulars, there's no afterlife like it in retirement.

There are very few executives anywhere who retire at fifty-five years of
age with an indexed pension equivalent to 70 per cent of their best six
salaried years. For most working civilians in Canada, Freedom 55 is nothing more than a catchy slogan of RRSP salesmen, and something few ever
dream of actually attaining.

Military generals, on the other hand, can enter their golden years a
decade sooner than everyone else, and they can do so with a pension that
is $23,000 higher than the average Canadian family income. Despite hav-
ing such a lucrative arrangement, our warriors rarely fade away into retirement. Instead, they often exert the power and influence to which their rank
entitles them, to guarantee their own continued employment at National
Defence as either "consultants" or civilian executives.

Even as DND publicly announced they were restructuring, downsizing and eliminating headquarters personnel in the 1995 White Paper, the top brass were preparing a special fund that would ensure their collective financial welfare would continue post-retirement. In fact, as a result of receiving their military pensions, these generals would practically double their personal income by retiring from the Forces in order to begin working for the Defence Department.

In order to implement the restructuring of personnel to match the manning levels of the 1995 defence policy, DND felt it was necessary to initiate four separate programs to analyse the impact of the reduction. Naturally, given the existing mentality at the National Defence Headquarters, the first step towards downsizing staff required expanding their own workforce. In the initial planning stages, the senior brass that had created the present bloated, top-heavy chaos determined that the only ones qualified to restore order were civilians with top-level military experience (i.e., recently retired generals).

On September 12, 1995, Vice-Admiral Larry Murray approved the establishment of a $14-million fund for "consultant" support to the downsizing program. Although such a sum being set aside by a department with 250 general-rank equivalents to hire additional executives may seem both redundant and excessive, in actual fact Murray kept his options open to increase the amount, if required.

In both Admiral Murray's approval and the original submission by Major-General George MacDonald, the underlying tone is that the "complexity" of the programs involved might require deadline extensions and/or additional funding as time went on. The original amount proposed for consultant support had been a one-year, one-time expenditure of $10 million. However, Murray and MacDonald had added $4 million to the pot to allow the program "a reasonable period of stability." In addition, MacDonald made it clear in his memo to Murray that the funding would be continued over the next two years at $10 million and $8 million, respectively. The note also mentioned that no reference would be made to these option years. In other words, only those with access to these consulting funds (retired generals) would have any knowledge of their availability and scope. No reference was made to obtaining Treasury Board approval, and all of the moneys allocated were to be drawn from various top officials' "reserve budgets"; that is to say, there would be no official mention in annual budget estimates.

It should be noted that this "special consultant fund" was not established to accommodate a new concept, but rather it merely expanded and exacerbated a growing trend of senior officers' securing themselves a second career. DND documents reveal that, between January and July 1995, "forty-seven different consultants and/or enterprises that employed former military personnel were awarded contracts" by the Department of National Defence.

Since the MacDonald/Murray pot of funds was authorized on September 12, 1995, such contracts have been let at three times that rate.

Because establishing a consulting business in itself takes a fair amount of labour and risk, many of these retiring generals are content to allow headhunter firms to outsource them as employees. Of course, this means the placement agency takes a 20 per cent commission off the top for their work, which usually involves nothing more than processing the invoices.

The rationale given by DND for senior military officers being rehired by their peers to do their old jobs is that this process "is enhancing DND's partnership with private industry as [DND] downsizes." Were it not for the retired senior military composition of these headhunter firms, this point might actually have some validity.

Probably the most unmistakable example of the abuse which is taking place is that of retired Rear-Admiral Peter Martin. The last post Martin held at National Defence Headquarters was that of associate assistant deputy minister of finances. As one of the top accountants for DND, Martin was aware of all the legal loopholes which existed in the post-retirement system, and he was also fully versed in the degree to which existing guidelines were flouted.

Before even officially retiring from the Canadian Forces, Rear-Admiral Martin had already secured a second income as a DND consultant. By June 7, when the first of his pension cheques had arrived, the ambitious former sailor had secured a total of three separate consulting contracts with three separate directorates within DND. At this juncture, he was making $12,210 a month as a defence consultant, plus his monthly pension of $5,400.

For some reason, Martin still felt he could be doing better, and his ambition soon paid another dividend. One of the DND contracts involved providing advice to the downsizing team know as Operation Renaissance. In his job description, he was ordered to establish the working team for this project, and as a former finance officer, he was to oversee comptrol-lership of the project.

It was about this time that Martin solidified his relationship with a Mr. Horbasz, the president of Horbasz Drysdale Management Partners Inc. (HDP). Originally, HDP had won a consulting contract with DND by low-balling a bid for a project they were unqualified to fulfil. After they ran into severe difficulties, Horbasz sought to remedy the situation by turning to Martin for help.

In spite of the fact that he was already managing a project which involved the hiring of "qualified personnel," Peter Martin accepted a senior partnership with HDP, and with it a large stock option in the management firm. Within one month of the signing of this illicit deal, an estimated $2 million worth of contracts was issued by DND to Horbasz for consultants, many of them to work directly for Operation Renaissance, and Peter Martin in particular.

Despite the potential conflict of interest, no one was prepared to blow the whistle on this scheme for the simple reasons that HDP paid the best per-diem rate for consultants ($800 to $1,500) and they were always will-ing to talk to a potential prospect. With the general officer corps targeted for downsizing, and a sizeable Force Reduction Plan (FRP) buyout now being made available, many of the top brass began to woo Horbasz with an eye on their own personal fortunes.

By December 1995, this incestuous situation had already become so blatantly apparent to workers at NDHQ that they gave these retread gen-erals the monicker "Horbasz's hordes." (In a letter faxed to *Esprit de Corps*, one whistle blower claimed that HDP's only purpose seemed to be the "rape and pillage of employment funds.") Horbasz himself was paid by DND as a consultant, but his only activity was to market his "executives" throughout the multitude of directorates and departments.

In some cases, retired generals prefer to keep the prestige and perks of their rank, and therefore shun the purely financial lure of consultancy. After decades of flaunting their status, it is often difficult for these high-ranking officers to contemplate being forced to assert themselves to achieve the respect the military system affords them automatically. For these officers, and they are not that numerous a breed, there are options available for con-tinued service, options to which no other service member is entitled.

When you happen to be a friend of the regiment, or a favourite of the government in power, things like mandatory retirement age mean nothing. General John de Chastelain set the tone for bending the age rules when he returned from retirement in 1994. De Chastelain often publicly defended the military's retirement at fifty-five policy against legal challenges, even though he himself was two years beyond that and still serving.

In 1994, when the Liberal government announced that there would be a public inquiry into the Airborne Regiment's deployment to Somalia, DND had more than 112 generals on their payroll. Nevertheless, de Chastelain saw fit to rehire his old friend retired Lieutenant-General James Fox to head up the military's Somalia Inquiry Liaison Team (SILT). For official purposes, SILT was nominally headed by Colonel Jean Leclerc. However, behind the scenes, this "dream team" for the defence had no less than two lieutenant-generals directing the show—James Fox and Jean Boyle.

At the time of his resurrection, Fox was sixty years old, five years past legal service. In order to bend the rules, and to accommodate Fox's wish to have the full authority of his rank, de Chastelain and Deputy Minister Bob Fowler arranged for him to be listed as a "reservist on a full-time callout."

Although unable to collect a military pension in addition to his salary, under this arrangement Fox was able to receive all of the benefits associated with a Regular Force officer being posted (the Crown paid him more than $13,000 in real estate fees alone). And he was back on a full lieutenant-general's paycheque ($129,000). In order to do this, Fox had to be posted to a militia regiment.

Since he had served in the armoured corps, the nearest available unit to Ottawa happened to be the Sherbrooke Hussars in Sherbrooke. The annual payroll for the entire Hussars Regiment had to be nearly doubled just to accommodate this bizarre arrangement. Despite Fox's advanced age, de Chastelain waived the regulation requiring his old friend, as a re-enlisting officer, to undergo a medical examination.

Another option for retired top officers intent on keeping their familiar trappings and perks is to take on various honorary appointments. A multitude of such positions is available throughout the military, and it must be pointed out from the outset that the overwhelming majority of the incumbents put "mission before self." Often they are concerned citizens who spend their own money in support of their units or regiments. However, when the pervading ethos of today's military high command comes in contact with access to tax-paid perks, the result is abusive waste and self-aggrandizement. Often these expenditures fall well outside of the existing DND support guidelines for such honorary functions, and they're only processed in deference to the former officer's previous rank and present circle of friends at National Defence.

Following his retirement from the Canadian Forces, former Army commander Lieutenant-General Jack Vance accepted the honorary appointment as colonel-commandant of the Royal Canadian Army Cadet Corps in 1991. From records obtained under the Access to Information Act, it would appear that General Vance took a great interest in his new charges. He flew far and wide to visit as many young cadets as he could. In a single seven-month period, Vance journeyed to Ottawa, Fredericton, St. John's, Petawawa, Ipperwash, Montreal, Banff, Vernon, Calgary, Quebec City, England and Wales, a total of twelve destinations in ten separate trips. While it was certainly noble of the former officer to be so generous with his personal time, the problem lies in the fact he billed the taxpayers for his travels.

Including airfare, Vance's ten trips in 1991 totalled more than $7,500. He submitted claims and was reimbursed for every one. Although the Army Cadet League of Canada receives an annual DND grant of $205,000 for their operations, this amount is in support of all 20,000 member cadets. With such a tight budget, it is improbable the cadets would condone such an extravagant expedition as the one week Vance spent (July 19–27, 1991) touring England and Wales to visit "Canadian cadets on exchange with their British counterparts" (fewer than one dozen in total). National Defence Headquarters, on the other hand, had no problem in funding such a venture.

By 1995, Lieutenant-General Vance was sixty-one years of age and had been out of uniform for seven years, but he was still willing to serve his country. His number came up when Canada had an opportunity to send a general officer to Australia to study their institutions as part of an officer development review board. Ironically, this ODRB had been established in an attempt to restore a sense of military ethos to the Canadian officer corps.

Rather than send one of the serving ninety-eight generals on this blatant junket to Australia, John de Chastelain decided to hire a retired officer, and

Jack Vance suited the purpose. In addition to the $3,501.79 in tax-paid travel expenses, Vance agreed to a $4,000 remuneration in exchange for his ten-day trip down under.

The contents of Vance's final report on Australia would be included in the 1996 training package taught to future officer cadets, which will stress military philosophies such as mission before self. And the responsibility that accompanies a commission.

Throughout his army career, Charles Belzile paralleled the achievements of Jack Vance. Both achieved the three-star rank of lieutenant-general. In retirement, the trend continued as Belzile replaced Vance as the honorary colonel-commandant for the Royal Canadian Army Cadet Corps.

By the summer of 1995, Belzile had been hired as one of three commissioners on the military's study to restructure the Reserves and he was a registered lobbyist for two defence firms, yet he still found the time to visit with young cadets in Europe. During a scheduled break in the commission hearings, Belzile travelled to England and France to check in on exchange cadets during a ten-day, $3,437 trip. Although he was long retired from the Forces, re-employed as a civilian at DND and working as an honorary appointment for an independent agency, National Defence paid the claims.

There is a popular phrase junior officers use to describe top commanders who are entering their golden years. They say: "Those who can—lobby. Those who can't—consult. Those who never could—teach at RMC (the Royal Military College)." The numbers and costs associated with the military's education system would more than bear out this theory.

Although our armed forces are slated to be reduced to 60,000 troops, as of 1996, DND spends $90 million on its own college system. The steady state population of 950 cadets at RMC are taught by more than 180 professors and lecturers, amounting to a staggering teacher-to-student ratio of 1 to 5.

A $1.6-million academic research program, staffed mostly by retired senior officers, is divided among seventy-four of these professors (equating to an average salary of $20,000 in addition to their pensions). The cost of all those professors and lecturers puts the cost-per-student upwards of $76,000 per year. By comparison, international students taking an undergraduate course at a Canadian university would spend roughly $17,000 for tuition, comparable accommodation and expenses.

General John de Chastelain received his education at RMC and was always a strong supporter of this institution and the cosy financial arrangement which it affords senior officers. In appreciation for his loyalty, RMC presented the retired CDS with an honorary honours degree on May 17, 1996. It is expected he will provide guest lectures at the college in exchange for honorariums plus travel expenses.

Even when retired general officers choose to leave the Defence Department environment and seek employment in another sector of the public service, the taxpayers end up footing an extra bill. Despite the fact that their executive salaries and perks are directly linked to those of civil servants, military officers (as with all service members) have a separate pension plan. At age fifty-five with thirty-five years in the Forces, soldiers can retire from federal government service and collect 70 per cent of their former salary. By then transferring to another department of the same public service, they can "double dip" by collecting a second government paycheque.

Lieutenant-General Ken Foster took full advantage of this when he turned in his army uniform in 1991. He was almost immediately appointed as an assistant deputy minister with the Department of Health and Welfare. Of course, it was the qualification of having been a three-star general in the Army that made such a top-level, direct entry into the public service possible. However, for the last ten years of his government career, Foster will be making 170 per cent of his lieutenant-general's salary (over $200,000). While, admittedly, very few service members can benefit from their military pension to such a degree, for the senior brass, whose military offices are already considered to be government appointments, it has become a growing trend. Such lucrative arrangements undoubtedly draw the ire and envy of even senior federal bureaucrats.

CHAPTER FIVE

The Grunts

Over the past decade, every time a new federal budget announced another cut to the Defence Department, it has been followed by a DND proclamation that this new reduction will be achieved "through a downsizing of headquarters." In 1995, Defence Minister David Collenette tabled a new White Paper on Defence, and, predictably, this latest military blueprint called for a drastically diminished "headquarters." Naturally, defence analysts have become cynical about these announcements. As one retired colonel was quick to point out, after eight years of this rhetoric, the number of personnel at NDHQ was larger than ever, despite the fact that, over this same period, on paper they had been slated for a reduction totalling 110 per cent of their strength.

On May 3, 1996, Deputy Chief of Defence Staff Lieutenant-General Armand Roy assembled his senior staff together for a "discussion" regarding the latest "targeted reductions" to headquarters staff. While General Roy was pleased to announce that some progress had already been made in trimming their numbers, he was afraid that any further losses might affect the "efficiency" of operations. The immediate suggestion was that they should, instead, make up their reduction quota shortfall by cutting more manpower resources from "field formations."

The whole objective of the 1995 White Paper restructuring had been to address the unwieldy imbalance of troops in relation to headquarters, yet the actual application of the cuts served to further underscore how deeply flawed the system has become—and just how out of touch with their *raison d'être* the senior command really are.

General Roy, as the DCDS, is responsible for all Canadian Forces "operations." As such, it is the job of his staff to co-ordinate all of the peacekeeping contingents and to prepare contingency plans. Given their role and task, Roy's personnel, perhaps better than anyone, would be fully aware of just how overstretched Canada's meagre field formations are. The operations centre at NDHQ is the first to receive support requests from our far-flung

UN commitments, along with status reports from those units in Canada preparing to deploy or just returned. Nevertheless, when faced with having to make some tough decisions, the operations staff at NDHQ still chose self-preservation at the expense of the frontline soldiers.

In a 1993 interview with *Esprit de Corps* magazine, Brigadier-General Michel Matte summed up this insular attitude with the statement that, in his opinion, even if the Defence Department were eventually to eliminate the entire combat function of the military, NDHQ would continue to operate on its present scale.

As ridiculous as this prediction may sound, few Canadians are aware of just how close our military already is to this becoming a reality.

When Paul Hellyer imposed his unification experiment in 1968, the proportion of officers in the Canadian Armed Forces stood at 16.7 per cent. At the time, this was considered to be excessive compared with our Second World War wartime officer strength of just 12.8 per cent. Naturally, a heavily over-officered force is an expensive force, but in practice it has also proven to be an inefficient one. Hellyer figured that by eliminating the redundancy existing in the three services and amalgamating the civilian and military headquarters he could dramatically reduce the ratio of officers to rank and file, thereby making a more cost-effective and field-efficient force.

What Hellyer did not take into account was the possible offspring of a marriage of bureaucratic principles with military authoritarianism—a gluttonous, uncontrolled, power-hungry monster.

As of 1996, the percentage of officers in the Armed Forces has ballooned to an unwieldy 22.6 per cent. To put this in perspective, if DND could even revert to the admittedly bloated pre-unification levels of rank distribution, it would mean the conversion of 3,982 Regular Force officers down to non-commissioned members. The annual savings of such a restructuring would be approximately $300 million and, with the additional 3,982 "troops," our understrength army battalions could be reinforced up to their wartime establishments of nearly 1,000 soldiers. This would effectively eliminate the over-rotation of our peacekeeping contingents, and consequently improve the morale of our hard-pressed army. Given such statistics, it is rapidly apparent that neither our country nor the Armed Forces has been properly served by the generals' "patriotic" subservience to bureaucracy.

The "rank creep" also illustrates the ever-widening gap between our combat units and Headquarters, which theoretically exists to support them. The staffing and manning levels of the basic combat formations have essentially remained fixed for centuries, and are fairly consistent in every armed forces of the world (including guerrilla forces). For example, the authorized strength of a Canadian infantry platoon remains thirty-two enlisted men, plus one officer—unchanged since the First World War. So, while infantry battalions are still commanded by lieutenant-colonels and brigades by brigadiers, our diminutive Armed Forces of 67,000 personnel have inexplicably come to be led by no less than a four-star chief of defence staff.

In war, a four-star general would command a field force of upwards of 500,000 troops, and a three-star lieutenant-general would direct an army corps of 125,000. In 1954, when Canada had a military force of 115,000 personnel, there were only three lieutenant-generals on the payroll. This ratio of one lieutenant-general per 38,333 all ranks was considered excessive at the time, but it would be comparatively modest by today's standards.

In the intervening forty years, the Canadian military has been virtually halved, down to a total strength of 67,000. Conversely, the number of lieutenant-generals has steadily increased over that same period. By February 1996, there was a total of sixteen on the books. This amounts to an indefensible ratio of one lieutenant-general for every 4,187 all ranks.

According to DND's 1996 organizational chart, each lieutenant-general presides over his own equally over-ranked, over-staffed human pyramid consisting of: 3 two-star major-generals, 7 one-star brigadier-generals, 35 colonels, 127 lieutenant-colonels, 407 majors, 896 captains, 269 lieutenants and 215 officer cadets, for a grand total of 1,960 officers. The full cost for this surplus of personnel, including pay benefits and indirect expenses, amounts to $49.7 million per year.

Over the past four decades, it is obvious that the civilian side of the department had its own internal growth agenda, which negated its ability (or willingness) to keep its uniformed alter egos in check. In 1954, DND had seven senior bureaucrats lodged in its top offices, which gave the department a mandarin-to-soldier ratio of 1 to 17,857. By 1996, a total of ten top-level civil servants resided at National Defence Headquarters, managing the affairs of a much-reduced Armed Forces at a ratio of 1 to 6,700.

At the bottom of this inverted and weighty pyramid are the few forgotten and misunderstood fighting soldiers whom we have left in the

Canadian Forces. In terms of their martial spirit and bearing, they stand in stark contrast to the departmental bureaucrats who owe their power and prestige to the very existence of this "combat capability." Nevertheless, in a world of self-interest, the concept of self-sacrifice as a virtue has no merit and is scorned by the non-warriors who control the Defence Department. Servicemen in combat trades (particularly the infantry) are mockingly referred to as "grunts" by those whom soldiers, in turn, refer to as "bean-counters" and "carpet-baggers."

In order to understand fully the extent of the moral failure of the military high command and bureaucracy, it must be measured against the martial ethos that still exists in these dwindling operational units. While it is distasteful that any senior public officials would abuse the taxpayers' trust, when the military leadership does so at the expense of the troops they purport to represent, it becomes an unconscionable act. Soldiers, unlike civil servants, take an oath to give their lives, if necessary, in the performance of their professional duty.

Very few, if any, young men and women in Canada join the Forces to serve in a combat unit simply because they need a job. Admittedly, some of the more technical trades in the military do provide the lure of professional training (a subsequent civilian career following a paid education). However, only those dedicated to proving themselves as combat soldiers will pass the rigorous training required of them.

Recruits are quickly indoctrinated into a completely different world, where previously held values disappear under the forceful training regimen delivered by non-commissioned instructors. All traces of individuality are erased, and even seemingly trivial lapses expose the new recruit to severe repercussions.

To be a minute late for parade is considered being absent without leave (AWOL) and, therefore, it is a criminal offence. A recruit wearing uniform trousers with a double crease is deemed "improperly dressed" and punished accordingly. Even personal hygiene, such as haircuts and shaving, are regulated and enforced with singular severity. Recruits undergoing training can be jailed for failing to have their hair cut.

Things the average teenager strives to avoid suddenly become the main focus of his or her life: achieving conformity, not standing out, not being noticed or singled out becomes the daily goal. Later in the training, whenever any recruit is guilty of an infraction, the entire unit is punished as a result. For example, if Recruit Jones is too slow in changing into his uniform following gym class, his entire platoon might be forced to miss their evening meal.

This strategy, which forces individuals to concentrate on the collective and to begin thinking as a team, is age-old and a proven formula throughout history. While conflict is naturally part of the human spirit, the disciplined art of modern warfare runs counter to our instincts. For soldiers to face life-threatening hostile fire and remain at their posts requires not only a high degree of mental conditioning, but also a measure of dedication to the mission.

History has shown that higher ideals, such as nationalism, quickly disappear in the carnage and terror of battle, and that most soldiers actually fight only for the sake and safety of their comrades. By contrast, school systems work on an inverse principle of rewarding students on an individual basis and encouraging competition among peers. The bond that is formed by soldiers training under such conditions is known as camaraderie, and it is an essential ingredient in forging a combat unit out of raw recruits. Although some civilians may think they have experienced a form of camaraderie at work or in school, the fact is, nothing can compare to the close quarters and interdependence of military training. During a six-month battle school course, fledgling infanteers spend virtually every minute within sight of their thirty-two platoon mates. All meals are taken together, they march everywhere in formation, showers are communal and even the sleeping quarters are without privacy dividers.

As fledgling soldiers, these recruits soon develop two distinct levels of authority and control. There is the formal version imposed by the instructors, and an informal pecking order within the ranks of the recruits. Normally this underground chain of command is established based on the natural leadership abilities of the individuals, and this is measured against their newly learned set of military virtues. Inevitably, these unofficial authorities find themselves unwittingly doing the work of weeding out the unqualified from their midst. As a result of the instructors' reliance upon the group punishment theory, it becomes the objective of the recruit leaders to eliminate the weaker members in order to strengthen the collective.

With the emphasis placed almost solely on mutual reliance, young soldiers quickly establish their own code, which invariably parallels the universal "warrior code." While there is no formal instruction given to recruits on this particular subject, the non-commissioned officers often give unofficial guidance to their recruits. Early in their training, new soldiers are also given extensive lectures on military traditions and regimental histories. Unlike the history lessons taught in high schools, these courses focus entirely on the heroic actions of individuals and the collective feats of the regiment at war. Recruits memorize and are tested on the dates and circumstances surrounding various battles and skirmishes.

What results from the indoctrination process is a unique subculture where courage is held in the highest regard and any act of self-sacrifice is considered the ultimate achievement. This credo is institutionalized in the awarding of medals and citations for valour. Although virtually valueless to mainstream society, these medallions are highly cherished and respected by soldiers. Few civilians could understand U.S. Admiral Jeremy Boorda's May 16, 1996, suicide after the media revealed that he had worn service medals which he had not earned. By contrast, veterans and serving soldiers realized that for this admiral to have done otherwise would only have exacerbated his misdeed. By falsely wearing combat decorations, not only had Boorda violated official regulations, but, more important, he had broken faith with his warriors.

Of late, Canadian generals have increasingly shown both a failure to live up to their own men's standards regarding this honour system and, in some cases, an inability to even comprehend the dangerous circumstances to which they have committed their soldiers.

General Jean Boyle, upon his appointment as chief of the defence staff, tried to bolster his thin operational résumé through claims he had commanded Canadian air operations during the Gulf War. Later, in an interview with the *Globe and Mail*'s Paul Koring, Boyle expanded upon this claim by intoning that he had been in personal danger during that war. Koring had asked Boyle about the low threat level of another high-intensity war, and the CDS responded, "I was in the [Persian] Gulf in 1991 and let me tell you, the threat was real."

The fact that Jean Boyle does not wear a Gulf War medal on his uniform led *Esprit de Corps* magazine to ask under access-to-information legislation for details of his wartime service. These files show that, other than a single visit to Qatar in 1990, the general was not deployed to the Gulf at all. As commander of the Canadian air division in Germany, he was 4,800 kilometres away, while Colonel Romeo Lalonde conducted air operations with his planes and pilots.

Caught out in his faked wartime credentials, Boyle did not have the courage to confront the media personally. Instead, he had the judge advocate general write a letter explaining what the chief of the defence staff "meant to say."

The tale of Brigadier-General Jimmy Cox and his visit to the former Yugoslavia offers a complete contrast. In September 1994, when Cox arrived in Croatia, the Second Battalion Princess Patricia's Canadian Light Infantry were hard-pressed to prevent a major Croatian offensive into the Serbian-held Krajina, on the Dalmatian Coast. It was the PPCLI's role to enforce the tentative ceasefire and to make the belligerents respect the zone of separation. They were fully prepared to fight if necessary. On September 10, that possibility became an inevitability as Croatian troops poured forward, occupying three Serbian villages, in the area of a town called Medak.

Sergeant Greg Trenholm was already on his third tour in Yugoslavia in eighteen months, and he was primed to start firing back for a change. He radioed back the details of the Croatian attack and then, without waiting for further orders, instructed his men to open fire.

For the next four days, the Princess Pats endured a severe bombardment and exchanged small-arms and machine-gun fire with the Croats.

General Cox made his way forward to the front line and made a dash for a Canadian bunker. Wild-eyed with adrenaline, General Cox turned to Trenholm and shouted above the roar of battle, "Sergeant, this is excellent *training* for the men!"

Trust and honesty are the cornerstones of the teamwork and mutual reliance that soldiers must embody in order to perform their profession. This ethical standard must be forcefully adhered to by the military authorities, but it is also strictly and often brutally enforced by the rank and file upon their peers. The strong bonds formed between soldiers are often verified with a rite of passage of some sort, which varies from regiment to regiment. In most cases, the ritual is a form of drinking game, which involves a certain amount of courage and competition. Many units adopt a game known as the "Zulu Warrior" or "Dance of the Flaming Arseholes." This involves two "players," each drinking a beer as quickly as he can to avoid being burned by the flames from a length of toilet paper tucked between his naked buttocks. Obviously this game is not meant to be conducted in mixed company and the participants are willing competitors—each urged on by his section mates to beat his opponent.

The videotaped hazing ritual performed by the Airborne Regiment, which was later broadcast by the media in 1995 and instrumental in the regiment's subsequent disbandment, was an aberration of this bonding ceremony. The excesses involved in that particular event, including the ingestion of faeces, vomit and urine, shocked other paratroopers who had never been exposed to such degradation. The fact that this particular sordid affair, despite its scope and scale, went virtually unreported for so long is easy to understand for the simple reason that soldiers will rarely "squeal" on their comrades— even when they themselves have been victimized. This is not because the system is perceived to be tolerant of such activities; in fact, it is quite the reverse.

As a result of the heavy punishments meted out for minor infractions, soldiers prefer to administer "barrack room justice" to their own peers, rather than involving the "system." One obvious reason for the reluctance to report an incident, especially during the training/weeding-out process, is that the soldiers are closely cohabiting in an open barracks. Since "the code" strictly prohibits and denounces "snitching," any such occurrence would undoubtedly result in dire consequences for the perpetrator at the hands of his own mates—regardless of the original provocation.

In the Somalia affair, one of the least-understood aspects of the whole scandal was the fact that Trooper Kyle Brown came forward on his own with the photographic evidence. In the thirty-six hours following the beating death of Shidane Arone, Major Anthony Seward had tried to persuade his paratroopers that the young Somali looter had been killed "during a rough apprehension."

Kyle Brown knew differently, as did most of the Airborne Regiment, but only Brown had the physical evidence which would implicate Master Corporal Clayton Matchee in the horrific torture death.

Prior to Trooper Brown submitting his photographs and statement, Master Corporal Matchee had warned him of the physical retribution he would suffer as a result of "ratting him [Matchee] out."

```
            THE BOOK BARREL
         2284 BLOOR STREET WEST
          TORONTO ON  M6S 1N9
            (416) 767-7417
         Transaction No: 50739
  01/08/97  11:18:27      CLERK:


   1*@  32.95 1895555930            32.95
      TARNISHED BRASS
  SUBTOTAL                          32.95
  TAX @ 8.000%                       0.00
  GST TAX @ 7.000%                   2.31
  TOTAL                             35.26
  DIR                               35.26
  Total Tendered          $        35.26
  DIR  Credit                        0.00


             THANK YOU!
   ASK ABOUT OUR PAPERBACK BOOK CLUB

      AND HARD COVER COLLECTORS CLUB
```

It took real guts for Brown to proceed, and even though his testimony thwarted the fledgling cover-up, Major Anthony Seward acknowledged that Brown had acted in a courageous fashion. Only those who understand and have learned the code would be able to appreciate fully the magnitude of such an action. For Brown to have suffered no violent consequence also clearly indicates that the men of 2 Commando collectively recognized not only the enormity of Clayton Matchee's crime, but also the necessity for the system to punish him, and thereby restore order.

Throughout the subsequent courts martial and public relations campaign to control the damage to the Forces' image, the senior management of the military banked heavily upon the public's ignorance of this unwritten code. Ironically, Trooper Kyle Brown was made the scapegoat by the military justice system, although his actions had originally been described as "courageous" by his own commanding officer.

To steal from another soldier or from your own comrades is viewed as a cardinal sin and, if identified, the thief is usually punished in a brutal fashion within the ranks. The rationale behind this is simple to understand when you realize that, because a soldier has to entrust his life in combat to his fellow soldiers, the act of stealing even a seemingly insignificant item of personal kit takes on a whole new dimension. Commanding officers understand that this trust must be maintained between soldiers and are quick to remove any culprits as soon as they are singled out.

A clear example of this sort of situation occurred in Winnipeg during the early eighties. A young corporal had been suspected of stealing wallets from other soldiers at the gymnasium. To catch him in the act, an elaborate ruse was prepared and, sure enough, the bait proved too great for the corporal to resist.

The trap was sprung and the culprit was roughly apprehended and manhandled by his captors back to his barrack room. Once there, a coat hanger was crudely bent to spell out the word "thief" and a propane torch was used to heat the primitive brand. Several soldiers then restrained the corporal while another applied the brand to his forehead.

The hideous scream that followed signalled a hasty exit for the vigilantes and drew the attention of several officers on duty.

Although in their haste to administer punishment, the mob had forgotten

to reverse the letters on the branding iron, the medical officer had no difficulty in ascertaining the meaning of the fresh burn. Within two days of the
incident, it was the "victim" who was tried before the commanding officer
and subsequently released from the Forces—for his own safety. There never
was a police investigation conducted into the vigilante process and no
charges were laid. While stealing from your mates for your own personal
advantage is severely punished, conversely soldiers are also expected to share
their few creature comforts with the collective. As a result, you will not find
more generous or hospitable hosts than frontline soldiers in their element
(suffering the hardship and deprivation of an operational environment).

In June 1991, thirty Canadian combat engineers were housed in a sunbaked Kuwaiti outpost. For three weeks they had been plying their dangerous trade, clearing unexploded ordnance (bombs and mines) in sweltering
60° Celsius heat. When a CBC film crew was brought out to tape their
exploits, the convoy escort thought to bring a cooler of pop out to their
comrades. It was the first cold beverage these troops had received since
manning their remote station, and only one can per man was the ration.

Nevertheless, as soon as the news team arrived, the combat engineers
were quick to play host and immediately offered their guests the only luxury item available: the newly arrived cold pop.

Even though the journalists had only been driving half an hour in
air-conditioned vehicles since leaving their breakfast tables at the fully
equipped international hotel, they gratefully accepted the proffered
drinks. Of the six-member camera crew, three actually helped themselves
to a second pop—meaning that nearly-one third of the engineer troop
sacrificed their luxury ration to the visitors. Admirably, there was
absolutely no resentment on the part of the young soldiers. In fact, one
trooper summed it up by saying, "It was lucky for us that [the escort]
thought to bring the pop, otherwise we'd have had nothing to offer [the
journalists] at all."

If soldiers are found to be hoarding goods from their section mates,
under normal circumstances the perpetrators will only be verbally
rebuffed. However, under extremely trying circumstances, such a self-interested attitude would likely draw a more physical response. In 1984, during
a winter exercise in Shilo, Manitoba, a rifle section had just completed three
days of gruelling forced marches and hasty bivouacs. Such a feat, in full

winter gear (including snowshoes), is incredibly physically demanding, and quenching their thirst became an almost maddening obsession.

It was at this point that a rifleman was observed drinking a can of Coke inside the section vehicle. Once discovered, the rifleman tried to conceal the evidence rather than share his beverage. Unfortunately, his clumsy actions only led to the revelation that he had an additional nine cans of pop stashed away in the carrier.

Enraged by this act of selfishness and possessed by their thirst, the other section members brutally beat the offender and appropriated his hidden stock. True to the "code," the incident was never formally reported by the victim, but from that day forward he was the most generous soldier in the platoon.

If and when a soldier is caught by the authorities for an infraction, he is expected by his fellow soldiers to admit his involvement and suffer any consequences—without attempting to mitigate his guilt through the implication of others. Troops also expect this responsibility of action to be reflected by their officers, once the soldiers themselves have confessed their own culpability.

Again the Somalia affair lends itself as a perfect example of how this simple system can break down if the essential ingredient—the courage of conviction—is lacking.

When Sergeant Mark Boland gave evidence to the military police and at his subsequent court martial, he never once shirked the responsibility of his rank. Nor did he try to involve his superiors to save himself. Although he himself had never struck young Shidane Arone, Boland had been the first one to guard him after his capture. It was Boland who turned over responsibility for the prisoner to Master Corporal Clayton Matchee, and then he went to bed.

The soldiers of 2 Commando had all been made aware of Major Anthony Seward's order to "abuse" captured looters, and Matchee had discussed his intention to "rough up" Arone with Sergeant Boland. Upon retiring for the night, Boland had cautioned Matchee with the, in retrospect, callous remark "Whatever you do, just don't kill him." The next morning was the first time Boland learned of the brutal beating death.

At his court martial, Mark Boland pleaded guilty to a charge of negligence, even though his crime had consisted solely of having allowed Clayton

Matchee to obey a standing order issued by their company commander, Major Seward. Boland's attitude towards accepting responsibility was unfortunately not mirrored by the officers of 2 Commando, and certainly not reflected in the subsequent actions of the high command.

Sergeant Mark Boland was the only one of the eight soldiers charged in the Somalia affair to plead guilty at his court martial. At the time, his original sentence of ninety days in a military jail was considered by the troops to be harsh but fair, and Boland himself was held in high regard for his honesty and sense of responsibility.

The military justice machine, however, driven by the desire to appease public opinion, appealed Boland's sentence and was successful in having him not only reincarcerated, but also dishonourably discharged from the service. By contrast, the three officers implicated in the same case pleaded not guilty to charges of negligence. Although there was overwhelming (and uncontested) evidence that they had issued orders for their troops to abuse prisoners, the strongest punishment issued as a result of their actions was a severe reprimand.

The message this sent to the troops completely violated the basic trust soldiers require in order to practise their unique profession. The principle under which combat troops operate is that the junior ranks must obey orders and that those who issue these orders are inherently responsible for any consequences. If a soldier feels that an order he receives may be unlawful, he has the right to request that his commander put the instruction in writing—but he does *not* have the right to disobey it.

If a soldier ignores or exceeds a directive, his punishment is usually swift and severe. However, it is still fully expected that an officer or non-commissioned officer will accept responsibility for the actions of his men (especially if they were only obeying a dubious order to begin with).

While the individual officers in the Somalia affair cannot be considered blameless (although they did plead innocent), it was the military justice system in this case which failed to hold them accountable. In so doing, they unwittingly underscored the negative impact of National Defence Headquarters' bureaucratic policies upon the strict ethos of frontline units. For the previous three decades, the trend at Headquarters had been to diminish individual responsibilities through overstaffing of the middle-management ranks and the micro-managing style of the senior leaders. By having the top brass control even the most minute details of all operations, the middle-ranked directors are effectively reduced to mere go-betweens, whereas the military, by its very nature, defines its chain of command in meticulous detail. Organizational charts are the first thing produced before planning any operation, regardless of its scale or scope. At the combat formation level, a vast array of regulations and standard operating procedures (SOPs) exist, so troops can rapidly work out a command hierarchy for even *ad hoc* units.

Junior commissioned officers are taught the intricate formulas of when "appointment" supersedes "rank" for purposes of command and control. For instance, when an armoured unit and an infantry unit are combined to form a battle group, normally the ratio dictates which of the two commanders controls the joint operation. However, this arrangement can be superseded by the particular mission or role, and a relatively junior officer can find himself temporarily responsible for the manoeuvre actions of a much larger formation.

Overall, the reporting chain is based on the strictly defined rank structure, and all possible exceptions are carefully formalized and recorded so that there is never any doubt as to "who is in charge" of a given organization.

However, once things get to the National Headquarters level, and the military component finds itself married to civilian counterparts, the only semblance of order that remains is the preponderance of organizational charts. It is, therefore, very difficult for many senior officers who first arrive in Ottawa late in their military careers to grasp just how things are really being run. Naively, many have been so steeped in their own experience that they are unable, or unwilling, to accept their new surroundings. These officers usually spend their tours at NDHQ loathing the environment and anxiously awaiting a return to familiar "military" surroundings.

Conversely, many ambitious junior officers who land a Headquarters tour early in their development quickly realize that the power base lies outside the published charts, and learn to swim in the fastest upward currents.

The rank and file are all too aware of this widening gap between themselves and their senior leadership and they voiced their concerns in the 1995 Phillips Study. In that poll, 83 per cent of the troops surveyed described the military brass as "self-interested careerists." By civilian standards, such a description of top executives may not raise many eyebrows, but in the military world it should have set off alarm bells.

"Any fool can be uncomfortable in the field" is an oft-heard jest among combat soldiers. Invariably, it is used by an individual attempting to ward off the scorn of his peers for having obtained a cushy job or a soft billet. To front-line soldiers, the more spartan the accommodation, the more gruelling the task and the more hazardous the mission, the more "bragging rights" they possess.

While soldiers will take immense pride in being immaculately turned out in their full dress uniforms, in field situations the reverse is true. Members of support units are often mocked for sporting crisp new combat clothing, and during an extended exercise, cleanliness would be viewed as evidence of a "slacker."

For most Canadians, accustomed to materialistic societal values, it would seem unfathomable that the endurance of hardship would be regarded as a measure of merit, yet for our troops it is a way of life.

Throughout the seventies and eighties, Canada's NATO contingent was consistently rated as being the "best soldiers with the worst equipment" in the sixteen-nation alliance. Instead of complaining about their neglected circumstances, Canadian soldiers took pride in their accomplishments with what was recognized by their foreign peers to be unsatisfactory support. It was a bragging right.

For decades, there has been a shortage of training ammunition and other vital supplies. And, unquestioningly, the troops accepted the explanation of tight budgets and meagre defence resources. Young soldiers still pride themselves on being able to keep armoured personnel carriers serviceable, despite the fact that they were probably manufactured at least ten years before the mechanics were born. Skilled weapons technicians often brag of their ability to keep Second World War–vintage machine-guns operable through their sheer ingenuity and resourcefulness.

To earn the respect of men in this environment, an officer must be prepared to sacrifice more, and to be seen constantly putting his men's welfare before his own. If a young lieutenant pulls rank in order to move to the head of a meal line, he is scorned. Yet, if that subaltern waits until all the men are served only to find there's no food left, his troops see to it that he doesn't go hungry.

Naturally, combat soldiers have naively assumed that the ethos by which they conduct themselves, and which they expect of their officers, is reflected all the way up the chain of command.

All too often they heard the media reports of budget cuts to the Defence Department, and the military analysts' subsequent chorus of woeful poverty. Since they themselves lived with shortages on a daily basis, it was easy to assume that the hardships were widespread and universal.

The rank and file's deepening animosity towards the high command began after the lavish excesses of their senior leaders were made public. Sure, soldiers always knew that their commander had a huge government residence. But they didn't realize that he paid no rent for it. Grown men, trained combat soldiers, often were forced to substitute for a shortage of blank ammunition by yelling "Bullet, Bullet!" during training exercises. Although such a practice was seen as humiliating, it was easier for these men to accept as belt-tightening under a tight budget before they learned that their generals were spending nearly $1 million a year on a luxury fishing camp.

In 1994, over-rotated peacekeeping contingents deploying to the former Yugoslavia were still content to exchange helmets with their homeward-bound comrades. They realized that the purchase of an additional 1,000 modern Kevlar helmets would cost the cash-strapped Defence Department nearly $500,000, and General John de Chastelain had repeatedly urged them to make do with less. These same soldiers seriously questioned the integrity of the Defence Department management when it was reported in the media that Deputy Minister Bob Fowler had spent $387,000 just in renovating his own office suite.

As morale plummeted throughout the Forces due to this "command crisis," the top generals and bureaucrats proved themselves to be completely out of touch with their own troops. Upon assuming the job of chief of the defence staff, General Jean Boyle announced that his first priority would be to get his soldiers a "pay raise." Boyle also conducted a leadership convention in Toronto to discuss the "perception" of a rift between senior officers and the rank and file.

It was decided there that General Boyle should conduct a "campaign" to visit all the major bases to meet the troops. Top brass thought that if Boyle could be seen announcing a 2.2 per cent pay raise, it would increase his popularity with the men. Unfortunately for the organizers of this "CDS tour," the soldiers had already seen through the obvious ploy to buy their loyalty and, instead, they had some difficult questions they wished to have answered by the new top soldier.

At his appearance in Calgary, General Boyle kept the troops waiting on the parade square for nearly two hours while he attended a reception at the officers' mess. After concluding his formal address, Boyle asked the troops to feel free to ask him some candid questions. With that invitation, a Master Corporal Murphy stepped forward and boldly asked the CDS, "Sir, just how do you think you're going to improve our morale by having us stand out here waiting for hours while you're in the mess getting drunk?"

Rather than address the question, or joke away the rebuff, an infuriated Boyle told the assembled troops: "Standing on parade is part of being a soldier and if any of you resent doing your job, then get the hell out of the service. There's over a million unemployed in this country who would gladly take your place."

Needless to say, the positive public relations impact the planners had hoped to achieve backfired miserably. Master Corporal Murphy spent three weeks on "extra duties" for his candour, and the battalion involved set a record for the number of voluntary releases in the following month.

As the new chief of the defence staff, General Boyle failed miserably in his attempt to win over "the grunts" by demonstrating that he does not understand them or the code they live by. And that lack of comprehension, not their frozen salaries, is why frontline morale has plummeted.

CHAPTER SIX

Going Bongos at Headquarters

The largest department in the Canadian government sits hunkered down in three cubelike, pre–cast-concrete buildings on the banks of the Rideau Canal in downtown Ottawa, literally in line of sight, or more appropriately in the line of fire, of the Peace Tower and Parliament. Architecturally, the three buildings that make up the Department of National Defence are more or less nondescript; their squat, recessed windows are more Chechen in character than Canadian. There's a standing joke in the capital that no one really knows how many people actually work in the Headquarters building.

Whatever the number, the fact is that the Department of National Defence is monolithic, a gigantic bureaucracy that has attained unmanageable proportions. Within its walls, as daily testimony before the commission of inquiry into Somalia confirms, it is possible to subvert the law, destroy evidence and literally almost get away with murder, and not be held accountable.

The remarks of the late Canadian filmmaker Donald Brittain made in 1979 on the eve of the première of his documentary masterpiece *Paperland: The Bureaucracy Observed* are prophetic in light of the trials and tribulations facing the brass and bureaucrats as they hunker down in Headquarters.

"My concern is for the monumental waste of money and high intelligence in bureaucracies," Brittain said to a *Toronto Sun* reviewer. "Good friends of mine have changed dramatically after a few years in the service. No longer are they outspoken and decisive. What I'd like to see is a return to first principles—the public good. An end to their quite desperate fear of making a mistake. It is this fear that leads to their proliferation and the absence of accountability that is the cornerstone of bureaucracy."

The truth is that the department is so byzantine in its structure and size that holding a person accountable is close to impossible, especially with a leadership lacking moral fibre.

According to the 1995–96 Defence Estimates, the personnel resources of the Department of National Defence included 97,727 full-time employees.

Of that number, 28,927 were civilians. In the Ottawa-Hull area alone, there are 12,500 civilian and military personnel spread out in 38 different buildings. As for the military, the Army listed 29,142, Maritime Command (the Navy) 17,181 and the Air Force 24,364 men and women. The figures do not include nearly 30,000 reservists.

Managing these resources from Headquarters are two chains of command, one military under the direction of the chief of the defence staff, the other the civilian bureaucracy under the control of the deputy minister of defence.

Serving the minister are six assistant deputy ministers, each with his own huge staff. The assistant deputy ministers are responsible for Materiel (the most powerful and influential), Policy and Communication, Personnel, Defence Information Services, Finance and Corporate Services, and Infrastructure and Environment. The PMO, the Project Management Office, comes under Materiel. Three of the six deputies themselves have associate assistant deputy ministers. Below them in vast numbers are chiefs, directors general and directors.

On the military side, reporting to the CDS, is the judge advocate general's office, the vice-chief of the defence staff, followed by the DCDS, and finally the chief of review services. Like their civilian counterparts, the military headquarters units also have chiefs, directors general, directors and one associate assistant.

Aside from assistant deputy ministers and chiefs, the staggering number of administrators consists of 10 chiefs, 59 directors general and 281 directors, along with their staffs of thousands. The telephone directory of the Department of National Defence is larger than that of most medium-sized Canadian cities. The sheer size and impenetrable nature of this bureaucratic jungle created an atmosphere of unaccountability and played a great part in the military's current loss of credibility.

Moreover, there has been a high turnover among the ministers of defence who have passed through the system since 1989, or as they joke around Headquarters "who have served under Fowler." First there was Perrin Beatty, who pushed for nuclear subs; then Bill McKnight, whose term was undistinguished; followed by Marcel Masse, a closet separatist, as it turned out, but who insiders say was one of the few who stood up to Fowler. Kim Campbell's June to January 1993 stint was ineffective. She claimed Fowler told her only what he wanted to, which wasn't much since the Somalia scandal broke while she was minister. Tom Siddon was more or less a caretaker minister whose term was also undistinguished. Last is David Collenette, who miraculously survives the mess by political instincts, but for how long is debatable.

The truth is, the ministers are at the mercy of the brass and the bureaucrats, who know they can chew them up and spit them out at will. It is ludicrous to think that someone can grasp the culture of this complex department in six months, as was the case for Kim Campbell, or less than this for Tom Siddon.

The heart and soul of National Defence is located on the thirteenth floor of the Major-General George Pearkes Building, one of the three bunkers disguised as office buildings. It is here that all the senior executives are housed and where the buzzwords "access" and "influence" take on new meanings.

The deputy minister of defence is seen as the resident authority, and his office suite is considered to be the epicentre of power within the department. It is said that you can determine an executive's level of influence by the proximity of his office to the DM's suite, and the importance of a directorate by its distance from the thirteenth floor, regardless of where it appears on an official organizational chart.

Up on the thirteenth floor, there is a unique atmosphere among the occupants almost reminiscent of an elite social club. It is here that all key decisions are made. In this world, where knowledge is power and power is currency, being in the know confers status in itself.

It soon became apparent following the arrival of Robert Fowler on the thirteenth floor that the "civilianization" of the department was paramount in Fowler's agenda.

Prior to 1989, the chiefs of the defence staff had jealously striven to maintain a division of responsibilities between uniformed appointments (Canadian Forces) and senior civilian executives (Defence Department). In this way, the thirteenth floor had its own two polarized power circles, and with that came an inherent checks-and-balances system.

With the appointment of General John de Chastelain as CDS and Robert Fowler as DM, the power was quickly consolidated into the office of the deputy minister. Fowler became involved in such matters as military promotions and discipline, which had heretofore been the sole purview of the top soldier. When he took over, de Chastelain had been only too willing to hand over his reins of responsibility.

One of the first actions de Chastelain undertook was to cancel the regularly held morning CDS operations briefings which normally preceded the daily executive meeting. It was here that commanders would brief their chief on operational matters, and while the deputy minister was often in attendance, he would rarely comment or give any direction. By cancelling these briefings, and covering their proceedings at the daily executive meetings, de Chastelain theoretically still held a co-chair position and retained some influence. In reality, the power shift was immediately evident to all involved. Fowler became recognized as the supreme unchecked power, barely thirty days into his six-year tenure as the senior mandarin at DND.

"Fowler knew he could play de Chastelain like a piano. He would cave in on anything," remembered Colonel Jim Allan. "De Chastelain was one of these guys who when unification came along, saw that the way ahead was not soldiering, but playing the political game and pleasing the political masters. He is a creature of unification."

Colonel Brian Reid added that "Fowler's intellectual strength cowed most opposition. De Chastelain would avoid confrontation in front of the staff, though he would discuss the matter afterward in private."

The daily executive meeting sets the tone for all that happens at Headquarters and, by extension, the entire Canadian military. To put the power structure in perspective, the minister of national defence does not attend these sessions.

It is here, following extensive background briefings, that the deputy minister determines what the minister will or won't be told on a particular issue—and in how much detail. The briefing book, which defence ministers cling to as their bible during Question Period, is prepared for them based on the direction of the deputy minister, gathered from the input he receives at the daily executive meeting.

Veteran politicians know that a powerful and ambitious deputy minister can make them or break them in their portfolios, depending on the status of their relationship. Characteristically, Fowler held an attitude of disdainful tolerance for each of the six defence ministers he served "under" while he was deputy. He had a "one-hundred-day rule." If the department seemingly ran squeaky clean for the first three months of a minister's appointment, he would have won the trust and support of the minister.

Although Fowler had no military background before being transferred to DND as an assistant deputy minister in 1986, his natural industry and work ethic combined to produce a consuming ambition to understand all things military.

He constantly demanded detailed intelligence briefings, and he diligently studied arms journals such as *Jane's Defence Weekly* to keep current with international technology developments. By working seven days a week and rarely heading home before 8:00 p.m., Fowler was soon able to challenge the senior officers who attended the daily executive meetings—even in their own fields of expertise.

By the time an officer reaches the rank of lieutenant-general, he is normally no longer challenged by either his peers—since they are from different services—or his underlings, due to the inherent authoritarianism of the command structure. Complacency among the top brass became commonplace, and this was mixed with their normal disdain for civilians, who generally fail to comprehend the intricacies of the military profession.

In Robert Ramsay Fowler, though, the top commanders soon found that they had more than met their match. Often these generals and admirals would base their decisions upon personal memories of operational command—on average, these were more than fifteen years old. Fowler, on the other hand, had a passion for assimilating and maintaining an up-to-date database. Frequently, he would catch out senior officers in a contradiction, and he wouldn't hesitate to embarrass them in front of their peers, just to demonstrate his superior intellect.

Rather than applying themselves to meet the challenge Fowler posed, the top brass quickly reverted to a more familiar and comfortable role of subservience. The only notable example of a senior commander attempting to stem the power tide during this period was that of Vice-Admiral Chuck Thomas. As the vice-chief of the defence staff, Thomas could see the increasing control Fowler was commanding and the resultant politicization of DND, which in turn was emasculating the Armed Forces.

In 1991, following another disastrous budget cut, Chuck Thomas decided he could no longer go on living a lie and misrepresenting the state of our forces to the Canadian public. In March, he wrote a personal letter to General de Chastelain outlining his position and bluntly stating the reasons for his early departure, not the least of which was the willingness with which de Chastelain himself had gone along with Fowler's proposed new direction for the Forces. Once de Chastelain received the resignation, he immediately conferred with Fowler on how they should deal with the problem. At this point, Admiral Thomas had not issued his letter to the media.

De Chastelain wrote an acceptance letter, which by its very tone and content undermined Thomas's position and belittled his arguments about the Armed Forces' future structure. The two letters were then leaked to the media on a wholesale basis. DND rarely airs its internal debates publicly and conflict makes for good news. Thomas, having committed his position first and not intending for it to be broadcast, was caught flat-footed. As a result, he was discredited by public affairs officers as a "grandstander, just weeks away from retirement" and the whole affair blew over rather quickly.

For insiders, the Thomas affair was to have long-term repercussions. The writing was on the wall, if you were a whistle blower.

As the old soldiers and sailors faded away, there came in their echoing footsteps a horde of civilian bureaucrats. By 1995, there were 151 civilian "generals" or senior executives on the payroll at the Department of National Defence, wielding power and influence in economic and political circles, and allotting money to questionable enterprises while often denying support to soldiers serving on operations.

In June 1991, 150 Canadian combat engineers were still plying their trade in the sunbaked and explosives-strewn sands of Kuwait. Although the Gulf War had been over for three months, Canada had agreed to keep a contingent of engineers in the region and a naval warship in the Persian Gulf. The men from 1 Combat Engineer Regiment (1CER) undoubtedly had the most dangerous job of any Canadian troops deployed to the Gulf (including those who served there during hostilities). Certainly, the extreme climatic conditions they faced were equal to the harshest ever suffered by Canadian soldiers.

Included in the U.S.–led Coalition Forces' strategy to liberate Kuwait from the Iraqi army was a prerequisite deadline—Desert Storm had to be concluded before the summer season began. The reason for this was the blistering 60° Celsius summer temperatures of this desert region. Therefore, the massive coalition air assault on Iraqi forces began on January 15, and only one month later, the whirlwind 100-hour ground attack was launched into Kuwait.

By June, although the oil well fires still burned voraciously and the blackened dunes of Kuwait were still littered with Iraqi corpses and unexploded ordnance, the CNN television crews had left. Without the constant media coverage, and with sailors and airmen enjoying yellow ribbon "welcome home" parades, the Persian Gulf War became a closed chapter in the minds of the Canadian public.

However, for Major Dick Isabel and his combat engineers, the hardships were just beginning to take their toll. The exhausting heat was inescapable. Even night-time temperatures at the regiment's bivouac dropped only to a roasting 45° Celsius. Because they were using open-topped metal water-towers, the only time Canadian soldiers could endure the scalding showers was in the hours well before dawn.

The operational task of these "sappers" was a dangerous and vital one. They were to mark and clear safe lanes through the desert. It was estimated that 40 per cent of the bombs dropped by the U.S. Air Force had failed to explode in the sand. Added to this overwhelming hazard were the vast quantities of stockpiled Iraqi munitions left behind during their retreat. For Major Isabel, there was a very real concern for the safety of his men as heat and fatigue took their natural toll on their abilities.

Isabel felt that if he could provide his troops with even a temporary respite from the heat, he could reduce the risks to his men. Because obtaining the necessary air-conditioning units through the United Nations bureaucracy was going to take four months, the young Major appealed to National Defence Headquarters for relief.

At the time, 1CER occupied a large Kuwaiti warehouse, which Isabel had acquired in an unconventional deal with its owner. Realizing that defence funds were "tight," the Canadian commander worked it out that a central air-conditioning unit would be installed at the warehouse owner's expense. All the Canadian government would have to pay was $42,000 in airfreight to ship the necessary machinery into Kuwait. Since all the details had been arranged in advance, it was estimated that the combat engineers could be relaxing in climate-controlled comfort within seven days of NDHQ approving the expenditure.

Alas, it was not to be. The message sent back to Major Isabel by Headquarters in Ottawa was a curt denial of his request. There were set budgetary rules and firm application guidelines which had to be followed—and the brass would not relent. As a result, the combat engineers were left out in the heat because their $42,000 "could not be rationalized."

To understand the absolute inversion of departmental priorities and the self-serving advancement of bureaucrats at the expense of the very uniformed soldiers they purportedly exist to serve, one must view the plight of 1CER in the light of the following episode.

At this very same time, the bureaucrats who control the "environment" at NDHQ, the Directorate of Facilities Management, were trying to unwind from the pressures of wartime service. Throughout the Gulf War, all personnel in NDHQ had put in some overtime hours, and the directorate's workers were no exception. However, as the maintainers and co-ordinators of DND's office facilities, their extra required efforts were far from Herculean, nor fraught with danger. Nevertheless, the charming and ambitious young executive director, Micheline Clairoux, decided that her forty-five civilian employees needed to take a break and relax.

At a cost of $86,000 to Canadian taxpayers, Clairoux contracted the private firm of Seagull Consulting to provide her stressed-out colleagues with a "mental retreat"—complete with a Californian guru. The five-day getaway was conducted at a resort hotel in Mont Ste. Marie, Quebec, an hour's drive from Ottawa. The schedule consisted entirely of such activities as sing-alongs, sports and a bongo-playing session, personally demonstrated by the Californian guru. The Canadian military had figuratively (and in this case literally) shifted its primary focus from bunkers to bongos.

Very few Canadians are even aware of the civilian component of National Defence, or that it comprises more than 28,000 individuals, representing roughly one-third of the total DND payroll. The role that these public servants perform is even less understood by the general public, but the natural assumption is that they provide "secure support for the 'fighting soldier.'" While ostensibly this is the basic premise, the reality of the present "civilian tail wagging the military dog" circumstances has evolved over years of empire builders using systemic flaws to increase their own power and prestige.

As one would suspect, there is a very distinct class division between the working-class civilians (rank and file) and the management cadre (officer and general equivalents). In many ways, the lower-ranking public servants have a greater commonality with our neglected troops than with their fellow civil servants in other government departments. One reason for this is the fact that, as employees of DND, all of these workers are subject to the independent justice system of the National Defence Act and they must adhere to the Official Secrets Act. Of course their bosses, in most cases civilian senior managers, have the authority to wield the absolute powers these statutes provide.

Unchecked power and unbridled ambition are a dangerous combination under any circumstances, and the senior civilian component of the Defence Department has taken full advantage of just such a situation over the past thirty years. The establishment of jealously guarded mini-empires within DND and the blatant careerism of these top bureaucrats—thinly disguised as "dedication" and "ambition"—have created, over a three-decade span, an enormous force of 150 civilian "general" equivalents. To put this number in perspective, consider the following.

Although the 1972 amalgamation of the Canadian Forces Headquarters with senior departmental staff admittedly created a greying of the previous black and white areas of control (soldiers commanded troops, while civilians managed public servants), this amounts to one civvy general for every 166 departmental employees!

This large group of senior executives have been highly effective in preserving their power through maintaining an extremely low public profile. The military general officer corps, itself horribly bloated in relation to the military strength it commands, have often been ridiculed in the media, and subsequently targeted for (minimal) reductions. By comparison, the senior general executives outnumber their uniformed counterparts by a ratio of 3 to 2 and, due to the occupational discrepancies in responsibility, they're in fact four times more overranked than the bloated Canadian general officer corps. One of the reasons for the invisibility of this high-priced echelon of bureaucrats stems from the very nature of the individuals who comprise it. Many of them, being veteran public servants, have long ago recognized that the true power in government circles lies behind the throne and not with the figurehead appointment established to represent any given department. From the top down in National Defence, this same principle applies: the minister fronts the department, but behind the scenes it is managed by the deputy minister. On military affairs, it is the chief of the defence staff who endures the flak or takes the credit, but under the tenure of Bob Fowler as deputy minister, even these matters were routinely controlled by the deputy minister, out of public sight.

Fowler understood and used four basic principles as the basis for his control over the department: access, power, knowledge and loyalty. He knew that in order to make people loyal to him, he needed to be able to hold power over their promotions.

That was how Carol Barrett, a relatively junior executive as the director general of classifications, came to be one of the most powerful people in Fowler's inner cabinet. Once the Deputy Minister realized that he could use the legitimate job classification process to upgrade, downgrade or move out individuals on a whim, Barrett had immediate and direct access to him (and vice versa).

Another individual who benefited from Fowler's control and manipulation of the job classification directorate was Nancy Wildgoose. To most senior officers and civilian executives, Wildgoose was an enigma whose power and influence defied comprehension. In 1989, she first joined the executive ranks as the director general of Policy and Operations. At the time, this position was regarded as relatively minor (level one, executive) but, even so, Wildgoose's education in library studies seemed an odd qualification for someone tasked with formulating military policy.

Once Fowler had singled out Wildgoose for his inner cabinet, the position she held remained unchanged, but her classification and power grew steadily. By 1994, Wildgoose was an executive, level three, or a major-general equivalent.

To outsiders, Wildgoose's appointment and the prestige she enjoyed seemed difficult to justify, given her lack of management skills and reliance on research rather than experience in her decision making. Admittedly, she was able to communicate in a very articulate manner, she was blindly ambitious and, more important, she was uniquely loyal to Fowler. Because her job involved organizing parliamentary matters and cabinet liaison, Wildgoose became Fowler's barometer for predicting any shift in the political winds.

She had Fowler's explicit trust and never failed to take the opportunity to demonstrate their close association, to the astonishment of senior officers. At daily executive meetings, she would frequently interrupt the proceedings, out of sequence, by addressing her questions directly to "Bob." Three-star generals still referred to Fowler as "Sir" in his presence and as "the DM" among their colleagues. Only when a senior officer was in company he trusted would the nickname "Teflon Bob" be used to refer to Fowler, and even then it was uttered with some trepidation.

Wildgoose relished her privileged position and wasn't hesitant in throwing her weight around, as shown by the following encounter with Chuck Thomas.

Vice-Admiral Thomas had spent thirty-three years in the Navy and had worked his way through numerous command and staff positions, both with the fleet and at National Defence Headquarters. He was widely respected by his peers and colleagues for his tough, no-nonsense approach to the profession of arms, and he possessed a keen intellect which allowed him to swim successfully in political seas. Nevertheless, despite his wealth of experience and powers of perception, Thomas was in for a rude awakening and quick re-education on the power structure when he was appointed vice-chief of the defence staff in 1989.

Shortly after he took up his new office as the "number two" soldier in the country, an imposing middle-aged woman breezed past his executive assistant and entered his office without knocking. In her hands were a number of forms and reports, which she brusquely instructed Thomas to have completed in time for the next daily executive meeting.

After her equally abrupt departure, Thomas summoned his assistant and demanded: "Who the hell is that woman?"

The aide replied, "That, sir, is Nancy Wildgoose. She is the director general of Policy and Operations."

"So that would make her just a level-one executive, or a civilian brigadier-general equivalent?" queried Thomas. "I'm a three-star admiral, second-in-command of a separate chain of command, yet she barged in here and treated me as though she were issuing me with an order."

"She was, sir," replied the aide. "Welcome back to National Defence Headquarters."

Physically, Wildgoose often appeared "tousled and harried, under pressure," according to Dave Statham, a retired naval officer. Her technique of authority was to "load it on people, to keep you off balance by being overbearing and authoritative." Statham added: "I would describe Nancy as the ultimate bureaucrat in both the positive and negative sense. I don't think that she will stand up to somebody and say, 'No, I want it this way.' She will bend, how far I'm not prepared to say. If she is rebuffed she will use other avenues; she's very good at that. She is very good at keeping herself in view and involved. There will be high-level meetings where people will say, 'How come Nancy's involved?'"

Yet it was this sometimes arrogant figure who became part of the ruling troika—Fowler, Wildgoose and Ken Calder. In 1986, when Fowler first arrived at DND, Calder was the associate assistant, and Fowler, as assistant deputy minister, was his immediate supervisor. The first project the two worked on was the ill-fated, grandiose 1987 White Paper on Defence.

The people Fowler selected for his inner circle were all hand-picked. When a ringer got tossed into the mix, the deputy minister was quick to get rid of the trouble-maker. Such was the case in 1989, when Fowler was promoted to deputy minister, and his old job of assistant deputy minister (policy) was filled by Louis Delvoie, who had served on the 1983 Trudeau peace initiative with Fowler. Since then, Delvoie had been at Treasury Board. For some reason the appointment did not sit well with Fowler, although Delvoie was a capable executive. Perhaps the reason was that Delvoie *was* a capable executive. Or perhaps the reason was that Delvoie was not beholden to Fowler for the appointment. Frequently over the next two and a half years, Delvoie and Fowler would have altercations at the daily executive meetings regarding policy issues. Unlike all of the senior officers in attendance, Delvoie was not afraid to match wits with the DM, and he would debate him authoritatively, to the amusement of all those present.

Needless to say, Fowler did not enjoy such exchanges, and he actively sought to undermine Delvoie's authority by granting Calder and Wildgoose direct access to his office. In 1992, when the first opportunity arose, he transferred Delvoie out of DND and promoted Calder to the position of assistant deputy minister (policy), thereby formalizing his control over the driving impetus of DND.

One of the more high-profile and potentially difficult senior appointments within DND is that of assistant deputy minister (personnel). With many contentious human rights policies being implemented and challenged over the past ten years, the ADM (Per) position has been frequently under fire, and very much in the public spotlight. Controversy has surrounded such issues as the acceptance of gays in the Forces, allowing women in combat roles, increasing the mandatory retirement age, establishing lucrative force-reduction buy-out packages, and investigating the rash of suicides in certain regiments.

Many of the press conferences regarding these subjects had been handled by the lieutenant-general, who happened to be the incumbent assistant deputy minister (personnel). Often the beleaguered general appeared poorly prepared for these events and was frequently shown to have no depth of knowledge under questioning. A clear example of this sort of unconvincing performance was the April 3, 1995, attempt by Lieutenant-General Paul Addy to rationalize the preponderance of suicides in the Royal 22nd Regiment (Vandoos).

Under the glare of the television lights, the hulking, bespectacled general quickly became visibly confused. Frequently consulting his scattered notes and running his hand through his crew-cut hair, Addy was obviously uncomfortable having his evasive answers shredded by a vigilant press corps.

Presumably, the department's public affairs team had hoped that the appearance of such high-ranking individuals would show their "corporate concern" for the issue and that they could effectively defuse the matter before it caught the public's imagination. Instead, even Defence Minister David Collenette rated Addy's performance as incompetent, and the whole affair blew up into a mini-scandal (mostly restricted to the French-Canadian press).

Nowhere to be seen throughout this entire debacle was the fastidious and diminutive Associate Assistant Deputy Minister (Personnel) Doug Lindley, another member of Fowler's "power club," whom he had personally recruited. Lindley had been an outsider, brought into his executive position at DND directly from industry. But he had quickly adjusted to his new civil service environment.

In fifteen years, Lindley worked for no fewer than ten different ADMs. Due to their rapid rotation in the job, few, if any, of the lieutenant-generals assigned to the position ever developed a solid grasp of the complex personnel world before they were promoted or replaced. Since he was the "constant," Lindley naturally became the power behind the throne. He knew where all of the skeletons were buried and which ones were likely to pose an embarrassment.

The ADMs he worked for came to trust his judgement, and when Fowler granted Lindley direct access, the military position diminished to little more than figurehead status, despite the authorized reporting chain.

When the chief of civilian personnel position became vacant, Fowler decided to leave the executive position unoccupied, with Lindley picking up the additional responsibility for that directorate's operations. Effectively, this simple manoeuvre doubled Lindley's power and gave Fowler direct influence over all DND personnel.

Like Bob Fowler, Lindley knew that in order to avoid taking responsibility, it is imperative to avoid being caught in the spotlight. Conversely, the military counterparts of these top bureaucrats, by virtue of their training, are readily accepting of the visible trappings which accompany these appointments. Although the present generation of top officers are just as reluctant as the civilian bureaucrats to take responsibility for their own actions (or those of a subordinate), their resplendent gold-braid uniforms and staff cars make them much easier for the media to target for ridicule.

Of course, the preponderance of civilian generals is no accident either, and the reason for this doesn't stem entirely from cronyism. Once again, it is arguable that a driving factor behind the swelling of the bureaucratic ranks is rooted in the avoidance of responsibility. When a ship has only one captain, it is easy to single out that individual for blame should any mishap occur. This is known in the military as command responsibility. However, if that same ship happens to have seventeen captains, all of whom have been entrusted with the full responsibility for her safe handling, it's a safe bet that a shipwreck would result in a lengthy inquiry with no conclusive results (i.e., everyone is off the hook).

To support this theory, one need only study the composition of National Defence Headquarters. The quickest way to do so is to thumb through the NDHQ phone book and to make a quick mental tally of the appointment titles. In many cases, the obvious redundancy and overlapping of high-ranking offices is compounded by an already microscopically defined area of responsibility. For instance, one could easily question the necessity of having both a director general for manpower utilization and a director general for force development when, by definition, their roles are indistinguishable.

While the responsibility of their offices may be shunned, and diffused by overstaffing, the top civilian bureaucrats certainly don't shun the privileges and perks afforded to their (military equivalency) rank. Although they don't have access to subsidized residences and chauffeured cars, the senior mandarins make up for these hardships by sending themselves on frequent all-expenses-paid government trips.

Whether they're flying or driving their personal car, the mode is always full fare at the public's expense. Air travel is naturally provided in business class, complete with free lounge memberships, and car mileage is reimbursed at the "high government" rate.

Deputy Minister Bob Fowler set the example for his top mandarins in terms of benevolence. This team of senior bureaucrats was incredibly generous to one another—with public money. Working lunches and farewell parties for co-workers would be lavishly catered with no regard to cost and, since the Deputy Minister was engaging in such practices, there was no fear of repercussions. Doug Lindley was probably the best example of both the lavish bureaucratic excess and the cheap personal pettiness that many of these executives displayed. As the man responsible for all of the personnel issues within DND, it was natural for Lindley to meet with the president of the Union of National Defence Employees (UNDE) to discuss a whole range of concerns. Everything from employees' frozen salaries, to force reduction packages, and even employer harassment cases, would have been on the agenda.

Lindley decided that the best way to iron out any differences with Ken Hawley, UNDE's president, would be over an expensive lunch every month. Naturally, since these were working lunches, the taxpayers footed the bill. One such tête-à-tête between these two gentlemen set the taxpayers back $142.42 in a pre-Christmas extended work session at the Canal Ritz restaurant in Ottawa. The relationship between Lindley and Hawley was so cosy that, when the UNDE president left his post in July 1993, Lindley splurged for a farewell dinner. The location was the prestigious March House restaurant, and both gentlemen brought along their spouses for this "working session." The total tab for the foursome was $183.06, and the taxpayers reimbursed Lindley the full amount.

On another occasion, Lindley entertained six guests from the Electrical Workers Union at the army officers' mess. Incredibly, the bill amounted to $254.06 for the seven participants, even though the price of a luncheon ticket at the subsidized mess is just $5.00. Alcohol at the officers' club is also very reasonable, at $1.50 per beer or shot. But since Treasury Board guidelines prohibit the use of tax money for the purchasing of alcoholic beverages (even on working lunches), it must have been assumed that Lindley and his guests ate six lunches each.

On June 18, 1993, Lindley treated his boss, Bob Fowler, and an Australian trade official, Ron McLeod, to a $145.58 snack at Le Café. Once again, work must have been discussed, because Lindley's claim was paid in full.

Doug Lindley also used the power of his position to take frequent trips abroad, notwithstanding that there are only a dozen or so civilian employees still working for DND in Europe. These week-long junkets would often involve just two or three scheduled meetings, offset with five days of off-time. Lindley would submit the maximum lodging and food claims, and he never missed recording the slightest incidental expense for reimbursement. In fact, when he travelled in Canada on the government tab, Lindley would record $0.25 local phone calls he made and submit a claim over and above his $4 incidental per diem.

For the DND bureaucrats, as with their military counterparts, the example of either fiscal restraint or abuse is established by the individual who occupies the top position. In the case of Deputy Minister Bob Fowler, the precedent for global travel and lavish claims had been set out in fine style. Fowler had an avid interest in photography, which he developed during his years at External Affairs and then travelling about with Prime Minister Trudeau. As deputy minister of national defence, Fowler would often venture out to visit far-flung peacekeeping locales, camera in tow. Usually, as witnessed by his whirlwind trip to Somalia, the troops themselves provided the justification for numerous visits to a variety of exotic ports of call. On other occasions, the rationalization for travel was even more transparent, but through clever manipulation of the military system, the whole trip could be classified as secret. One clear example of this was the junket Fowler and his two top aides took to watch the launching of a space shuttle in Cape Canaveral, Florida.

At that time, the Canadian military was assuming the responsibility for a national-level, highly trained anti-terrorist and security force in the Canadian Forces. Code-named Joint Task Force Two, it was to replace the RCMP's Special Emergency Response Team. The whole affair was classified top secret by the military brass, and no one without the proper clearance was even to know the role or composition of the new JTF II. Fowler was instrumental in the transfer of responsibility for the anti-terrorist squad from the RCMP, and it was his instruction to keep the squad out of the public eye. It also allowed him, his top mandarins and favoured officers to travel about the world without disclosing the purpose of their travel. As long as the name JTF II was on the claim, that was all that could be disclosed.

The Cape Canaveral launch was one example of this being used. Fowler shot some great photos of the launch, the Florida temperatures were a welcome midwinter break from a frosty Ottawa and one member of Fowler's party even managed to take in a dog-breeding show in Texas—all at taxpayers' expense, all in the name of national security and all buried in highly classified documents as a defence secret.

Senior defence bureaucrats, including the deputy minister, would normally have little reason to travel abroad on official business, given their role and responsibilities. However, once the standard had been set, it became simply a matter of using one's initiative to obtain travel clearance, even on the thinnest of pretexts. A training course in a foreign country was frequently the grounds for approving sizeable sums from the Defence Department's budget to send a senior executive touring about on federal funds.

Certainly one of the best (or worst?) examples of such abuse is the case of Micheline Clairoux, of bongo fame, who had been brought into NDHQ as an executive by Fowler in 1991. Coming directly from a clerical job at Environment Canada, Clairoux seemed to her new co-workers to wield an enormous amount of clout with the Deputy Minister.

According to a submission for reimbursement, Micheline Clairoux had official clearance to take a one-week communication course from Anthony Robbins in Del Mar, California. The cost to taxpayers was $5,741.97, not including Clairoux's salary for the week. Although it may seem outrageous that the Canadian public would pay for their senior government officials to take these sort of personal advancement lessons, the incredible twist in this story is that Clairoux had already taken the same course in 1990, when she was working for Environment Canada. Taxpayers had forked out $970 for her to take the same Anthony Robbins course in Toronto.

The reasons for Clairoux's seemingly straightforward case of excess going unpunished result from the same systemic flaw that enabled the general officer corps to perpetuate similar abuses with impunity. When both the military police and the judge advocate general answer to departmental senior management, it is impossible for the system to monitor and correct high-level corruption if, as was the case, the very top officials are involved in similar activities. Inevitably, those trusted individuals who worked closely with these men and implemented their will knew exactly what was transpiring. Once compromised, the top officials were in no position to punish those underlings for their indiscretions or excesses for fear that they would in turn be able to point the finger back at them.

It would be impossible to detail in this book all of the questionable activities that occurred throughout the Defence Department during Bob Fowler's reign as deputy minister. However, the examination of just one core sampling of a single directorate throughout this period will illustrate the deep-rooted and pervasive practices which crippled DND.

At first glance, the rather innocuous-sounding Directorate of Facilities Management (DFM) and its governing office, the Director General Executive Secretariat, would make little impression on the average citizen. The names do not conjure up a mental image of anything even remotely military, and therein lies the secret to the power of the organization: they are unobserved by the outside world.

However, to those familiar with the labyrinth of power corridors running through NDHQ's thirteenth floor and cutting into the political circles of Ottawa, DFM is a veritable treasure chest.

The reason this directorate attracts so little public attention, yet attracts so much internal interest, lies in the very function of DFM. As the acronym and title suggest, this organization manages the "facilities" or office spaces at NDHQ. This entails the negotiating of building leases, contracting of renovations and purchasing of new furniture. In a private corporation, such a role would be considered minimal in importance, especially once the company was firmly established in its head office. What keeps DFM in such a vital and lucrative role is the fact that National Defence is the largest single tenant in Ottawa. Many people wrongly believe that the military's epicentre of operations is tucked neatly into the three office towers at 101 Colonel By Drive, right in the heart of the nation's capital. Given the overall strength of our tiny and thinly dispersed military forces and the impressive facility at Colonel By, one would think that such a large structure would be sufficient.

It is evident only when one looks at the NDHQ phone book that the Department of Defence actually rents additional office space in no fewer than thirty-eight separate locations in Ottawa alone. Naturally, the arrangement has been far from optimal in terms of effectively managing a military headquarters; however, it has also made it very difficult for outsiders (and even insiders) to visualize clearly the actual size of DND's more-than-12,000-personnel-strong administrative empire.

In some cases, the federal government actually owns the buildings DND occupies, so only maintenance costs would be processed through DFM. In many instances, however, the Crown leases the office properties in which the military is housed. In these situations, it is the staff at DFM who negotiate the leases and oversee the landlord–tenant relationship, even though the actual contracts are issued by Public Works Canada. To convey an idea of the financial power DFM controls, it should be noted that the annual rental fees processed by this directorate were in excess of $75 million in 1992.

There is also a separate budget established for renovations and furniture procurement, and this provides DFM with an additional $8–9 million in spending authority. All in all, including salaries and overhead, this small directorate is, in fact, a $100-million-a-year mini-empire within National Defence. And because of its rather mundane function, DFM rarely attracted any notice.

It did, however, cater to the fancy of Bob Fowler, who, as deputy minister, directly controlled DFM's activities through the Executive Secretariat. Shortly after being appointed deputy minister, Fowler in turn promoted his executive assistant, Denys Henrie, and placed him in charge of the challenging and complex Executive Secretariat.

Barbara Shore, who worked in the Deputy Minister's suite, had a fondness for the handsome and personable Henrie, but she admitted that the job of director general for the Executive Secretariat was too much for the young man to handle. She also believed that Fowler knew this when he put him in charge of this vital position. Shore reasoned that, by having a loyal and likeable but relatively incompetent manager in charge of the secretariat, Fowler could retain control of its power and at the same time distance himself from any fall-out. As events unfolded, Shore's assessment was to prove true.

It was in 1991, shortly after Micheline Clairoux was brought in by Fowler to run the newly created post at the Directorate of Facilities Management, that the trouble first began. Denys Henrie had not been pleased with the selection of Clairoux ahead of two other qualified candidates. Although he was to be her immediate supervisor, Henrie knew enough not to cross Fowler over his selection. Even so, very little research was done at the time to confirm Clairoux's credentials before putting her in charge of a $100-million directorate, with a personal signing authority of up to $250,000.

Despite her credentials, or rather lack thereof, Micheline Clairoux soon found herself part of Fowler's inner cabinet. One of her first major projects for Fowler involved DND's purchase of the Louis St. Laurent Building in Hull. This office tower had been completed in 1985 by the well-known Ottawa developer Pierre Bourque. It had been arranged that, upon its completion, DND would lease the entire structure. It had cost Bourque, including the land purchase, $41.5 million to construct the Louis St. Laurent, but this investment had been secured with a signed ten-year lease by National Defence.

Although the rental agreement with Bourque was not due to expire until May 1995, Fowler called in Clairoux in 1991 to examine the feasibility and cost of purchasing the building. The DFM employee who managed the facility was Rick Williams. Clairoux consulted with Williams as to the suitability of the office tower, now that DND had had a full five years of experience with it as tenants. Williams immediately rejected the idea and presented Clairoux with a list of structural faults and shortcomings which had been noted by DND inspectors. For example, the air circulation and heating systems had always been a source of complaint among employees at the Louis St. Laurent. According to the blueprints, there should have been no problem, so a thorough inspection was conducted. What they discovered was that many of the air vents were simply a façade, with no corresponding duct work behind them.

Williams not only recommended against purchasing the building, but also advocated not renewing the rental agreement. Armed with this information, the newly hired Clairoux went back to see Fowler. The Deputy Minister requested further evaluation. No fewer than three times this scenario was played out between Fowler, Clairoux and the staff at DFM, each time with the same result. After the delivery of a *fourth* report, the Louis St. Laurent was deemed satisfactory for DND's needs.

The actual contract for the purchase of this building was negotiated by Public Works Canada; however, when the auditor general examined the details of the deal, he was quick to note some serious discrepancies. In his 1992 report, the auditor general noted that, at the time of purchase (in 1991), the replacement value of the Louis St. Laurent would have been only $53 million. Two separate market value appraisals, which had been conducted that same year, concluded that the office tower's sale value was $64 million and $66 million, respectively. Despite this research, Public Works Canada had signed a lease-to-own purchase agreement with Bourque valued at $73 million. Although the auditor general concluded that Public Works had inexplicably and knowingly paid $6–10 million more than market value for the Louis St. Laurent, no investigation was launched to determine why. The auditor general's report caused barely a ripple in the House of Commons, there was no negative press coverage, and the whole affair was seemingly closed.

From that point forward, Clairoux made no attempt to demonstrate even the semblance of fiscal restraint or any adherence to regulations. She bragged openly about having "the goods" on the Deputy Minister's lavish $387,000 office renovations. This particular file, however, was to spark the tinder-box of corruption that DFM had become, creating in the process nearly two years of explosive internal investigations.

Once the top official has compromised his integrity, the system can't help but disintegrate, and the example of Bob Fowler and DFM between August 1991 and July 1993 clearly illustrates this point. During this twenty-three-month period, no fewer than seventeen separate investigations were conducted into DFM's activities by no fewer than twelve different agencies. The range of allegations involved everything from kickbacks, theft and fraud to sexual harassment and the use of illegal hiring practices. But despite the nature of these allegations, at no time were the military police called in. In the middle of all this probing, the man responsible for the whole directorate, Denys Henrie, committed suicide. In his note, Henrie listed five top officials, including Fowler, as being "responsible" for his death. Yet even this desperate cry for help went unheeded as the police were once again kept out of the investigation. Despite Henrie's senior position in National Defence and his accusatory final statement blaming other top officials—many of whom were and had been subject to subtle internal DND investigations—there was not even an inquest.

Once the whole mess in DFM started to erupt, Fowler desperately tried to distance himself from the scandal. He even attempted to put in some stricter controls; however, he no longer had the moral authority to enforce his will against those who were aware of his indiscretions.

CHAPTER SEVEN

Milking the Cash Cow

Every time the debt-ridden federal government announces yet another cut to its defence budget, military analysts and associations collectively howl in indignation that our Armed Forces are already underequipped with outdated weaponry. Invariably, the Defence Department's response has been to "rewrite" their defence policy to match the available funds: manpower levels are reduced and major procurement projects are cancelled. The end result is that we have fewer and fewer soldiers left working with increasingly aged equipment, and a defence industry unusually dependent on government subsidies rather than military contracts.

The myth arising from this repetitive cycle is that a lack of money is the major stumbling-block, and that more cash is required to rectify the situation. In reality, over the past ten years there's been more than enough money spent, billions in fact, to purchase absolutely nothing tangible. The simple truth is, the procurement process, like the rest of the Defence Department, has been mismanaged. Just as pumping massive amounts of foreign aid into a Third World country does little to benefit the inhabitants when the recipient government regime is corrupt, so until the present procurement system at DND is modified to make it wholly accountable, capital acquisitions programs are destined to be subverted.

Of course, the top bureaucrats and generals are loath to admit that there's anything wrong with the way things are being run. However, their recent track record proves them wrong. The much-publicized and -politicized cancellation of the $5.5-billion EH–101 helicopter program is probably the best example of how the defence budget is used up in massive expenditures that acquire nothing in return. Over the course of this controversial project to replace the Navy's ageing Sea King helicopters, the Defence Department cut cheques to a total value of $627 million to pay for requests for proposals, research funds and cancellation costs. For its part, the Navy didn't receive so much as a quart of oil out of the deal. Not to mention the fact that their old Sea Kings are now seven years older, and we're no closer to finding or financing a replacement. In public, DND-funded defence analysts will argue that these costs-for-nothing-in-return should be blamed on political interference. After all, it was the Liberal party that turned the whole affair into part of their election platform, and it was Prime Minister Chrétien himself who gave the cancellation notice.

Although frustrating for the long-suffering defence industry, they dare not admit the truth about who is really to blame. Their future livelihood still depends on the whims of those who failed to implement the project the first time around. The fact is, had the EH-101 program been properly managed by defence officials, it never would have become the vulnerable political football that it did.

One need only look at all of the major equipment projects the Defence Department has undertaken over the past ten years. In virtually every case, whether the program ends in cancellation or completion, the record shows the same pattern of managerial ineptitude and political interference.

When Robert Fowler and Ken Calder wrote the 1987 White Paper on Defence, it consisted of a top-to-bottom shopping list for army and navy hardware. In the early 1980s, the Canadian Air Force had undergone a complete modernization with the acquisition of new CF-18 fighter air-craft, so the procurement priorities were redirected to the other two ser-vice branches.

Topping Calder and Fowler's blueprint was the controversial purchase of nuclear submarines and main battle tanks. Both of these high-profile programs bit the dust for reasons of fiscal restraint in Finance Minister Michael Wilson's 1989 budget. Of those equipment acquisitions projects that survived the initial axing, many reached their infancy prior to a costly (to taxpayers) cancellation and others still floundered their way to a dubi-ous fruition (for the servicemen and women who must use them).

At the time of the 1987 White Paper, Canada had a NATO commitment to protect Europe's northern flank with a brigade group and a fighter squadron dedicated to the defence of Norway. The vehicles and equipment for this field force were kept in Bardufoss in northern Norway. The Canadian troops involved would annually conduct an airlift exercise to this remote region of Scandinavia, and then spend several weeks training with their allies. Due to the unique demands made by the rugged (and often frozen) terrain, the NATO high command had selected the novel

Hagglunds BV 206 All-Terrain Carrier as the vehicle best suited for service in Norway.

In the interest of logistical compatibility and inter-operability, the Canadian Defence Department had purchased some two hundred of these excellent transport vehicles directly from AB Hagglunds & Soner in Sweden. They were then permanently stationed at Bardufoss. The members of the assigned Canadian battle group were issued only a half dozen of the new vehicles in order to conduct driver training prior to their deployment.

A fundamental part of Fowler and Calder's White Paper was to refurbish and revitalize the militia and to increase its ties to the regular army. This new concept was given the deceptively martial monicker "Total Force." On paper, the total number of reservists was to be doubled, from 20,000 to 40,000, and since the militia traditionally operates with whatever hand-me-down equipment is available from the regulars, new vehicles and weapons would have to be purchased.

For transportation, it was felt that the Hagglunds BV 206 would make an ideal choice for a militia personnel carrier. The reasons for this choice were not found in the militia's military operational requirements, but rather in the BV 206's political expedience.

As an all-terrain amphibious carrier, designed for crossing wetlands and soft snow, the BV 206 is an excellent vehicle. Its design is based on a split cab, single-drive-train system, which allows it to negotiate tough cross-country conditions without increasing the ground pressure beyond that of a walking man. However, in order to achieve this, the BV 206 relies upon a lightweight fibreglass chassis and extra-wide rubber tracks. In actuality, the vehicle provides its occupants with absolutely no armoured protection, and only a few BV 206s are even equipped with weaponry.

As a Scandinavian battlefield taxi, operating on the roof of the world, the BV 206 has no equal. The proposal for this same vehicle to equip the Canadian militia had no merit whatsoever. Nevertheless, it was announced in 1990 that Canada would purchase 800 of these carriers at a total cost of nearly $200 million. If the vehicles had been bought directly from Hagglunds, their manufacturer, the costs would have been less than half that. Instead, it was decided this program would help stimulate industry in western Canada. To that end, an assembly plant, Foremost Inc. of Calgary, Alberta, was contracted under the joint working title of Hagglunds–

Foremost, to produce a Canadianized version of the BV 206, known as the Northern Terrain Vehicle.

By the time this grand scheme was cancelled in the 1991 federal budget, land for an assembly plant had been purchased by Foremost, and work was already under way on the new facility. Although the cancellation costs were never publicly announced, analysts estimated that the total cost to taxpayers on the Northern Terrain Vehicle program amounted to more than $45 million.

Despite this expenditure, the militia never did see an increase in the numbers of vehicles (in fact, they were to be further reduced in 1995), and there's been no specific program announced to replace the cancelled Northern Terrain Vehicle: however, the term "Total Force" is still in use.

The Naval Reserve, like its militia counterpart, was promised a revitalization and refurbishment in the 1987 White Paper. At that point, the part-time navy had a motley collection of small, wartime-vintage training ships. The slow speeds of these vessels and lack of any armament made them suitable for nothing more than basic seamanship training. Fowler and Calder decided that they would give the Naval Reserve the full-time mission of coastal defence, thus freeing up our regular surface fleets for "blue-water" ocean patrols. A new class of ship would be developed and built, but in the meantime the reservists could take on their new responsibilities, using their existing resources.

Under the new mandate, the Naval Reserve would be capable of conducting mine-sweeps and surveillance as well as regular patrol functions. The twelve new coastal defence vessels were each to be outfitted with four different high-tech electronic centres, enabling the ships to be transformed to best suit each mission.

The requests for proposals were issued in 1989, and two Canadian shipyards put in strong bids for the $600-million contract. At that stage, politics intervened, and the bureaucracy proved its ineptitude. For both shipyards, Halifax Dartmouth Industries (HDI) and Canadian Shipbuilding and Engineering (CSE), failure to win the contract would mean having to shut down their facilities, whereas the successful bidder would achieve a shaky extension to its livelihood.

The two companies lobbied their respective political representatives heavily, with the threat of massive job losses if they didn't get the contract. In an effort to appease the Tory caucus, who had been pressuring their defence minister, Bill McKnight, and, subsequently, his flamboyant successor, Marcel Masse, Deputy Minister Robert Fowler and his procurement staff put forward a plan to "split the contract." Obviously, both shipyards understood more about the potential business impact of doubling their start-up costs while simultaneously halving potential profits than the government planners did, and this badly flawed idea was quickly rejected. Still looking to keep the politicians and shipbuilders happy, it was decided that the "loser" in the coastal defence vessel bidding would be awarded an untendered consolation contract.

At this time, HMCS *Protecteur*—an ageing replenishment ship that had just seen hard service in the Gulf War—was overdue for a refit. A hasty $30-million deal was signed between DND and CSE to perform the overhaul on *Protecteur*, and it was simultaneously announced that HDI had won the coastal defence vessel contract.

Unfortunately for Canadian taxpayers, and ultimately the Naval Reserve, Robert Fowler and his managers had made a huge error in their haste to find a political solution. The CSE shipyard is located at Port Weller, at the south end of the Welland Canal. DND's procurement officials were embarrassed to learn that HMCS *Protecteur*'s beam and displacement would not allow her to navigate the narrow locks and channel.

This $30-million oversight obviously had the potential to create tremendous political embarrassment, so another hasty solution had to be found to make good on the contract with CSE. In a rash move, HMCS *Nipigon* was pulled from active service and sent in *Protecteur*'s stead to the CSE yard. There was no need to measure the *Nipigon*; she had been completely refitted at CSE just twenty-four months earlier (and was not due for another overhaul for another eight years). Unfortunately for Navy planners, the work to *Protecteur* could not be delayed and was recontracted to a West Coast shipyard.

The $30 million taken out of their budget to perform unnecessary work to the *Nipigon* had to be accounted for from the Maritime Coastal Defence Vessel Program. As a result, it was necessary to reduce the shopping list of mission suites for each vessel. Instead of giving each of the twelve new ships four possible configurations (a total of forty-eight suites), the

Navy is now able to procure enough electronics to allow each vessel only one role (twelve suites in total). Incredibly, despite its outright waste of $30 million and the shortfall in expectations, the Maritime Coastal Defence Vessel Program is actually regarded as a success story by the Defence Department—at least the Navy received a dozen new ships and some modern technology. The Naval Reserve should consider itself lucky.

In the case of the Army's new Light Support Vehicle, Wheeled (LSVW), politics and profit played even more of a part in ensuring that the end users (the grunts) did not get value for what the taxpayer spent. The controversial $200-million contract was awarded to Western Star Trucks of Kelowna, British Columbia, in 1992. At the time, Al Horning, the Progressive Conservative MP for the Kelowna riding, proudly boasted to his constituents that he had played an active role in the lobbying for Western Star.

Even though an election was around the corner, and new jobs meant votes, Horning was unwise to have made a public comment on this particular contract. Already the other bidders (a total of four bids were submitted) had begun to ask questions as to the impartiality of the assessment by DND in what was supposed to be an open and fair process.

Documents released under access-to-information legislation show that the Western Star Truck, an Italian design to be built under licence, was rated fourth in virtually every category. Overall, the military assessment determined the Western Star vehicle was suitable but not recommended. At the time, only the Italian air force was employing these IVECO trucks, and they were used as runway repair vehicles. Meanwhile, the Canadian Army was looking for a robust, general-purpose pick-up truck to replace their worn-out five-ton fleet.

Despite the fact that the IVECO model was largely untried and incompatible with other North American vehicles (it requires purpose-built tires to fit its wheel rim), Robert Fowler and his assistant, Raymond Sturgeon, recommended its purchase to the Tory cabinet.

Unfortunately for Fowler and Sturgeon, once the contract was signed with Western Star the problems began in earnest. Over the next eighteen months, the IVECO/Western Star prototype failed twice to pass the military's acceptance trials. In fact, Army engineers at the Land Engineering Test Establishment (LETE) test site found more than 200 major deficiencies with the new trucks. Despite repeated requests from senior management, these engineers refused to issue the new light trucks a clean bill of health.

Already the Army high command had voiced their displeasure at the choice of the Western Star Truck. At that point, the appeasement offered to commander Lieutenant-General Gordon Reay was that these unproven Italian vehicles would still have to be approved by army mechanics—and any flaws detected would then be corrected prior to their entering full production. By the spring of 1994, the Liberals had replaced the Conservatives in power. With LETE refusing to co-operate, Fowler soon faced the possibility of another of his major procurement programs falling victim to political cancellation. (The EH-101 helicopter fiasco was still a recent event.)

At this critical juncture, the decision was taken by Fowler and Sturgeon to include LETE with the 1994 list of base closures announced following the federal budget. It's a wise move to hide a body during a massacre, and as expected, the shutdown of LETE generated little media interest. Internally, however, Army Headquarters was furious and quick to realize the magnitude and implication of Fowler's hasty decision. A top-level aide to General Reay sent a letter at this point to *Esprit de Corps* magazine encouraging its staff in their efforts to expose the high-level corruption in DND's bureaucracy. He wrote, "Bob Fowler and Ray 'we don't need no stinkin LETE' Sturgeon are not skeletons in our closets, they are vampires and true to their nature, they are sucking the very lifeblood out of our army." Despite their outrage, army officials were powerless to stop the bureaucrats.

Without the stubborn impediment of a military test establishment, the Western Star Trucks were soon qualified fit for service by a civilian firm in Nevada and the production lines began to roll. In all, nearly 2,500 of these vehicles will be delivered to the Army by mid-1996, and there is a follow-on purchase of 315 additional trucks in the works.

Since entering service, these trucks have been plagued with sudden engine fires, bedevilled by poor cross-country performance, criticized for a lack of tactical capability (their metal-on-metal brakes can be heard for miles) and generally resented by the troops that operate them. Because of the lack of dependability of these trucks, most units have issued a strict set of guidelines restricting them to speeds of not more than eighty kilometres per hour on the highway and no off-road driving.

Incredibly, the unit price (to taxpayers) for these pick-up trucks amounts to approximately $80,000. By contrast, the U.S. army vehicle, the ubiquitous, wide-bodied Hummer (originally considered "too rich" for the Canadian Army's budget), now retails in civilian stores for just $40,000. Obviously, a fleet purchase of Hummers would entitle the buyer to a volume discount, but even paying full list price, the Canadian Forces could have saved more than $100 million purchasing this proven and respected vehicle "off the shelf."

In fact, because of its size and versatility, the Hummer would have also effectively eliminated the need to replace the Canadian Forces' worn-out fleet of Iltis utility vehicles, thereby saving additional hundreds of millions of dollars. Instead, these lightweight jeeps are, as of 1996, overdue to be retired from service, and already bids have been sought on a whole new Light Utility Vehicle, Wheeled (LUVW) project.

This time around, however, Fowler and Sturgeon's successors will not have to worry about their vehicle choice not passing its trials: only the soldiers will.

Whenever a military supply system breaks down under stress, either in combat or during training, the inevitable result is that unwanted goods arrive in huge quantities while vital necessities are nowhere to be found. Although these sorts of inevitable logistical complications are understood and tolerated by the troops, there should be no such occurrences in the peacetime procurement process. Through the mismanagement and corruption of the system, feast or famine has become the standard of inconsistency under which the Canadian Forces operate. In most cases, the rationale for the excess or absence of equipment can be traced to politically motivated origins, but nevertheless it is the bureaucrats and generals who willingly accept these pressures.

Most Canadians are blissfully unaware of the vast quantity of resources the Defence Department squanders on "non-essentials" while at the same time maintaining (currently) that our soldiers remain woefully equipped.

There is no other army in the world that issues uniform clothing on a scale even close to Canada's. Our service members all have sets of combat clothing, work dress and dress uniforms. If they are in a field unit, they also receive full arctic gear. Since the Canadian Army conducts peacekeeping operations and training missions in temperatures that range between

−60° and 60° Celsius, they receive a wide variety of everything from head-gear (Tilleys to tuques) and footwear (sandals to snowshoes). When soldiers being transported from base to base found they had difficulty packing all of this kit, new barrack boxes were purchased and issued.

This is not to say that our soldiers don't deserve to be properly outfit-ted. It is essential, though, that the niceties be put into perspective and measured against the shortages. Although our troops have been conduct-ing dangerous peacekeeping tours in the former Yugoslavia since 1992, the Army still does not possess enough modern Kevlar helmets and flak vests to equip two contingents at once. It has now become a routine drill for sol-diers on rotation to exchange helmets and vests at the airport, and then sort out the sizes later when time permits.

By comparison, in the late 1980s, it was decided for the sake of morale to improve the Army's self-image by issuing a new work dress uniform to all personnel. The project cost was more than $10 million to equip 20,000 troops with the new camouflage-pattern jackets and patent leather "com-bat" boots. The whole thing was regarded by the troops as being purely for cosmetic reasons and as simply a way to make Headquarters staff appear more martial. In fact, by 1995, these "hunting costumes" had become so detested by the troops that Major-General Clive Addy, commander of Land Forces, Western Area, prohibited his men from wearing them. Nevertheless, the camouflage jackets remain an authorized uniform item and, as such, soldiers will still have to pack them in their new barrack boxes.

Of all the modern shortcomings facing our army, the ability to deal with enemy tanks is certainly not a pressing concern. For twenty years now, Canada has been equipped at the unit level with highly effective tube-launched, optically tracked, wire-guided missile (TOW) systems. After 1988, our anti-armour vehicles were improved with an upgraded TOW turret, and they still remain state of the art by international standards.

At the section level, Canadian soldiers employ an 84-mm rocket-launcher known by its designer's name, the "Carl Gustav." Although it is relatively dated in terms of technology, the delivery system was given a new lease on life in the mid-eighties with a new, improved rocket, which gave it an effective range of from 100 to 700 metres.

Since the TOW system's optimum range is between 400 metres and

2 kilometres, tactically the Canadian Army should have been all set. However, in 1989, immediately following the Canadian government's decision to cancel the nuclear submarine program, DND began negotiations with the French firm Aerospatiale for a new anti-armour system, the Eryx missile. France and Britain had been the two bidders on the submarine program, but whereas Canada was still at that point working with the British on the EH-101 helicopter deal, France had no such consolation package. Although the Eryx missile itself showed great promise, it was still in development and, more important, Canada had no tactical niche for it to fill. Nevertheless, DND entered into a costly program (the initial buy was announced at $208 million in 1992), spending the Army's budget on weaponry which, however efficient, was undeniably unnecessary.

The official rationale at the time of the purchase was that the Eryx, with its range of 200 to 500 metres, was necessary to close the anti-armour tactical gap left between "the TOW and the Carl Gustav." The problem with that argument is that anyone familiar with those weapon systems knows there was no "gap" to fill.

The $208 million spent acquiring the new missiles easily could have been put to better use outfitting our soldiers with such tactical capabilities as a modern rifle grenade or a new submachine-gun. Unfortunately, DND's procurement process is not so much a means for serving our own military's needs as it is a handy pot to curry national and international political or industrial favour.

For the past ten years, the senior command has realized that a replacement was necessary for their burnt-out, thirty-five-year-old armoured personnel carriers (APCs). In fact, even before these old tracked vehicles started rattling themselves apart on constant peacekeeping patrols in Yugoslavia, they topped the Army's annual wish list at the procurement meetings.

Obviously, such a major program would require a large chunk of the Defence Department's annual equipment budget over the entire period of its implementation. Therefore, one would think that this would be actively planned for over time, and all available resources would be carefully husbanded during the preparation.

Unfortunately, such was not the case. As the result of a whim decision taken by then defence minister Marcel Masse—and subsequently implemented by Robert Fowler and his procurement directors—the APC replacement program was delayed by three years.

Although seemingly unrelated, it was Masse's 1992 public proclamation that DND would purchase one hundred new helicopters at a cost of $1 billion that set back the armoured vehicles. Originally it had been proposed that fifty of these utility choppers be purchased from Bell Helicopter in Mirabel, Quebec. However, given the proximity of the aircraft company to his own electoral riding, Masse took a personal interest in the project.

It was his idea to increase the number of helicopters and virtually double the cost, despite the fact that such a number could not be tactically justified. Nevertheless, once the decision was made by Masse, Robert Fowler and his spin doctors were quick to lend it their support. In their public releases, the claim was made that these 100 new utility helicopters would be replacing 109 existing choppers in three different aircraft fleets. As the new 412s were a modernized version of the Twin Hueys already in service, it was easy to see how they would effectively replace this aircraft. However, DND's statement that the 412 could also replace the Chinook (heavy-lifting) and Kiowa (light reconnaissance) helicopters would not have withstood close scrutiny.

Fortunately for Fowler and Masse, the media were already busy shooting down the EH-101 helicopters and this project proceeded unscathed.

For the Army, the bad news came when Marcel Masse proclaimed that the Bell 412 purchase was in fact an "army program." So, $500 million more than budgeted was spent on something the Air Force didn't need, and the Army ultimately paid the price through the delay to their much-needed APC project.

Another example of this sort of inexplicable overbuying of resources would be the Army's new ten-ton trucks, or Heavy Logistic Vehicle, Wheeled (HLVW) as it is known to military procurement officials.

These trucks were also part of the 1987 shopping list and were given a top priority because the Army's old five-ton vehicle fleet was on the verge of collapse. At the time the request for proposals went out, the defence policy called for substantial growth to our military in terms of personnel and capability. However, by the time the contract was awarded to the Austrian–Canadian consortium of Steyr–UTDC in 1988, many of the planned increases had already been targeted for cuts for budgetary reasons.

Nevertheless, Steyr–UTDC were issued a DND purchase order to produce 1,200 of these heavy transports. At the time of the announcement, much political mileage was made of the job creation this contract would provide in the Kingston, Ontario, area. UTDC, the Canadian partner, was to provide the assembly line for Steyr's parts and design. Although UTDC had never produced trucks before—they traditionally manufacture train cars and subway cars—the project was fairly successful in terms of both the product produced and the overall timetable.

The problem with the HLVW project lies in the fact that the whole concept was based on an unrealistic scale of issue. While even to construct an entire assembly line for a total vehicle run of 1,200 would be considered wasteful, the simple truth is that our tiny army of just 20,000 troops doesn't need that many heavy trucks.

In fact, in 1991, when Defence Minister Marcel Masse announced that Canada would be reducing the NATO commitment (it would later pull out of Germany altogether), the military brass were faced with a glut of these logistical vehicles. UTDC was still in full production, and their parking lot was already full of brand-new but already surplus vehicles. As an interim solution, it was decided to equip the Airborne Regiment with these trucks—even though they're not even transportable by air.

As for the job-creation aspect of this $160-million project, when the last truck rolled off the assembly line, the pink slips were issued and the chain was put on the gates.

The largest Army purchase program already under way is the $1.8-billion purchase of new radios and communications sets. This massive contract was won by the Ottawa-based firm Computing Devices Canada back in 1990, yet despite the huge size of the dollar figure involved, the various delays and the cost overruns, very little media attention has been given to this project. At the core of the Tactical Command Control and Communication System (TCCCS) acquisition is the purchase of 10,000 new man-packed field radios. The scale of issue was determined, like those of many other projects, based on the erroneous presumption that manning levels would increase to match the 1987 White Paper's recommendations. Despite the fact that top DND officials knew, even before Computing Devices had entered the definition phase of the TCCCS project, that those personnel numbers would never materialize, nobody downsized the purchase order.

If one were to count every cook, accountant, dentist and clerk in the Canadian Army, it would be difficult for them to muster 20,000 hearty individuals at any one time. Of that number, fewer than 8,000 soldiers would ever actually be involved in field exercises or operational missions. As for those who would be tasked (even hypothetically) with conducting dismounted manoeuvres or patrols using a tactical radio, the tally would be somewhat shy of 3,000. Even if the militia's entire combat element were to be added to this total, the overall number would still fall short of the 10,000 mark. Under normal tactical conditions, radios are distributed, one to each platoon of thirty-two soldiers or, in rare cases, one per section of nine soldiers.

When the $1.8-billion TCCCS program is complete, our soldiers will enjoy a 1 to 1 radio-to-soldier ratio—the highest ever deployed by any army in the world. Ever.

Sadly, for soldiers and taxpayers, this sort of artificial industry stimulation has become the cornerstone of today's military procurement. In fact, in some incredible instances, like that of the Oerlikon ADATS program, the civilian jobs and industry subsidies actually outlast the weapon systems they produce.

The air defence anti-tank system (ADATS) was also part of Fowler's ill-fated 1987 White Paper, and like most of the grandiose schemes it tabled, the ADATS was destined for cancellation. This particular project ended up costing more than $1 billion before it was mothballed in 1995.

The original hope had been that Canada and Oerlikon Buehrle, the Swiss manufacturer, would establish a North American arms plant outside Montreal. DND and Industry Canada would split the start-up costs with Oerlikon on this developmental missile system, and the Army agreed to buy, as an initial purchase, thirty-two of these high-tech units. At the time, it was Oerlikon's intention to market the ADATS to the U.S. military; the preliminary interest by their army was encouraging. If a major sale of ADATS to the United States was signed, then the Canadian government's speculative interest in this industrial project would result in hundreds of high-tech jobs. Instead, the Berlin Wall came down, the Cold War was over and the militaries of the world began to rethink their requirements.

By 1991, Oerlikon Canada had established its plant in St. Jean-sur-Richelieu, Quebec, and completed the Canadian prototypes. At this stage, the parent company, Oerlikon Buehrle in Switzerland, decided to cut their losses (no U.S. sale was forthcoming), and they pulled their funding of the ADATS program. The Canadian government, using DND's budget, continued to support Oerlikon Canada, even after the thirty-four units had been built and delivered. Maintenance and upgrade contracts for ADATS were issued along with additional research funds in order to keep the foundering company afloat.

In 1992, after a training accident destroyed one of the Army's ADATS (the tractor-trailer which was transporting it rolled, crushing the turret), it was determined that these systems were too expensive for use during field exercises. Shortly after they had been "shelved" by the operational units, National Defence Headquarters decided to mothball the whole project. Although the systems are officially no longer in active service, DND still set aside $40 million to be spent on the ADATS in their 1996 budget estimates.

Our air force has not been involved in any major acquisition projects since receiving their fleet of modern CF-18 fighter jets in the mid-eighties. However, by virtue of the high maintenance costs of these planes, the Air Force, like the other Canadian service branches, have seen their budgets victimized by political and bureaucratic waste.

Despite being outbid by Winnipeg's Bristol Aerospace, Montreal-based Canadair won a $1.2-billion lifetime contract to service and maintain the Air Force's 138 CF-18 aircraft, a fleet that is now reduced by flying accidents to 120, of which only 60 are kept operational.

At the time, there was a considerable amount of political debate surrounding the contract, as it was felt that Quebec was receiving more than its share of aerospace and defence contracts already. As part of an industry restructuring, the federal government had proclaimed various cities as "centres of excellence" and Montreal was chosen as the aerospace capital of Canada. As such, Canadair, located at Mirabel Airport, found itself well positioned for DND's CF-18 contract. Nevertheless, the Winnipeg-based Bristol Aerospace was soon threatening to close its doors and lay off hundreds of workers as a result of losing the bid.

With political pressure mounting, the Defence Department bureaucrats quickly sought a consolation package to offer Bristol. The result was a $350-million contract to refurbish and upgrade the Air Force's fifty-four

CF-5, single-engine fighter aircraft. The contract was later reduced to $79 million for forty-four planes. After twenty years of service as part of Canada's NORAD commitment, the CF-5s were increasingly viewed as trainer aircraft, as opposed to frontline fighters. They took over this operational role shortly after the CF-18s became fully operational. Ironically, Canadair was the original benefactor of the CF-5 acquisition. The Montreal company built eighty-nine of these aircraft from 1968 to 1971 only to see most of them go directly into storage.

Since more than a thousand of these planes operate in the United States, and all of them will inevitably require refurbishment, both Bristol Aerospace and the Canadian government were confident this project would produce long-term benefits. In fact, initial sales were encouraging, and then the bottom fell out of this ambitious scheme. It was only shortly after Bristol Aerospace announced a CF-5 refurbishment deal with Singapore that the legal troubles began to brew. Northrup, the original manufacturer, had never granted Bristol the world-wide marketing rights for the CF-5 avionics, and naturally they didn't want to end up competing with their own subcontractors. Since the Canadian government had been instrumental in arranging the Singapore–Bristol deal, the Defence Department was named as a co-defendant in the eventual Northrup claim.

With future foreign sales potential effectively stalled, DND began to distance themselves from the CF-5 project altogether. In tabling his 1995 White Paper on Defence, David Collenette announced that the entire CF-5 fleet (just upgraded at a cost of $350 million) would be mothballed in order to save DND money.

By May 1996, it was announced that twelve of these fighters had been sold to Botswana for a price of $67 million. Obviously, the government press release didn't mention that this sale further contributed to an arms race in southern Africa, but it was also deliberately misleading in another way. While citing the sale as a cost-recovery to the Crown, it failed to mention that Bristol Aerospace received a 20 per cent commission on the deal. That's a $13.4-million paycheque for selling off government (taxpayers') assets.

Also in May 1996, DND issued a press release announcing that they had just purchased two new Lockheed CC-130 Hercules transport aircraft. The rationale for this $108-million expenditure was cited as being the necessity to replace the two Hercules our air force has lost due to mishaps since 1991.

The announcement also stated that Canada's strategic airlift is facing an ever-increasing demand due to our UN peacekeeping commitments. Given both the timing and the content of this military press bulletin, no coverage was afforded this major purchase, and, more important, no one in the media even questioned the basic premise or the startlingly high costs. If they had done their homework, it would have been apparent that, over the same five-year period, strategic airlift demand had decreased significantly, while our available resources had increased dramatically. Once again, the Defence Department, while pleading poverty and restraint, was spending an enormous amount of money to fulfil a non-existent need.

Since 1991, the Canadian Forces have been reduced by more than 15,000 personnel. Our NATO brigade group and air division have been pulled out of Germany, thereby freeing up a tremendous number of aircraft. During 1992–93, Canadian peacekeeping commitments were at their zenith, with nearly 5,000 troops posted overseas on five far-flung global deployments. However, since that time, Canada has discontinued its long-standing commitment to the UN mission in Cyprus; the peacekeeping operation in Cambodia was successfully completed; the scale of our commitment to the former Yugoslavia was reduced from two battle groups to a single contingent; the Somalia deployment was not renewed beyond a single tour; and the force we sent to Rwanda has been downsized to a handful of observers. Admittedly, Canada recently committed our Armed Forces to an increased presence in the UN mission to Haiti. However, there is no question that the Canadian Air Transport Group had only recently seen far busier days.

Also not included in DND's $108-million press release was mention of our air force's five brand-new A310 airbuses. Although care was taken to identify the two planned replacements for the two destroyed Hercules transports, curiously no reference was made to the $440 million that had already been spent in the past three years to increase our airlift capacity.

In 1992, DND had been quick to use their budget to bail out the Progressive Conservative government and a cash-strapped Canadian Airlines. At the time, the Tory cabinet was under a tremendous amount of political pressure from Western Canada. Canadian Airlines, headquartered in Calgary and at that juncture on the verge of financial collapse, was lobbying hard for government support to stay afloat. Its rival, Air Canada, was based out of Montreal and until recently was a government airline, so even a hint of favouritism would be enough to spark east–west, franco–anglo debate. Since Prime Minister Brian Mulroney was at this stage trying to create a suitable national climate to ratify his Charlottetown constitutional agreement in a referendum, the airline issue took on great significance.

One of the major liabilities on Canadian Airlines' accounting books was the unpaid costs on five new airbuses. These aircraft had been acquired unused from the now-defunct Wardair and had never been brought into full service by Canadian.

While the Defence Department still operated an ageing fleet of five Boeing 707s, Deputy Minister Fowler had rewritten the defence policy in 1990 to eliminate their role as passenger carriers. From January 1991 onwards, the transport of service members was to be chartered out to Air Canada (a contract valued at $100 million annually), and the Boeings would be used strictly for the purpose of air-to-air refuelling.

In early 1992, however, Robert Fowler and his policy assistant Ken Calder found themselves rewriting the defence blueprint yet again. Apparently, they had just discovered that there was an urgent need to increase the Air Force's strategic airlift capability. Not surprisingly, it was determined after a short study, that five second-hand but nearly new airbuses best suited the Defence Department's needs. They were readily available (to fill the urgent need), and the sale price was reported as being too good to pass up.

Undoubtedly, other procurement programs had to be delayed or scaled back to accommodate the hasty airbus purchase, but somehow Fowler and Calder managed to find the extra $427 million in their budget to complete the deal. In fact, they even managed to scrounge up enough defence funds to convert one of these new airplanes to plush VIP standards. (This lavishly appointed jet was later referred to by a scornful Liberal Opposition as Mulroney's flying Taj Mahal.)

For Air Force planners, the airbus purchase was not only a surprise, but it also marked a 180-degree turnabout in their policy towards passenger aircraft. Air crew had to be trained to fly the new aircraft and a whole support base had to be established, while, simultaneously, a viable role had to be sought for this new "asset."

What was eventually decided was that it was cheaper and more effective for DND to charter civilian airlines to carry service members than it was for them to try to do it themselves; in other words, the same rationale that had led to the 1990 decision to privatize this service still applied. After an attempt to sell off their five airbuses in 1994 met with a glutted market and no takers, DND decided to convert these underutilized passenger jets to air freighters. It was subsequently announced, as part of the Liberal government's 1995 budget, that another $80 million was being budgeted to have Aerospatiale, the plane's manufacturer, modify the airbuses to accommodate cargo instead of people.

Incredibly, this costly proposal to transfer five air freighters to our air force's strategic airlift inventory was made just ten months before the $108-million purchase of two Hercules was announced.

Obviously, the question is, how was it possible for this level of abuse and mismanagement to develop to such a deplorable state virtually undetected and seemingly unchecked? The answer, in part, lies in the absence of a firm defence policy. This makes such waste possible, but under the shrewd control of self-interested individuals, it becomes inevitable. Without a strictly defined blueprint for the structure of our armed forces, resistant to the winds of political change, the defence budget is nothing more than a pork barrel free for the plundering. With no consistent yardstick by which to measure progress or judge any shortfalls, procurement funds for our military have become subject to the discretionary whims of the senior bureaucrats who write up "interim policies" as required.

The cancellation of most of the 1987 White Paper's equipment purchases actually freed up huge amounts of defence procurement funds which had been earmarked for those various long-term projects. As a result, individuals like Robert Fowler and his assistant became greatly empowered through their control of the defence budget. Every subsequent defence policy paper drafted by Fowler and Calder reflected their desire to increase and solidify their newfound power. Vague buzzwords and catch-phrases came to replace anything resembling a solid direction. It was Fowler's stated intent that, throughout the downsizing, DND was going to retain a "multipurpose combat capability." In other words, it was "anything goes" in terms of acquiring equipment, and certainly the pattern of procurement throughout this period reflected that attitude. Even though our navy possessed only three old diesel-electric submarines, and hopes were waning for their eventual replacement, Fowler spent millions on air-independent research. This revolutionary development would allow a submarine to operate its diesel engines while still submerged through the use of liquid oxygen. The diesel engines are then used to recharge the batteries which drive the main electric motors. With this technology, even conventional subs would have a limited capacity to patrol beneath the Arctic ice pack. In fact, two Canadian firms, Allupower and Ballard Systems, thanks to DND funding, actually became world leaders in this experimental research which our own navy would never acquire.

By keeping "all the doors open," Fowler and his senior buyer, the assistant deputy minister (materiel), gained incredible international power and prestige. Foreign officials from Australia to France all had files opened on Fowler to catalogue everything from his likes and dislikes to his personal quirks. Overseas, there was no doubt in the mind of any arms merchant that Robert Fowler ran the Canadian Defence Department, and it was necessary to woo him successfully in order to make any large-scale sale.

Meanwhile in Canada, experienced politicians quickly learned it didn't pay any dividends to run afoul of the bespectacled Deputy Minister of National Defence. Rather, it was deemed to be worth currying his favour if one hoped to satisfy one's constituents with federal job creation. Robert Fowler had direct control over massive amounts of discretionary funds, and everybody in Ottawa paid him homage accordingly. Yet to the Canadian public in general, and even the majority of his own department, Fowler remained virtually an unknown entity.

Traditionally, government buyers have not been known for their ability to negotiate shrewd business deals, and often in the past taxpayers have chided officials for their excesses, in all departments, of all levels of government. What makes the defence budget difficult to subject to public scrutiny is the fact that its role and mission are unique and therefore poorly understood. This cloak of deception has been cleverly manipulated over the past decade by individuals such as Deputy Minister Fowler and his communications officials to the point where it has become almost ludicrous. For example, if the federal Department of Natural Resources requires a fleet of pick-up trucks for field work, presumably they would choose a commercial model and pay the standard retail cost (approximately $20,000). Common sense dictates that once a vehicle's life expectancy has been established, then a pattern of purchase/retirement can be developed;

for example, should a ten-year expiration be used, then every year 10 per cent of a fleet would be scrapped and an equivalent number of new vehicles acquired to replace them. Such a system allows for a relatively fixed annual expenditure, prevents the eventuality of trying to maintain an "old" fleet, and enables the buyer to have the flexibility necessary to meet any short-term changes in scope or mandate (i.e., drastic personnel cuts would equate to fewer vehicles purchased).

As illustrated by the examples of the HLVW and LSVW procurement projects, DND does not apply any of these theories, even when purchasing what is essentially a non-defence item. Instead, by insisting upon developing their own truck designs (slightly modified from an existing model) and purchasing them on a full-batch basis, procurement officials deliberately turn what should be a routine purchase into a political magnet.

By using the parameters of the recent LSVW project, we can clearly see the flaws of this process. Simple arithmetic shows that the cost of keeping a 2,500-vehicle fleet of $20,000 trucks at a ten-year currency level would cost about $5 million annually. After twenty years of implementation, the total program cost would be $100 million and our army would still have 2,500 trucks aged one to ten years with only 250 due to be replaced—at a cost of about $5 million. Instead, the DND senior management decided to buy all 2,500 trucks at once. The very scale of the purchase attracted political interference, with politicians seeking to use the program to artificially stimulate the auto industry, thereby creating short-term jobs. The initial cost therefore ballooned to $200 million and included the start-up cost of establishing a now unused assembly line. Twenty years from now, the Army will have an entire 2,500-vehicle fleet overdue for replacement. This will undoubtedly cost taxpayers millions in life-extension repairs while a new $200-million batch purchase is negotiated.

When it comes to an actual weapon system, the Defence Department plays even more heavily upon the public's ignorance of such issues to push the costs to unrealistic levels. In the case of the $5.5 billion for fifty EH-101 helicopters, the excessive numbers led to the project's eventual downfall. In fact, DND's last-minute, pre-election attempt to reduce the numbers actually helped to expose the duplicitous accounting of defence procurement officials.

Kim Campbell's Tories were at that juncture rapidly losing their lead in the 1993 election polls, and the EH-101 purchase was seen as a major liability. Following a top-level cabinet meeting, Deputy Minister Robert Fowler was tasked with scaling down the purchase in some way to make it more publicly acceptable—but without making it appear the Conservatives were giving credence to the Opposition party's charges that the EH-101 was a gold-plated luxury item. Bob Fowler, Ray Sturgeon and the top procurement officials met with various lobbyists and contractors, and soon a revised proposal was announced.

Unfortunately for fledgling Prime Minister Kim Campbell, she had not spent a long enough period in the defence portfolio to second-guess its bureaucrats (even though she'd been at the helm during the initial stages of the Somalia scandal). Campbell trusted the numbers she had been given, and she quickly announced the project cuts at a press conference in the autumn of 1993.

Shortly after she claimed that DND would shave $1 billion off the price tag by reducing the number of EH-101s ordered by a total of seven aircraft, editors and journalists quickly calculated that, using those numbers, the Defence Department could scrap another twenty-eight machines and still get fifteen EH-101s for free.

The cost figures made absolutely no sense, and despite the levity in most editorials at the time, serious questions were being asked. The Tories were badly embarrassed by the miscue (what had been intended as a public relations effort backfired horribly), and the procurement officials at DND closed ranks to avoid further scrutiny.

To try to salvage the situation and to save political face, Kim Campbell had to explain that included in her $1-billion-announced savings was nearly $400-million worth of program contingency funds, which were (for PR purposes) no longer being included in the total cost.

Incredibly, it alarmed no one at the time that these top-level defence buyers lacked confidence in their own ability to manage a program to the extent they built at least $400 million into the budget for expected "cost overruns."

Similarly, very few people thought to question the enormous cost of the Army's new armoured personnel carriers when the project was announced in 1995. While no one could deny the urgent necessity of equipping our troops with new combat vehicles, the price tag of $800 million for 200 new APCs should have sparked serious interest.

In their press release, DND trumpeted the virtues of these new General Motors (Diesel Division) armoured cars, describing them repeatedly as a defence system. Presumably, the jargon used in the official announcement was intended to disguise the fact that the unit price of these "systems" is a staggering $4 million each. Because private citizens cannot purchase armoured vehicles, it is very difficult to conduct cost comparisons to establish a relative value. However, when one realizes that for the $4-million price tag of a single new APC you could purchase more than thirty customized, fully loaded tractor-trailers, it begins to put the Defence Department's procurement process in perspective. Eighteen-wheelers with their 500-horsepower engines are far more powerful than these armoured cars, their construction is far more complex and they are designed to run, virtually non-stop, over a fifteen- to twenty-year lifespan.

So why does it cost thirty times as much for each of these APCs—particularly as part of a bulk-quantity purchase?

The answer given by Defence Department public affairs officers invariably is based on the formula of obfuscation and deceit: "The cost includes spare parts and training packages expected over the lifespan of the vehicle." Most journalists will accept this explanation without question and assume it is their own lack of experience or naïveté which led them to question the dollar figure in the first place. In other words, this clever deception works most of the time.

One has to wonder, though, why on earth DND officials take the time to compile such massive dollar figures for their programs when obviously the far lower upfront purchase price would be to their advantage in obtaining both cabinet approval and public acceptance. The answer, of course, lies in their almost manic obsession to divest themselves of accountability. Building a twenty-year maintenance projection into a program's cost means that everyone involved will be long retired before the final tally of cost overruns can be assessed. Since by then the original equipment purchased will itself be due for replacement, presumably the media would be preoccupied with the new program.

Conversely, if DND were to announce a specific fixed cost per unit, and a strict delivery schedule, then shortly after the completion of each major

The former chief of the defence staff, General John de Chastelain, retired in December 1995 amid reports that his colleagues at DND concealed information about the murder of sixteen-year-old Shidane Arone in Somalia. (Credit: Canadian Forces)

Deputy Minister of National Defence Robert Ramsay Fowler. During his stewardship, greed and corruption flourished in Canada's military high command. (Credit: Canadian Forces)

Colonel Michel Drapeau was one of the few brass at DND headquarters who began reporting cases of fraud to his superiors. For his efforts, he became the victim of a smear campaign. (Credit: Canadian Forces)

Micheline Clairoux, left, director of Facilities Management at NDHQ, spent $86,000 after the Gulf War on a "mental retreat" for stressed-out employees. Part of Clairoux's agenda included importing a "guru" from California to lead the DND workers in bongo-playing sessions to soothe their nerves. (Credit: Author's archives)

In 1995, Minister of National Defence David Collenette announced that the entire fleet of CF-5 fighter aircraft was to be mothballed just after $350 million was spent on an upgrade. (Credit: Canadian Forces)

Although he was earning more than $125,000 a year, Lieutenant General Gordon Reay spent his soldiers' money to buy himself a television set and a VCR. (Credit: Canadian Forces)

There was no inquest or autopsy into the death of thirty-nine-year-old Denys Henrie, the director general of DND's Executive Secretariat. Henrie left a suicide note that read, in part, "For my death, I hold responsible [Bob] Fowler... [Micheline] Clairoux" and others. (Credit: Canadian Forces)

Jean Boyle, left, was picked to succeed John de Chastelain as Canada's top soldier because he was not tainted by Somalia. Yet, in April 1996, evidence emerged that Boyle had misled military investigators by claiming he knew nothing of the destruction of documents. (Credit: Canadian Forces)

The handsome Colonel Serge Labbé, commander, Canadian Joint Forces, Somalia, was reported to have offered a case of champagne to the first paratrooper who killed a Somali. (Credit: Canadian Forces)

Deputy Minister of National Defence Robert Fowler, centre, visited Somalia barely a month before the murder of civilians by Canadian paratroopers. Here he meets with local clansmen. (Credit: Canadian Forces)

ABOVE: *Captain Peter Gunther and his wife, Dominique, at a memorial service for their son, Corporal Daniel Gunther. Gunther was murdered while on UN peacekeeping duty by Muslim militiamen in the former Yugoslavia. Officials at headquarters conspired to make Gunther's death seem an accident.* (Credit: Le Soleil)

BOTTOM RIGHT: *Private Kyle Brown, who witnessed the brutal beating of Shidane Arone, tried reporting the incident to a number of NCOs but found them all drunk. He willingly helped investigators but ended up as an accomplice to the crime, was court-martialled, found guilty and jailed.* (Credit: Author's archives)

LEFT: *Lieutenant Colonel Carol Mathieu, who commanded the Canadian Airborne in Somalia, changed the rules of engagement with Colonel Labbé's approval. Suspected looters could be shot "between the skirt and flip flops,"* he said. (Credit: Canadian Forces)

Captain Jim DeCoste was killed in a jeep accident on September 18, 1993, in the former Yugoslavia. His body was robbed by the Serbian soldiers in the truck that collided with his vehicle. The Canadian miltary concluded DeCoste's driver was at fault and compensated the Serbs, who had also looted guns and ammunition from the jeep. DeCoste was known as "the soldier's soldier." (Credit: Katherine Taylor, *Esprit de Corps*)

program a thorough audit could be done and subsequently accessed by the media. In this situation, not only would defence contractors be subject to the watchful scrutiny of the taxpayer, but senior bureaucrats would also have to face the dreaded threat of accountability for their actions.

In all of these tales of defence purchases, the end users, the soldiers who are destined to receive this equipment, appear to be singularly absent from the equations. The reason for that can be traced back to the senior officer corps' breaking faith with traditional values and putting their own personal interests ahead of that of the service.

Nothing else can explain the fact that it has taken nearly a decade to procure new helmets for our troops—despite the urgent requirement created by dangerous peacekeeping operations such as Yugoslavia, the selection of a proven design (U.S.) in 1986, and the price tag for a Forces-wide scale of issue of less than $15 million.

The same neglect of basic needs has been illustrated by the delayed implementation of a new pay system for reservists. When the original contractor failed to deliver a useable product, a new software firm had to be selected. The resulting five-year period of costly experimentation has meant that, young soldiers often go unpaid for months. In many cases, their unit commanders resort to paying their troops from private canteen funds and donations.

For two years in a row (1995 and 1996), a young militia captain has stood up at an Ottawa defence conference and asked the Chief of the Defence Staff, "Sir, when are my men going to get paid?"

In total contrast, one could compare the ease with which Defence Minister Marcel Masse frivolously gave an NHL hockey team a $250,000 gift. In October 1992, Masse met with Marcel Aubut, president of the Quebec Nordiques, and promised him this substantial sum from his Defence Department's budget. Over the ensuing weeks, DND officials were hastily dispatched to Quebec City to meet with Mr. Aubut to determine exactly what the Canadian Forces would receive in exchange for the money. In the end, the Defence Department spent a total of $250,000 in order to fulfil Masse's benevolence. To account for the expense, the Nordiques allowed two small Canadian Forces crests to be painted outside their centre-ice face-off circle.

The paper trails documenting this largesse were leaked to *Esprit de Corps* magazine in 1996. It shows everyone involved in processing this payment objected to it, with the exception of Robert Fowler. Richard Burton, the executive assistant to Fowler, finally intervened and directed that the money be transferred into the public relations account from the vice-chief of the defence staff's "reserve" fund. On the paper detailing the budget transfer, this expenditure of $250,000 was listed as part of the EH-101 helicopter program.

Although the policy directives which control these programs and their priority came directly from the Deputy Minister, it was a cowering and coveting cadre of top officers, collectively shirking their responsibilities over a ten-year span, that allowed such rot to take hold.

Despite the apparent conflict of interest, it has become the norm for retiring general officers to find themselves an executive placement with a defence-related firm. Their distinguished title is usually vice-president of government relations. Their real role is to exercise power and influence over their old friends to solicit contracts for their new employer.

Naturally, soldiers have become cynical about any equipment deficiencies they are forced to endure, blaming the shortcomings on a sweetheart deal orchestrated by a former general. While this is not always the case, as the number of retired generals–cum–defence executives proliferates, the cause for concern is becoming increasingly justified.

In 1990, Lieutenant-General Larry Ashley was the commander of Air Command. Just prior to retiring, he was instrumental in pushing through the purchase proposal of three Lockheed Arcturus aircraft. At the time, the deal was being billed as a too-good-to-pass-up final sale. Lockheed had announced they were shutting down their Arcturus assembly line, and this was to be the last batch produced.

Shortly after the deal was signed, Larry Ashley turned in his uniform and moved to Ottawa. Within months, it was announced that he was the new president of Lockheed Canada. Nobody challenged the potential conflict of interest. However, soon after assuming his new executive office, Ashley found himself earning his keep by smoothing things over with his old comrades.

According to the 1995 auditor general's report, the Arcturus aircraft Lockheed delivered to the Canadian Air Force were badly deficient in several key areas. The main glitch was that the electronic surveillance equipment didn't function well in inclement weather. Since these aircraft were purchased to provide maritime patrols on Canada's Atlantic Coast, this was no minor setback.

Although Lockheed did manage to sort out the problem, the delivery dates were subsequently delayed by several months. What the auditor general noted in his report was that DND, in spite of the obvious legal grounds for compensation, had failed to pursue Lockheed for $52 million in penalties and rebates. Despite the findings of the auditor general and DND's own internal reports from the chief of review services, the Defence Department senior management chose to let the whole affair drop rather than seek compensation.

Whether or not the presumption is grounded, the perception remains among the rank and file that former Lieutenant-General Ashley's appointment as president paid off a handsome dividend to his new employers.

Were it an isolated occurrence that a senior officer retired from the Forces then reappeared in the defence industry, the problem would be restricted to each individual in question. Regrettably—for the integrity of the entire defence procurement process—it has become only the rare exception who chooses simply to fade away from military service. All too often, the employment link comes as the direct result of a buyer–client relationship, and non-senior officers have come to regard managing a procurement project as a springboard to a post-retirement executive position.

Suppliers and lobbyists are fully aware of this attitude and, consequently, the fifteen-year salary and expenses of a "redundant" executive (or more, depending on the value of the project) are built into the contract costs. For the Defence Department, the practice creates problems during the implementation phase of these programs, as the representative who negotiated the deal on their behalf is now working for the supplier. Any contractual discrepancies that arise would need to be clarified with the original signatories, both of whom are now on the same side of the dispute.

Colonel Paul Coderre was the Defence Department's manager of the $1.8-billion Tactical Command Control and Communication System (TCCCS), the new radio program. After signing the contract with Computing Devices of Canada in 1990, and overseeing the definition phase of the project, Colonel Coderre announced his intention to retire from the Forces. Less than one year later, Coderre was named vice-president at Computing Devices.

Colonel Ralph Genest's last military posting was as the project director for a $289-million computerized supply system for the Armed Forces. Shortly after this major contract was awarded to SHL Systems in January 1995, Genest accepted an executive position with this same supplier. By mid-1995, however, delivery dates had been delayed. In fact, an American firm was tentatively contacted by DND about the possibility of taking over the project, in case SHL failed to produce the specified product. Throughout these tense negotiations, Ralph Genest was dealing with his successor and long-time friend and colleague, Colonel W.J. Rance, on behalf of his new employer.

One of the more ambitious senior military officers to leave DND and seek his fortune with a private enterprise was Colonel Tim Sparling. In 1994, this gentleman found himself working at National Defence Headquarters as the director of international policy, and one of his responsibilities was to liaise with the new Pearson Peacekeeping Centre (PPC).

The $10 million in federal seed money for this venture had been approved in February by Prime Minister Jean Chrétien; however, DND was not quite sure how to support this independent facility. While the Canadian Institute of Strategic Studies (CISS) under the directorship of Alex Morrison was nominally responsible for the PPC, all of its financial support and tuition for its students would be drawn from the budgets of DND and Foreign Affairs.

In August 1994, the vice-chief of the defence staff wrote to Alex Morrison at CISS to officially appoint Colonel Tim Sparling as the military's "point of contact" for the peacekeeping college. From that point until his early retirement from the Forces in August 1995, Sparling worked directly on DND's submission for funding to Treasury Board—not only for the original start-up allotment, but also for the annual training budget necessary to make the PPC functional.

In September 1995, after hanging up his old uniform, Mr. Tim Sparling was proclaimed as the new "Executive Director" of the Pearson Peacekeeping Centre. Even though official complaints were registered with DND and Treasury Board for alleged violation of guidelines, officials at both these institutions failed to see a conflict of interest in Sparling's actions.

Former Air Force Brigadier-General Ron Slaunwhite took matters of divided loyalty to even greater depths. Slaunwhite finished his military time as the project director for the CF-18 program and then promptly retired in 1984. Immediately following his release from the service, Slaunwhite was offered the presidency of McDonnell Douglas Canada (the F-18's manufacturer). His move between offices was so quick that he had the $50,000, chrome 1 to 10 scale CF-18 replica model moved directly from NDHQ to his new corporate suite. The expensive gift had been presented by McDonnell Douglas. However, what should have become a decorative public foyer display at NDHQ was "appropriated" by Slaunwhite as his own personal property.

If any man can be seen as a rival to Robert Fowler in terms of the damage he has done to the Canadian military institution, retired Vice-Admiral Ed Healey would be at the front of the line. His power in defence circles is second only to Fowler's, and in the world of defence lobbyists he reigns supreme.

When Fowler was appointed deputy minister of defence in 1989, Admiral Healey was the incumbent assistant deputy minister (materiel) (ADM[MAT]) or senior buyer. Having occupied the post since 1985, the ambitious Healey had created a comfortable empire, and he surrounded himself with like-minded individuals.

From 1987 to 1989 it was high times for defence procurement officials in Canada as world-wide arms dealers aggressively pursued the elusive pot of gold promised in Fowler's grandiose White Paper. General Paul Manson had been the chief of the defence staff throughout this period, and he had clearly set the tone for his officers to embrace the offerings of industry. During this period, Manson strengthened DND's long-standing relationship with publisher Bill Baxter. With Manson's blessing and Ed Healey's active participation, Baxter was contracted to produce the lavish annual arms exhibition known as ARMX.

The would-be Defence Department contractors spent millions of dollars exhibiting their wares, but far more was expended unseen in the hosting of exclusive hospitality suites at downtown Ottawa hotels. With the program cancellations of 1989, the writing was on the wall that these good times were going to come to an abrupt end. (DND officials had cleverly waited until four days after ARMX 1989 before they made the announcement, thereby guaranteeing they would not miss out on any of the freebies.) At this juncture, Ed Healey retired from the Defence Department and immediately began marketing his knowledge of procurement strategies as a senior partner with the lobby firm CFN Consultants.

CFN's partners were all retired senior officers. However, once Healey came on board, he soon took them to previously inconceivable levels. Arguably what made Healey so effective was his close ties to Robert Fowler, and the access he still had to his old offices. As of May 1996, Healey was still issued with an identification pass, which allowed him to enter NDHQ buildings without an escort and without having to register.

Healey often relies on his "outside" credentials to gain access to media outlets. Since 1990, he has been an executive with the Canadian Defence Preparedness Association (CDPA). The directors of this non-profit organization of "concerned citizens" are traditionally CFN partners.

When the Canadian government was actively debating the virtues of purchasing four modern diesel-electric submarines from the British Navy, Healey often described himself either as a retired admiral or as the president of CDPA. He was able to have his "pro-submarine purchase" editorials published in all of the major daily newspapers. Had editors thought to check out the lobby register, they would have discovered Vickers Shipbuilding and Engineering Limited (VSEL) had long retained CFN on its behalf. As the shipyard that designed and built the four British Upholder Submarines, VSEL stood to make millions on the operation and maintenance contract if the Canadian deal went through.

Of course, such obvious linkages are not always possible to make when researching the client list of CFN Consultants. However, it is generally known throughout the Ottawa lobby community who is selling for which defence firms.

According to Jim Eddy, Ed Healey invited him several times to participate in a social function known as "Hawks and Eagles." This sort of get-together took place roughly ten times each year, and the venue was invariably the prestigious Hunt Club Golf and Country Club near the Uplands Air Force Base in Ottawa. Eddy's firm had secured a multimillion-dollar subcontract on the Canadian patrol frigate project, yet they were relative newcomers to the defence industry circle of old boys.

Prior to retaining CFN Consultants as their registered lobbyists, potential clients would often be invited by Healey and his partners to sample their access and influence by participating in a "Hawks and Eagles get-together."

The price of inclusion in this cosy club was not cheap; up to ten prospects would pay between $3,000 and $5,000 for their inaugural appearance. The steep entry fee was recompensed by the knowledge that the ADM(MAT) of DND and the Chief of Supply would be in attendance. Usually CFN clients would manage to meet these two influential figures and spend a few minutes each peddling their wares.

The food and beverages at these functions were lavish and the client list was strictly screened; however, the only reason clients paid the steep costs to Healey was to gain access to the DND officials. Attending such functions does not constitute a clear conflict of interest, provided the government official receives no direct cash benefit and is unaware that access to him is being peddled to prospective clients.

There is nothing to suggest that at the time that he was attending these functions as ADM(MAT) between 1992 and 1994, Ray Sturgeon knew that Healey was using the occasion to solicit clients for CFN Consultants. Nevertheless, once Sturgeon himself crossed over from the public service to join Healey's lobbyists, he was soon engaged in arranging client access to his successor, Lieutenant-General R. Fisher.

In October 1993, one of Sturgeon's professional responsibilities as ADM(MAT) was to chair a NATO procurement committee on unmanned surveillance aircraft. The job entailed several trips to Brussels every year, and a fair amount of detailed research was required on the subject. Sturgeon felt that the time commitment to this project would be excessive, and although the chairmanship for Canada indicated a certain amount of prestige, he wanted to second his duties to someone else. Despite the fact that DND has an abundance of senior supply officers and bureaucrats, Sturgeon decided to hire a private consultant from CFN Consultants to sit in for him on the NATO committee. It is indicative of the amount of influence CFN has with senior DND managers that no one questioned Sturgeon's actions.

Through negotiations with Ed Healey, retired Major-General Dick Oldford was awarded a personal service contract to fulfil DND's unmanned-surveillance committee obligation. The original value of the contract was established at $48,000, plus all travel expenses. For those familiar with such consulting contracts, the dollar figure will come as no surprise. The majority of these "old boy" arrangements are initially authorized at just below the $50,000 government cut-off limit for sole-source contracts. Once the incumbent is safely ensconced in the position, the total value can be revised upwards with relative impunity.

Six months after hiring Dick Oldford as his personal stand-in at NATO, Sturgeon received a job offer from Ed Healey to become a senior partner with CFN. Dutifully, on April 12, 1994, Sturgeon wrote a letter to Bob Fowler explaining his intention to leave DND and to seek his fortune with the lobbying community.

In his letter, Sturgeon explained that the conflict-of-interest guidelines should be waived in his case as he was not involved in any direct dealings with his new employers. Four days later, before any response from the deputy minister, Dick Oldford's contract was amended upwards. The rationale given for increasing the value to $150,000 plus expenses (a $102,000 raise) was that two additional meetings had been added to the schedule, bringing the total to six conferences for the year. To put this in perspective, Ray Sturgeon as ADM(MAT) was an executive level five, receiving an annual salary of up to $129,000. Yet for taxpayers to hire a stand-in for him was now valued at $150,000 by Sturgeon himself.

Fowler responded in writing to Sturgeon's employment request and conflict waiver on April 22 by wishing him all the best in his new career. He also took the opportunity to remind Sturgeon not to involve himself in any direct dealings with CFN Consultants between then and his retirement.

When the CFN letters between Ray Sturgeon and Bob Fowler were publicly released after an access-to-information request had been made, Dave Rider, a reporter from the *Ottawa Sun*, filed a story outlining the details of this incident. However, when he was contacted for comment, Ed Healey scoffed at the suggestion that anything improper had taken place. "If Sturgeon was going to feather his nest, he would have taken at least $2,000,000, not just $100,000" was the defence Healey offered the reporter.

Although the *Ottawa Sun*'s story received little attention (page 32, second edition only), behind the scenes at NDHQ there was a mad scramble to conduct damage control before the more serious conflict of interest was exposed. Journalists at *Frank* magazine had followed up on the Dave Rider story and began making some potentially damning links, which posed possible international repercussions for our government.

The trail of corruption started back in 1988 with an experimental project developed by Canadair-Bombardier and funded by the Defence Department. Work had been started and prototypes were built of an unmanned surveillance aircraft, which was given the working title "Sentinel." Canadian troops and sailors conducted trials on this "flying peanut" during the late 1980s and early 1990s, but the express hope was that the United States would show an interest, thereby creating a market for this unique product.

Usually, surveillance drones are deployed to gather battlefield intelligence, but they are rarely issued to any formation smaller than an army corps (50,000 to 125,000 men). Because the largest field unit deployed by the Canadian Army is a brigade (3,500 troops), the Sentinel should have been considered too rich an asset for our small forces.

When sea trials with the U.S. and Italian navies in 1991 failed to spark a serious interest in the Canadair Drone, the federal government decided to pull the plug on the project's funding. By the time of the Sentinel's announced cancellation in the 1989 budget, DND had already spent $3.6 million on its development. Although this project had just been cut, Canadair was determined to keep it alive. Between the spring of 1989 and January 1993, the marketing executives at Canadair decided to switch tactics and they retained CFN Consultants as their lobbyists.

Since 1989, Ed Healey's successor as ADM(MAT) had been Rod Gillespie. In the summer of 1992, Gillespie retired (at forty years of age) from DND and started work as vice-president at Canadair. His job was to market Canadair to his previous employers, where as ADM(MAT) he had gained an intricate knowledge of their budgets and procurement strategies. Having worked at Healey's old empire for the previous three years, Gillespie was only too aware of the power and influence CFN Consultants carried throughout the procurement world of National Defence. The recommendation to retain Healey's services would indeed turn out to be a sound investment.

When Ray Sturgeon contracted Dick Oldford to chair the NATO committee in his stead, CFN Consultants were no longer just providing Canadair with a simple lobbyist for their project: their man was now actually on the inside. Since Canada was too small a market for the Sentinel, if the project were to be resurrected, it would have to attract some international interest. Whether by coincidence or by design, just a few scant months after Dick Oldford began his chairmanship, there was a flicker of hope for Canadair's Sentinel. Canadian defence procurement officials placed enough stock (albeit faint) in the fledgling NATO interest to recommend that the research funding to Canadair be reinstated.

No public announcement was made to the effect that this cancelled program was being renewed; it was simply tabled in the 1995 budget estimates as a $30-million annual expenditure.

Following the publication of the *Frank* magazine article that made all of the above connections, Lieutenant-General Fisher, Sturgeon's successor as ADM(MAT), was forced to prepare a briefing note on the subject for the Minister of National Defence. In a two-page memo to David Collenette, Fisher confirmed the essential facts and figures as being correct. In his defence of the situation, Fisher noted that, although it was realized that CFN was Canadair's lobbyist, Dick Oldford had signed a non-disclosure agreement before he assumed his chairmanship duties.

With that line of defence, the DND bureaucrats battened down the hatches in anticipation of a media storm that never materialized. Canada had knowingly sent an arms salesman, disguised as a bureaucrat, to pitch a defence system to our NATO allies; and the Canadian taxpayer paid for it twice (CFN's $150,000 contract and the renewed $30-million funding to its client).

Without any public clamour, there was no investigation launched into this affair, and no corrective measures were taken. The DND senior management had dodged a bullet.

The NATO committee/CFN Consultants scandal was not the only close call that the DND procurement officials had to sweat through in 1995, and it certainly wasn't the most (potentially) damaging. A top-level annual threat assessment, known to senior DND executives as the Kipling Report, points out areas of concern which could possibly impact negatively on the Canadian Forces. True to the corrupt nature of the present defence establishment regime, the focus of the Kipling Report has become increasingly centred on media issues and unreported scandals.

What the top brass identified as the most serious threat to the integrity of the Forces in 1995 was the Canadian Patrol Frigate (CPF) Training Program. Although two years later very few people would even be aware of this story, at that crucial juncture the DND officials involved recognized the magnitude of its implications. To put it in perspective, the Somalia affair was listed as being a "moderate" threat, whereas the CPF trainers project was given an "ultra-sensitive" rating.

While some media outlets did touch on this story, DND was successful in limiting the damage through an immediate counter-offensive. In fact, internal DND memos show that the two top public affairs officers, General Jean Boyle and Ken Calder, were directly involved in the communications strategy to deflect and subdue any wider coverage. Boyle and Calder were successful in managing the issue off the front pages before it could attract further interest.

CHAPTER EIGHT

A Law unto Themselves

Until the Somalia scandal threw a glaring public spotlight on the internal workings of the military, few Canadians even realized, or cared, that Canadian soldiers were subject to a different justice system than civilians.

After months of disturbing media revelations emerging from the Somalia inquiry, Canadians probably wonder just how the top brass managed to keep a lid on this boiling pot of injustice for as long as they did. For two years now, brave officers have broken ranks to tell their tales of top-level abuse of authority, obstruction of justice, interference with police investigations and destruction of evidence.

Eventually, the whole military justice system came under critical review. Under this independent scrutiny, it began to fall apart. It rightly seemed the Canadian military was singularly incapable of investigating itself and administering justice in a fair and equitable manner. Internal reports had already pointed out the shortcomings and potential abuses that could occur under DND's authoritative top-down structure, which has no inherent checks and balances. Outside experts were asked to analyse the military police and judge advocate general directorates within DND, and repeatedly they proclaimed urgent reforms were required to prevent senior officers from interfering with the administration of justice. Unfortunately, these reports and alarm bells fell on deaf ears. The recipients of the warnings had already found they enjoyed the full control the systemic flaws of the military justice system afforded them.

Just as the popular television show *Law and Order* depicts, police functions and the judicial process fulfil two distinctly separate roles in the administration of justice. This is the case in almost all systems, and the Canadian military is no exception. However, because of the unique function soldiers perform, and the conditions under which they are expected to operate, a different value system from that of mainstream society must be used in the judicial process.

Historically, armies have been known for having a far stricter code of discipline than that of the civilian populace whom they undertake to defend. Due to the very brutal and spartan conditions which the profession of arms entails, the punishments required to maintain order among the ranks have to be swift and harsh. Under combat conditions, desertion from duty is still punishable by death, even in the Canadian Army. (Few Canadian civilians realize that the death penalty is still on the books of the National Defence Act.) Disobedience and disloyalty are seen as a severe threat to the maintaining of discipline and are chargeable offences under the Queen's Regulations and Orders. Virtually anyone in a position of authority, including a master corporal, has the power invested in his rank to lay charges upon a subordinate for even slight violations of standing orders.

Depending on the severity of the alleged crime, enlisted soldiers are paraded in front of their commanding officers to face a summary trial, or they may elect to have their case heard at a court martial. Senior NCOs and officers facing serious criminal charges and whose crime may warrant punishment longer than ninety days in jail (the limit for a summary hearing) face court martial. As for all criminal acts perpetrated by an officer, or senior NCO, it is mandatory that a court martial be convened to hear the charges.

The stringent rank structure not only creates the cohesion necessary to maintain tactical command under wartime conditions, but also manifests itself in the strict written regulations that constitute the basis of military justice. Under most circumstances, a combat unit is self-monitored by its own chain of command and, in turn, self-regulated through severe punishments for any offenders. Military police attached to field units are theoretically tasked with the wartime role of processing prisoners of war and traffic control only. Even in peacetime, only drastic circumstances would warrant a commanding officer's calling on the military police to conduct an investigation into his own soldiers. In such cases, the imperative remains keeping the chain of command intact, thereby retaining the unit's cohesion.

In most cases, investigations are initiated by a battalion or formation commander, and the police officers assigned would then report to him directly while keeping their own military police superiors informed of their actions. At all times during their operations, the military police remain subject to the same service code of discipline that applies to all soldiers. In other words, they must remain rank-conscious and pay the proper respects (salute, stand at attention, etc.) to all commissioned officers, even if they happen to be suspects.

Obviously, this allows the mostly non-commissioned junior-ranking police force to be fully effective only on very low-level probes. A clear example of this inherent flaw and lack of investigative flexibility was captured on videotape during the Somalia investigations. Master Warrant Officer Paul Dowd was the police officer who conducted the initial interviews in Belet Uen regarding the torture death of Shidane Arone. Being a senior non-commissioned officer, Dowd had no difficulty in asserting authority over the junior ranking soldiers involved in the incident during his interrogations.

However, eventually it came time to question Captain Michael Sox, the platoon commander whose men were implicated, and who himself had been accused of assaulting Arone during his capture. At this point, Dowd became a subservient, almost cowering individual, and completely lost control of the interview.

The only real investigative independence the military police can exercise, lies in their secondary chain of command, which is topped by the director general of security and military police (DGSAMP). Complaints and objections regarding abuse of authority and interference in police operations can be sent from the DGSAMP directly to the deputy chief of the defence staff. However, the most senior rank in the military police is only that of colonel, so obviously this in itself limits the "clout" in a strictly rank-structured environment to those at the unit level (lieutenant-colonels commanding battalion-sized formations).

In such cases, often the pattern had been for the Army senior command to use their rank to protect their own subordinate officers. In 1993, when Lieutenant-Colonel Carol Mathieu was being investigated by the military police for his involvement in the Somalia operation, a warrant was obtained to search his house for any supporting evidence. Colonel Mathieu protested to his own commanders at the manner in which he was being treated by the military police.

Major-General Brian Vernon was one of the three senior commanders who took it upon themselves to express their opinions to the investigating officer, Major Vince Buonamici. When Buonamici went public with allegations of this interference in January 1996, Vernon was incredulous at the accusation. In an interview with *Esprit de Corps* magazine, he essentially confirmed the facts as being correct. "Yes, I called him. Yes, I expressed displeasure at the way he was conducting his investigation," Vernon admitted. It was Buonamici's conclusion that Vernon had trouble with. "How can you call that interference? I just expressed my opinion." He added, "What is the point of being a general if you can't express an opinion [to a junior officer]?"

Although complaints were lodged by the DGSAMP with the DCDS over this incident, no action was taken against the generals involved.

With a military justice system designed to be self-policing at the combat-unit level (service crimes) and a police force with its effectiveness limited to the junior ranks, there is obviously a systemic deficiency in an organization as top-heavy and bureaucratic as the Canadian Armed Forces. What works effectively at keeping soldiers at their firing posts in the heat of battle has little usefulness in monitoring civil servants and senior officers. Yet, of the 97,727 personnel subject to the National Defence Act (military and civilian), fewer than 8 per cent actually serve in anything resembling a combat unit.

Naturally, the majority of the offences committed by the DND staff, given its composition, are white-collar crimes such as fraud and theft. Though the military system is completely ineffective in dealing with such matters, the senior management at DND have resisted all pressures to adapt to their new circumstances. The main reason for this reluctance to divorce martial law from the reality of their present environment is that it would mean relinquishing the absolute control they presently enjoy.

No one understood power and control better than the duo of Robert Fowler and John de Chastelain. During their tenure as deputy minister and chief of the defence staff, Fowler increasingly took over the reins of the entire military justice system, and de Chastelain all too willingly allowed him to do so.

The daily diaries for the Deputy Minister, obtained under access-to-information requests, show that the Director General of Security often met Fowler in his office to discuss individual investigations. Normally such a function would be passed up through the chain of command from the deputy chief of the defence staff to the CDS, and eventually (in extreme cases only) the DM would be informed as to the progress of a police probe.

Unlike his predecessors, Fowler had a thirst for the knowledge that he knew equalled power. Being a micro-manager, all too familiar with the bureaucratic process of "filtering" information up through the various levels of command, Fowler drank directly from the various faucets of information. The key to managing an issue depended on the timely flow of important information directly to him, so that he could structure a timetable for responsive action without being subject to any external interference (i.e., take care of the mess before anyone else even discovers it).

During his time as DM, Fowler became increasingly cognizant of and driven by media pressures. Any press at all, regardless of the slant, was unwanted because it would end up shining a bright light upon the tattered façade DND had become. Fowler frequently told senior staff his personal motto of "no surprises" applied to both good news stories and bad news stories. If something was going to be released by DND, then it was going to have his personal stamp of approval.

Often public disclosure of any impropriety became viewed as a larger crime than the original infraction. Internally, if an officer was turned in by his own staff for abuse of authority, the charges would rebound upon the whistle blowers with dire consequences. Charges of insubordination and disloyalty would often be the basis for the system to crush honest underlings, in order to protect senior-ranking culprits.

The pervading attitude for this oppressive atmosphere was generated right from the very top, and because of this, the limited effectiveness of the military police/justice system was powerless to tip the balance.

There is probably no clearer example of this unchecked (absolute) control than the investigation into one of the Somalia cover-ups. On April 15, 1993, Major Vince Buonamici had been tasked to investigate the irregularities of a shooting death in Somalia, which had occurred more than six weeks earlier, on March 4. Buonamici had been aware of the unusual circumstances of this particular incident as early as March 5, the morning after the shooting, because he had been briefed and put on immediate stand-by to fly to Somalia.

The lengthy delay between the original report of the alleged murder and the dispatch of his investigators had always puzzled Major Buonamici. Despite the senior level of the personnel involved in such a decision, Buonamici took it upon himself to investigate this aspect of the overall case. Following a rather blunt interview with DCDS Vice-Admiral Larry Murray, the officer in charge of all operations, the young military police major filed a report in August 1993 that was a damning indictment of Admiral Murray and the "tardiness" he had demonstrated in not launching an immediate probe. During the intervening six-week period, Buonamici claimed that all key witnesses had the opportunity to collude on their stories, and most of the incriminating evidence had been destroyed. The victim's corpse had been buried without a coffin; as a result, the cadaver had turned to a soupy texture, making the autopsy difficult. In Major Buonamici's opinion, the actions on the part of Murray were "inexplicable."

As with all military reports, Buonamici's assessment was passed up the chain of command to those in higher authority. Since the military police branch report went directly to the DCDS, Admiral Murray was the first senior general to see the damaging file. At that point the media were already levelling allegations of a cover-up. And at the same time, the hapless and newly appointed Defence Minister Kim Campbell was being badgered almost daily with similar attacks from Liberal Opposition members. Despite the tremendous external pressure and the fact that a military police officer had named him as the culprit, Admiral Murray wasted no time in informing his superiors of Buonamici's report. In a letter to Chief of Defence Staff Admiral John Anderson, Murray denied the allegation of an "inexplicable" delay by claiming that he, indeed, had had his reasons. Instead, Deputy CDS Murray complained to Anderson about the inappropriate manner in which Buonamici had phrased his "strong" comments and conclusions.

Bob Fowler, as a close friend and mentor of Murray's, was sent a copy of the letter that had gone to Admiral Anderson. Fowler wasted no time in reassuring his top officers as to where he stood. In the margin, Fowler scribbled "The DCDS' response [to Buonamici] is remarkably measured. Mine would be less." And the notated copy was sent back down the chain of command.

The message this simple note sent was registered loud and clear. No further action was taken against Murray; in fact, he was subsequently posted to command the Navy, and then promoted to vice-chief of the defence staff in 1995.

For his part, Vince Buonamici found himself under surveillance by his own peers. It was feared that Buonamici might leak his cover-up report to the media, and that made him virtually *persona non grata* among members of his branch.

When power is absolute, it also sets its own, oft-changing course. Two military policemen in Halifax discovered this when they showed leniency towards a senior officer—and were still punished for their actions.

This bizarre tale begins in the early hours of November 10, 1994. CFB Halifax Base Commander Navy Captain R.W. Bowers had attended an RCMP function at the chief petty officers' mess on the evening of November 9. After having consumed a large quantity of alcohol, Bowers decided to take a staff car from the motor pool without authorization, and then he drove downtown to Dartmouth. Military police later spotted the Canadian Forces vehicle, which they realized had just been reported "missing" by CFB Halifax authorities.

After following Bowers for a short distance, the police saw him stop and let a well-known prostitute exit his staff car behind a video store. Shortly after that, the MPs pulled Bowers over and ordered him out of the vehicle. It was only at this point that the police recognized Bowers as their base commander. His formal dress uniform was in disarray, his eyes were glassy and he reeked of alcohol. When asked about the hooker, Bowers claimed she was just a well-dressed hitch-hiker, and he had only been concerned for her safety.

The MPs advised Naval Captain Bowers he was in no condition to drive home, so one of the officers took it upon himself to transport the drunken base commander to his residence, and then secure the "missing" military vehicle back on the base.

Later that morning, a military police DND sergeant went to the home of his superior to inform her of the incident. However, based on the information received from the duty sergeant, it was decided that no further action was to be taken. No investigation conducted, no charges laid. In order to cover herself, this young officer chided the duty NCO for not advising her of the incident while it was still in progress (i.e., the middle of the night). In future, all incidents such as this one involving senior officers were to be brought to the security's officer's attention immediately.

At that time, everything seemed to be under control, and for the next six months the Bowers file seemed to be closed. Then on April 10, 1995, came a dreaded surprise as the original police report was leaked to *Frank* magazine. A journalist from this notorious publication telephoned the police officer who had apprehended Bowers on the night of November 10, in order to confirm the authenticity of the leaked document. At this point, all hell broke loose at Navy Command Headquarters, and a Significant Incident Report (SIR) was dispatched immediately to Ottawa. By contrast, no mention of the Bowers incident had been reported to Ottawa at the time it occurred.

Press lines, or public relations reports, were generated at once to deflect any wider media coverage. The strategy applied was to launch an immediate summary investigation. That way the brass could officially refuse to comment (as is DND's policy) on any case under investigation. Of course, this meant proceeding down a path which the senior brass would sooner not travel, so the mandate of the investigation was strictly limited in its terms of reference. In a letter written by Naval Captain R.W. Allen, it was made clear to investigators that both Vice-Admiral Murray and Lieutenant Claire Gardham, the officer to whom the MP reported, understand "the aim is not to find fault, but to profit from the experience."

To make matters easier, when the *Frank* story broke and mainstream journalists began probing for answers, Captain Bowers was away from Halifax and unavailable for comment. Fowler and Murray had decided on a swift and effective course of damage control. And in this instance, their skill and experience in deception paid them a welcome dividend.

Without anything substantial to bite into, media interest faded and the story was dropped before it could be picked up. Without a public spotlight to pressure the investigators, the focus of the military investigation became centred on how the story of Bowers was leaked, rather than the Base Commander's bizarre activities.

The testimony of the principals in the investigation, obtained later through access-to-information requests, contradicted the MP's report. Captain Bowers claimed he was not drunk and that the woman was just a hitch-hiker. Bowers pleaded ignorance to the regulation that forbids anyone from driving a military vehicle less than eight hours after drinking alcohol. He even commended the MPs for their tact in handling the situation and for not reporting the incident, which he regarded as a non-starter.

The investigators accepted Bowers's statements as fact and cited him only for the minor infraction of violating the rule regarding alcohol and military vehicles. His punishment was a written reproof, which would stay on his file for only twelve months.

By contrast, the military police corporal and the base security officer received stiffer punishments for "not following proper procedure" and "not handling the media properly." Obviously, PR was the driving factor in this case, since the whole affair had been known "unofficially" throughout the ranks of top Navy Headquarters officials for months, and no action was taken until *Frank* magazine got hold of it. Even the press lines prepared at the summation of the Bowers probe indicate how the top brass were prepared to sacrifice all integrity for the sake of image.

Incredibly, the official response line read: "Captain Bowers is pleased that the summary investigation confirmed he is not guilty of any legal or moral misconduct." This response made no reference to the fact that Bowers had, in fact, been issued a reproof.

The same powers of authority also issued a reproof to Lieutenant Gardham for having "willingly misled the public" when she originally told *Frank* magazine that no alcohol had been involved. She admitted she had done so only "to protect Captain Bowers's reputation." In DND's eyes, her crime wasn't the lie she told, but rather the fact that she was caught. (A condition of her reproof was that she receive counselling in the handling of the media.)

The documents from the Bowers case also revealed a far more sinister side of enforced loyalty, which became the practice under Bob Fowler's tutelage. At the same time they ordered the showpiece summary investigation in the Bowers incident, the brass deployed another task force to discover the real culprit: the whistle blower who had leaked the report to *Frank* magazine. Other than admitting such an investigation had been initiated, there are no records of the Special Investigations Unit's activities in this case, and no final report has been released under Access to Information.

The military police members questioned during the summary investigation do make reference to the SIU investigation of the leak, and all expressed an element of fear as a result.

Secrecy and fear are the two main weapons the SIU possess, and their clandestine operations have given the unit the reputation of being "above the law." The fact is, they are.

ᓚ

In 1989, the Special Investigations Unit was headed by Lieutenant-Colonel Peter MacLaren, a blindly ambitious officer who revelled in his unit's task of "maintaining internal security" within DND. Bob Fowler had just been appointed as deputy minister, and John de Chastelain was the new CDS. As newcomers to their jobs, they had relatively little to do with overseeing the operation of the SIU, but all of that would soon change.

Lieutenant-Colonel MacLaren's undercover cops were virtually without a controlling agency. In theory, they answered directly to the DCDS (not through police operations), but in actuality they were used by various commanders up to and including the deputy minister.

Their access to high-tech surveillance equipment and absence of strict controls naturally led the SIU collectively to abuse authority. In 1989, they went over the edge in the case of Lieutenant Michelle Douglas, a military police officer. It was suspected that Douglas was a lesbian, and the SIU were called in to obtain proof. She was put under close surveillance and, once enough evidence had been gathered, she was brought in for "questioning" by the SIU team. It was during these videotaped interviews that the investigators crossed the bounds of propriety. They used their power and authority to ask Douglas questions which had no relevance to the case, but which were purely derogatory and voyeuristic in their nature.

At this time, homosexuality was still grounds for dismissal from the Canadian Forces, and Douglas was released from the Army following the SIU's investigation. However, she chose to fight the ruling under the Charter of Rights and Freedoms, and she filed her case in a federal court.

Senior management team were singularly nonplussed by this development, as it seemed to be an open-and-shut case. The Canadian Forces regulation pertaining to homosexuality was still valid, and it appeared as though they had strong evidence. However, when the judge advocate general (JAG) viewed the "evidence," namely, the videotaped interview, DND's case disappeared.

Instantly, it was recognized that the SIU had gone too far and that, if the public became aware of its actions, it could cause serious embarrassment and political pressure upon DND. No time was wasted in issuing damage-control directives; first off, the JAG was to offer to settle with Douglas—whatever the cost. The idea was to keep the case from going to court, where under full disclosure the video would become court evidence, and therefore publicly accessible. Although the actual settlement was never released, DND sources put the "hush money" payment at between $100,000 and $150,000.

The second phase of the plan was to order a complete review of the SIU's activities by an outside agency, along with a board of inquiry into the Douglas case.

Heading up the independent review was a former provincial court judge, René Marin, and his 1990 report has a scathing indictment of the entire Special Investigations Unit. In his forty-two recommendations, Marin essentially called for a massive reduction in the renegade unit's scope, scale and powers. Its criminal investigation mandate was to be revoked, and it was to be relegated to nothing more than conducting security clearances. Even the name was to be changed to the Security Clearance Unit in order to distance itself from the infamous reputation the SIU had earned for itself.

Given the number of Marin's politically sensitive findings and the indefensible actions of the SIU, DND's senior management willingly agreed to accept all forty-two recommendations. Even Bob Fowler, "the Volvo Man," seemed paralysed with fear over the backlash the Marin report could generate in the media. As it happened, events turned in his favour as the crisis developed in Oka, Quebec, over a land claim by the local Kanesatake Mohawks, and the Gulf War escalated. In the midst of all the patriotic and sympathetic outpouring of support for our troops, Fowler and de Chastelain quietly let the Marin report slip into the public domain—completely unnoticed.

At the same time that René Marin was conducting his review of the unit, Brigadier Jim Hansen had been put in charge of a board of inquiry into the Michelle Douglas case. In the testimony heard before this board, the transcripts show that several individuals were clearly culpable of abusing the special privileges bestowed upon police officers. In addition to that, two key characters were found to have given false testimony in an attempt to cover up the actions of their investigators. At the time Warrant Officer Paul Dowd, who had conducted the Douglas probe, and Lieutenant-Colonel Peter MacLaren, the SIU commander, were clearly criticized by the findings of Hansen's board of inquiry. Although there is no record of any punishment being administered to Dowd and MacLaren, the ambitious Lieutenant-Colonel was relieved of his SIU command before Marin completed his report.

When the whole Douglas incident vanished from the headlines because of Oka and the Gulf War, Fowler and his senior associates must have breathed a collective sigh of relief. Although they had told Marin that all forty-two of his recommendations would be accepted, the ink on his report was not even dry before DND reneged. Without missing a step, the SIU marched on to their same irregular and uncontrolled beat. The name change was formally rejected, and the criminal investigation mandate was deviously maintained by the formation of a new secret and unauthorized sub-SIU force called the National Investigative Service. Inexplicably, given what had transpired in the Douglas case, both Dowd and MacLaren were promoted to master warrant officer and colonel, respectively.

In both cases, the promotions were to newly created positions of increased authority. Although only a senior non-commissioned officer, Paul Dowd was put in command of the new NIS force. MacLaren, as the second full colonel in a branch which is authorized to have only one such officer, became the heir apparent to his boss, Al Wells. (In July 1993, MacLaren ascended the military police throne upon Wells's sudden retirement.) Virtually everyone in the military police branch had watched with interest when it appeared that Deputy Minister Fowler (by virtue of commissioning the Marin study) was going to clip the SIU's wings. Morale in the police ranks plummeted when the unit emerged unscathed, and its two prime detractors became further empowered. According to one senior police officer, the message that was sent down from Fowler's office was that not only would such questionable covert activities be tolerated, they would be rewarded.

When Judge Marin had tabled his report, he had stipulated that his recommended changes be in fact implemented—and be seen to be working. Yet for the subsequent four years, DND officials successfully warded off Marin's unwelcome interest in following up the SIU report. Correspondence between senior generals and the retired judge indicated such a review was unnecessary as all was proceeding well.

By 1994, DND had run out of delaying room, and reluctantly Marin was allowed to bring in a fresh team to examine the military police operations. The new danger consisted of two former RCMP commissioners, and the focus of this audit was widened to include all aspects of DND's self-policing capability. The new report was more damning than the original, and it recommended that the whole concept of the military maintaining a separate police force be examined in detail. René Marin noted that while civil police are held accountable to the public they serve—not only by the courts, but also by various external committees, boards and commissions—the military police respond primarily to their own internal command structure. This lack of external controls seriously undermines the objectivity of military police conducting investigations into military personnel, and Marin recommended drastic changes be made as quickly as possible.

Instead of action being taken upon the advice of this independent review, the Marin audit was buried. Despite media requests under Access to Information, the 1994 report was not released until January 1996. In condensed briefing notes for the minister of national defence, Fowler made the Marin audit sound like it had been a thumbs-up approval from the judge. As a consequence, no further action was taken.

From that point forward, MacLaren and Dowd gave blind, unswerving loyalty to Bob Fowler, in return for his giving them all the toys and gadgetry they desired.

Documents leaked to *Esprit de Corps* magazine in 1995 showed purchase orders for a new seven-car fleet for MacLaren's SIU operations section. With the NIS up and running, albeit as an unofficial unit, the operations section of the SIU should have been restricted to conducting security clearance checks. However, according to the justification for the $275,000 purchase of these seven new cars, they were up to an awful lot more than researching school records.

It was stated that all seven automobiles should be different makes to enable the SIU to conduct round-the-clock covert tails and surveillance. One had to be a van to accommodate video listening and photographic equipment. A four-wheel-drive model was necessary for mounting cross-country chases (the work order says that suspects had been "lost" in the past as a result of this shortcoming). All of the vehicles had to have powerful engines and excellent handling characteristics to enable the SIU to conduct high-speed chases. New cars were needed reportedly because of the excessive usage that the old fleet had been put through. Unfortunately, this argument was not substantiated by the work tickets, which showed the vehicles' odometer readings ranging between 10,000 and 22,000 kilometres. Such low readings could not possibly have created the "life-endangering condition" of the cars outlined in the request form, yet the funds were readily approved for the SIU.

Hard-pressed troops in Yugoslavia were sharing helmets, but the secret police had money to burn because as far as the senior management were concerned, the real battle was being waged on their doorstep. While the enemy was seen as the media, the real threat was the growing legion of willing whistle blowers. MacLaren and his heavily funded covert unit were the fear-factor necessary to keep things in check, and Fowler spared no expense.

One massive SIU operation was code-named "Apostle," and it was conducted during the spring of 1994. The Land Engineer Test Establishment (LETE) had failed to approve the new army light trucks. In unexpected retaliation, the entire facility was ordered closed as a cost-saving measure (in the budget of 1994).

Engineers working at LETE made the connection between their stubborn refusal to rubber-stamp the truck and the closure of their brand-new $20-million workplace. Shortly thereafter, several contacts who had worked on the Light Support Vehicles, Wheeled project began leaking the test results to *Esprit de Corps* and, in turn, to Peter Worthington of the *Toronto Sun*. After a spate of articles and editorials in both publications, the vice-chief of the defence staff, Lieutenant-General Paddy O'Donnell, prepared a written rebuttal.

Generals rarely prepare their own homework and, in this case, O'Donnell made a tremendous error in judgement when he assigned LETE to produce the facts and figures for his case. But before the vice-chief could even post his official response, a draft copy of his letter was faxed to *Esprit de Corps* complete with a cover sheet detailing all of the inaccuracies it contained.

Once *Esprit de Corps* had advised O'Donnell by fax of the mistakes it contained, he never did mail his complaint. Furious at being undermined, Fowler ordered his loyal secret police to descend upon LETE to make sure this wouldn't happen again and, if possible, to identify the culprit. In Fowler's eyes, the leak to the media constituted a breach of national security, and MacLaren's high-tech spies readily accepted their task without question.

Since it had been LETE mechanics who modified the SIU van into its covert surveillance configuration, it was easily spotted parked on the long approach road to the LETE facility. And that was the whole idea.

Gerry Jette, a long-time LETE employee, thought he was being followed home by the sinister-looking vehicle after work one night. To confirm his suspicions, he picked up speed and began weaving through the thick rush-hour traffic. The van did likewise, all the way to Jette's rural-route address some forty-five minutes south of Ottawa. After the SIU agents had set up their "clandestine surveillance" in his neighbour's driveway, Jette snuck out his back door. He approached the darkened van and observed two agents inside busily videotaping the front of his house. After photographing the pair of "secret agents," Jette pounded on the van door. He invited the startled occupants in for a cup of coffee, but they fled without saying a word.

Operation Apostle lasted over three months and cost taxpayers an estimated $300,000 in military police resources. In return, three private houses were searched, because Apostle had detected "suspicious" activity on the part of LETE employees. What the Crown recovered was a government container of window cleaner, a wooden shelf (rescued from the LETE wastebin) and three old metal lockers (later discovered to have been delisted as scrap). No charges were ever pressed as a result of the investigation.

On paper, and to any other police force in the world, Apostle was a huge failure and an embarrassing revelation of SIU's lack of professionalism. However, the operation's real mission of intimidation had proven to be a resounding success. LETE was closed down with barely a media whimper. In fact, the majority of the coverage focused on who was going to take over the vacated property—the RCMP or the Canadian War Museum.

Documents detailing SIU activities are heavily edited when released under Access to Information, for national "security" reasons, but even the portions obtained by *Esprit de Corps* detail a multitude of questionable practices and abuses of the purpose of this unit. For example, a retired officer from the legal branch was "followed" home by the SIU to obtain his personal address, under direction from the judge advocate general. Such information was already on file.

When *Ottawa Citizen* reporter David Pugliese broke a story about the military's ultra-secret anti-terrorist squad conducting counter-sniper missions in the former Yugoslavia, the SIU were immediately sent to shut down the leaks. The Joint Task Force is the highly specialized national response team dedicated to countering terrorism. In 1993, DND took over responsibility for this mandate from the RCMP. Fowler had been more than instrumental in ensuring that this role was passed to National Defence, and he was almost obsessed with its training and operations. Since the unit itself was a "national secret," all purchases associated with its function could be known to only a very select few (and were entirely unaudited).

Because the JTF was a special pet project of Fowler's, and because he followed operational developments in microscopic detail, there can be little doubt that the Deputy Minister was fully aware of this anti-terrorist squad's activities in the former Yugoslavia. For the generals involved, the thin pretext for the JTF's deployment was the fact that they were protecting Canadian citizens (albeit trained troops). In reality, they were "cowboying" it, despite a deadly risk for all of the Canadian troops involved. The *Ottawa Citizen* report threatened Fowler and his generals with further unwanted media probing, which would eventually lead to politicians posing questions that could not be answered.

The day his story appeared, the *Citizen* reporter believed he was being tailed by a white panel van as he walked to work. After realizing the driver's actions were unusual if not deliberate, he took note of the licence plate number. At an intersection, a second white van appeared and joined in the slow-paced pursuit of the pedestrian journalist. Both drivers wore sunglasses, were young and muscular and had close-cropped, military-style haircuts. The licence plate on the second vehicle had an identical number except for one sequential digit.

Somewhat intrigued by the encounter, David Pugliese called the police vehicle registry to check the plate numbers. Both white vans were registered to Campbell Ford Leasing in Ottawa, and there was no way of obtaining the name of the lessees.

Nearly twelve months later, however, when the dates and details of various SIU operations were revealed under Access to Information, it became apparent that senior staff had ordered a hunt for the "JTF leak." The documentation shows that most of this SIU activity was centred on the troops in the former Yugoslavia who may have spoken to the reporter. Although little was released regarding the incidents in Ottawa, *Esprit de Corps*, which had provided the *Citizen* with quotes and information on the JTF, was also approached by a Canadian Intelligence Security Service (CISS) operative the same day the counter-sniping story appeared. She wanted to know "who had blabbed" and to warn *Esprit de Corps* that "the boys [JTF] are really in a mess over this one—so watch yourselves."

The caution she issued was meaningless, until notes were compared with the *Citizen* reporter on his adventure with the white panel vans. The two incidents, combined with the SIU team's being dispatched to Yugoslavia, indicate that all the stops were pulled out to keep the JTF under wraps. Presumably, it was one of their "training missions" to intimidate the reporter who had so damagingly exposed them.

Even when the National Investigation Service (or VIP police, as they're mockingly referred to) don their kid gloves and narrow blinkers to begin looking into an allegation against a top officer, sometimes the stench of corruption is too strong or the howls of protest too loud for senior management to ignore.

In these cases, where a top official's guilt is pretty much a certainty, given the evidence uncovered, a board of inquiry is conducted with a hand-picked panel. Under the National Defence Act, commanders are authorized to conduct a board of inquiry (BOI) into any significant incident. Usually this does not include criminal activity because a BOI, by definition, is not authorized to lay charges, and any testimony given at such a forum is inadmissable in any subsequent trials which might result.

For incidents such as training accidents, a BOI is probably the most expeditious manner in which a commander can examine the circumstances. The objective in those cases is to find the fault in order to prevent a reoccurrence. Since offenders will not be charged, a more honest picture can be painted by the participants without fear of self-incrimination or of "blading" anyone. (To fingerpoint in the Army is considered stabbing someone in the back, or a "blade.")

However, in cases where a senior individual is accused of personal wrongdoing following a police investigation, the board of inquiry is a convenient ploy to protect the guilty. Probably the best case study of this sort of obstruction of justice through abuse of authority would be the inquiry into Brigadier-General Gary "Sky" King, whose case has taken on almost legendary proportions. The truth was actually far worse than what anybody had imagined, and the miscarriage of justice even more blatant.

As a young flight-lieutenant flying CF-104 Starfighters in Europe, Gary

"Sky" King had an early taste of the military's ability to cover up embarrassing misdeeds. Stationed in Lahr, West Germany, King's squadron was on an exchange visit at an Allied Danish air base. On July 18, 1967, King was flying a photo reconnaissance mission over the Baltic. His assignment was to record any suspicious Soviet shipping activity. But on his return flight, King decided to have a little fun.

In the vicinity of the Danish airfield was a well-known nudist resort, and King thought he would amuse his colleagues by making a low-level pass over the beach to snap a few dirty photos with the CF-104's high-powered telephoto lens.

What King hadn't counted on was the abundance of seagulls, which he flew into at barely 100 feet above the wave tops. Almost immediately the CF-104 air intakes started sucking in the large birds, causing the engine to sputter and die. Since the Starfighter had virtually no gliding capacity, and at barely 100 feet there was no time to restart the engine, King ejected from his doomed plane. The startled nude bathers, who had witnessed the entire spectacle, notified authorities immediately, and King was rescued within minutes.

King recalls that he was "debriefed into the wee hours" when he returned to his squadron. Yet, his superiors decided to list the embarrassing $1-million aircraft loss as "routine," and no disciplinary action was taken against the young pilot. King, however, was soon transferred out of fighter command to fly transport planes. With no note in his personnel file to reveal this infraction, King started fresh in this new command and soon rose through the ranks.

From July 1988 to October 1989, Brigadier "Sky" King was the chief of staff at Air Command Headquarters in Winnipeg. Throughout that period, this Air Force general ran his office in a manner that Sergeant Bilko (of television and movie fame) couldn't even dream of. A handsome and cunning individual, King used all of his wiles to keep his activities in sync with his military duties.

Eventually, his finance officer and secretary grew worried about being implicated as King became more and more brazen. Since they had to sign the actual claims, and then process them, their own positions were becoming more tenuous, and loyalty to a boss can go only so far. When these two subordinates went to the SIU with their information, it was too detailed for the unit to ignore. The copies of travel claims, phone bills, itineraries and statements should have been enough to warrant an immediate arrest.

Instead, due to the "high-profile" nature of this case, Ottawa got involved and the senior management team decided to convene a board of inquiry. It was John de Chastelain in conjunction with Bob Fowler who decided not to lay charges against a brother general officer, despite the overwhelming evidence. The intent was to keep the whole matter an internal one, and in this regard their strategy was wholly successful. Had Sky King been court-martialled with media present, the testimony he gave would probably have created a demand for a public inquiry into the Armed Forces a full five years before the probe into Somalia was launched.

In their findings, the board declared King to be guilty of ten major offences, many of those including multiple infractions of the same rule. The cost to the Crown in unauthorized personal aircraft usage and service support would have totalled more than $400,000. His duplicated claims and padded expenses were close to $40,000.

While the results of the BOI were damning enough, given no charges were laid, it is the testimony of King throughout the proceedings that provides a window into the general officer (collective) mind-set.

King's first instinct was self-preservation at all costs, regardless of who else might be implicated for his own abuses. His first defence was to blame his subordinates (the ones who turned him in). Throughout the eighteen-month period that he was chief of staff at Air Command, King scheduled unnecessary trips to Ottawa or Trenton predominantly for personal reasons. All the claims were billed to the Crown. The Brigadier acted incredulous at his hearing, saying that his staff should have stopped him sooner as he had no idea that this was not allowed.

One particular Toronto trip took place over the period December 28–31, 1988, and King claimed it was justified because he had done "research" at the Command and Staff College and had met with the president of the International Committee for Air Shows (ICAS). Given the dates were over the Christmas–New Year holiday, the board did some digging, only to discover the CF Staff School had been closed. Under cross-examination, King calmly stated he had had the commissionaires let him in. A quick phone call revealed no such access had occurred, so King changed his story. He had borrowed a key from a friend and let himself in.

Again this didn't check out, and King was forced to confess: he had never been to the CF Staff School on those dates.

As for his meeting with the ICAS president, that didn't withstand scrutiny either, because the man had spent the Christmas holiday in Florida. When pressed to explain, King maintained he did have a conversation with the official, but it had been from his Toronto hotel room.

Even with all the evidence in, King still saw nothing wrong in his actions.

When ICAS paid for King to fly to Las Vegas, the Brigadier submitted a $905.52 (U.S.) claim to the Crown for the same travel expenses. His defence for this was to say he had forgotten that he'd received the cheque from ICAS and that his finance officer should have checked before finalizing his reimbursement. His claim that he'd provided her with the cheque stub did not bear up under investigation.

There were many deliberate abuses by King, ranging from using a Hercules transport aircraft to ship his own furniture, to lying to an air traffic controller in order to land his plane on an unauthorized strip (he faked an emergency). One by one, King tried to deflect and diminish the charges by either lying or blaming others, but finally even he realized the game was up.

At that juncture, King switched his tactics and took the offensive. Self-preservation kicked into high gear as his angle became "If I'm guilty, then others of higher rank are more so." In a rambling statement, King outlined a litany of abuses by top Air Force generals that made his "crimes" pale in comparison.

He cited a May 1989 incident where Brigadier-General Al DeQuetteville had taken three dual-seater CF-18s and two T-33 jets to Torremolinos, Spain. The airplanes contained passengers who were non–air crew, and the drop tanks were filled with golf clubs. The idea had been for these ten top officers to spend four days on the Spanish Riviera playing golf. When this five-plane formation landed at Torremolinos, there was already a Canadian Forces Hercules parked on the airstrip. By sheer coincidence, Lieutenant-General Larry Ashley, the commander of Air Command, had already brought his own entourage over to Spain and they too were out on the links.

Obviously, no disciplinary action could be taken against DeQuetteville, so Ashley just laughed the whole thing off and the two generals played a round of golf together. Taxpayers paid for all of the hotels and meal receipts for both parties. (Just five years later, Al DeQuetteville had been promoted twice and he himself became the commander of Air Command. The Spanish golf holiday did not impede his career.)

As for the personal use of transport aircraft, King described how General Ashley's wife and her friends would use the Commander's Cosmopolitan passenger plane to go on shopping trips. The Brigadier detailed Mrs. Ashley's latest "cross-country training trip" as having been a two-day jaunt to the West Edmonton Mall. The officers' wives who accompanied her on this "spree" all submitted hotel and meal claims.

The message King gave to the board of inquiry was quite clear: if they tried to scapegoat him, he would squeal like a stuck pig and bring the whole upper Air Force echelon crashing down. His message was obviously received loud and clear. Although Sky King was told to (voluntarily) hand in his uniform, no charges were laid against him and he would keep his pension. The DND official response line quoted only the last of eleven board recommendations, which was that "the air force's financial procedures needed to be tightened up." Once again the whistle blowers got the blame.

Gary King had no trouble finding a new job with the Edmonton airport, based on his "General" credentials and his honourable discharge. In an interview with the *Toronto Sun* in 1996, he said the Air Force had been unfair to kick him out over this issue. He claimed "just because he had shown six months of bad judgement was no reason for them to have terminated his twenty-year career." He also said he could have gone on to become chief of the defence staff.

While boards of inquiry are conducted by senior officers of various backgrounds, depending on the issue and individuals involved, they are normally advised by an assistant judge advocate general (AJAG). These legal officers would prepare the terms of reference for a BOI and guide top officers through the difficult procedures of the National Defence Act. As a result of their background and status as lawyers, naturally the AJAGs involved would have far more clout at these hearings than the published organization chart would indicate.

Like the military police, these AJAGs answer to two separate chains of command, which converge at the level of brigadier-general. This is the rank the judge advocate general holds and he is the senior legal adviser in the Canadian Forces. It is his responsibility to oversee the application of the National Defence Act and, by extension, to impose military justice.

Since the JAG's appointment, like all those of general officer rank, is subject to the personal recommendations of the chief of the defence staff and the deputy minister, the concept of "impartiality" is questionable. Added to this conflict of interest is the fact that the JAG is also the personal counsel of the CDS, the deputy minister and the minister of national defence on matters pertaining to the military.

This glaring systemic flaw was exposed in April 1996, when Colonel Geoff Haswell made a public statement alleging that John de Chastelain, Bob Fowler and the serving CDS, Jean Boyle, had been involved in a plot to alter and destroy Somalia-related documents. In the following weeks, Haswell himself was charged under the National Defence Act and was to be court-martialled by the very same judge who, by appointment, represents as legal counsel the same three men the Colonel had just implicated.

Although the system has always been structured in this manner, it wasn't until recently that the inherent faults were exposed.

In 1990, Robert Fowler directed, on his own authority, that the JAG would attend the daily executive meeting and monthly defence management committees. From this point forward, senior officials' views and input on all issues, including legal matters, were now made known to the JAG on a daily basis. Somewhat reluctantly, the incumbent, Commodore Peter Partner, would make frequent appearances at the daily executive meetings, but on slow days he would send a junior officer in his stead. In June 1993, Partner retired and was replaced by the overtly ambitious Pierre Boutet. Traditionally, the position of JAG is a three-year-term contract, which, since it is the senior legal post, terminates with the retirement of the general who holds it. Boutet was still six years from retirement age in 1993, and DND's military justice system was approaching a very critical period. Fowler needed a loyal ally and Boutet needed an unprecedented two-term (six-year) contract. Both men got what they wanted.

Boutet actually agreed to Fowler's proposal of moving his office (from a separate building where his legal officers all work) to the thirteenth floor of NDHQ. The rationale used for this move was to provide the CDS and DM with easier access to their legal counsel.

When a court martial involving a senior officer attracted media attention, Fowler would assign a trusted general—usually the associate assistant deputy minister for Policy and Communications—to monitor the proceedings and report back to "senior management" on the potential public relations fallout. These briefings were stamped "SECRET," and the handling instructions stated they were "to be hand carried only" and "not to be posted to any files"; in other words, they were to be destroyed after reading. As a major-general, Jean Boyle wrote many of these reports during the Somalia courts martial, and in all cases the JAG was one of the five top-level addressees. Bob Fowler, John de Chastelain, Ken Calder and Larry Murray were the others who received these daily "threat assessments."

In a system like the military where the authority is top-down and absolute, under the guiding hand of the obsessive Bob Fowler justice became a passing consideration in deference to the "big picture" (the public relations impact an incident could have upon the department). As a result, those senior officers who had to be charged and court-martialled were rarely found guilty. Even on the rare occasions where top officers were judged by their peers to have been at fault, the punishments were a slap on the wrist.

While no media outlet ever picked up on the trend, there were a staggering number of Canadian commanders who were found wanting when challenged with the increased demands for peacekeeping commitments over the past five years. During that period, as Canadians found themselves deploying more troops abroad than they had done since the Korean War, many Canadian officers—contrary to the claims of most analysts—failed to make the grade.

Many of these unit COs were quietly relieved of command without fanfare or charges of negligence, and most of those found wanting on operational duty have since been promoted. Of those whose poor performance had dire results or criminal overtones, some were court-martialled and found guilty, but none received more than a reprimand under the military justice system. (Major Anthony Seward was sentenced to three months in jail by a civilian court of appeal in May 1996 for his part in the Somalia scandal. Ironically, it was non-military judges who better understood the responsibility that accompanies rank and command.)

In addition to the Airborne Regiment's fiasco in Somalia, Bob Fowler had to manage such potential crises as a destroyer captain in the Persian Gulf being declared incompetent (for alcohol-related reasons) and shipped home by his own crew; a company commander being dispatched back to Canada from Cambodia for a lack of leadership ability; an Air Force colonel who flew his plane while drunk after frolicking in a pool with a topless female master corporal; and a battalion commander who allegedly made more than just homosexual advances on one of his young captains.

In the former Yugoslavia, an armoured squadron major lost his command for letting his soldiers disobey a standing order and consume more than two beers per man, and a young infantry company commander was relieved of his duties for lying to his battalion CO. (His men had been instructed to return confiscated weapons to Serbian militiamen, but they had taken the initiative to drive their armoured personnel carriers over them first.)

In keeping with the recent inversion of military values, it was the latter two examples that received the most punishment and media attention, even though the mitigating factors in the "crimes" involved were operational circumstances and the necessity to provide field officers with some latitude. The officers who had shown personal initiative with a view to their men's welfare and safety were chastised by the system (though lionized by their troops), and those who abused their rank and subordinates were protected by the system.

In cases involving field formations, NDHQ's influence on the legal proceedings would be somewhat delayed if charges were laid by a contingent commander before Headquarters could become involved directly. By contrast, the destroyer captain deposed by his sailors was a good example of the military high command's ability to keep potential scandals under wraps. Documents obtained under Access to Information show that the admirals exchanged two separate sets of memorandums on the subject. One was the real situation, and one was a deliberately falsified "clean audit trail." The originals were to be destroyed upon receipt.

Inside NDHQ, the will of the institution pervades all functions, and the military justice system has been entirely corrupted. Officers guilty of crimes are protected almost at all costs, and those in the clubhouse confines of the thirteenth floor openly flaunt their imunity.

In 1991, the public affairs branch decided they should improve their own image by sprucing up their dress uniforms. Most regiments, trades and branches in the Canadian Forces have their own distinctive cap badges, shoulder flashes, collar dogs and buttons which adorn a standard pattern uniform. Those units without their own accoutrements wear the Canadian Forces buttons and Canada flashes instead.

Although only one hundred officers in number, public affairs decided to purchase the works, with the Latin motto *veritas* (truth) emblazoned in brass on their tunics, cummerbunds and branch ties as well. The cost for all of these items, including gold cloth cap badges (usually only worn by general officers), was a hefty $19,952. In all other regiments, it is the soldiers who purchase these items with their own money, as such uniform items are not government issue. However, Colonel Geoff Haswell decided that the taxpayers would cover the cost of his branch's new "jewellery." He had the money transferred from the budget for displays and exhibits and, to avoid scrutiny, ties and cummerbunds were listed as "skirting cloth" and public affairs shoulder flashes featuring the word "truth" were deceptively labelled "giveaway pins."

When the supplier of these items forwarded the two sets of purchase orders to *Esprit de Corps*, the magazine ran the whole story in the July 1994 issue. For the six months following, each edition carried an update on this case (nothing was being done), and the articles made it clear that the magazine would fully co-operate with military investigators (provide both sets of damning correspondence).

Documents finally released following an access-to-information request in 1996 revealed that the senior brass at NDHQ had been concerned about the first revelation in *Esprit de Corps*. However, their concerns lay solely with the public relations impact and not with the crime itself. Bob Fowler, Ken Calder, Jean Boyle and Ruth Cardinal all exchanged a flurry of correspondence on the subject of how to keep the lid on the story. Internally, the public affairs branch knew that Geoff Haswell had been forced to pay back out of his own money $12,000 of the $19,952 that had been misappropriated. He then recovered the funds from his branch kit shop. While this action cleaned up the audit trail, it did not deal with the fact that a senior officer had deliberately attempted to abuse the Defence Department.

Nevertheless, Calder and Boyle feared that even acknowledging the repayment would be hailed by *Esprit de Corps* as a victory over corruption, which would lead to other whistle blowers forwarding their documents, so Ruth Cardinal, Haswell's immediate supervisor, signed and sent a letter to *Esprit de Corps* falsely stating that because of the passage of time "no action could be taken" against Haswell or any other officer. Despite this officer's conduct, senior management protected his reputation, and he was never punished for this crime.

Whistle blowers and honest military police have on occasion jointly forced the system to go through the ponderous motions of laying charges and eventually court-martialling a senior officer, but the resulting farce of a judicial hearing only serves as further condemnation of today's military justice.

Colonel Mike O'Brien (not to be confused with the publisher of the newsletter Fowler held in contempt) was long known to his peers as an operator and was distrusted by many. When he had been the commander of the Canadian Forces Base Cornwallis, he had run the camp as his personal fiefdom. When NDHQ became suspicious of O'Brien's activities, Colonel Jim Allan was sent down to the Recruit School to conduct a thorough audit. Allan recalled that O'Brien had treated the investigative team with casual disdain until Allan asked to see "the books." After some discussion, Colonel Allan returned to his transient quarters to find his bunk lavishly adorned with a gift of wine and foodstuffs. Attached to it was a welcoming message from O'Brien.

Although now retired, Allan still refuses to give out specifics of O'Brien's activities at CFB Cornwallis. However, within a few weeks, the suspect colonel was relieved of his command and brought to NDHQ. Ironically, his new job was to replace Jim Allan. During the changeover, Allan says that O'Brien's "fat ass hadn't even warmed the chair before he started to receive calls from his investment brokers."

Many senior officers at NDHQ hitched their rising financial stars to O'Brien's sideline business of peddling real estate development, and since they were making money off the arrangement, nobody questioned his use of time and government services.

Bob Fowler liked O'Brien because of his ability to get things done. The portly, pseudo-intellectual colonel soon had direct access to Fowler at all times, and he was placed in charge of the vital operations centre.

In addition to his love for making money, O'Brien also bred and raced greyhound dogs, and this hobby also occupied much of his time (and government travel claims). In 1992, while the Airborne Regiment was preparing for its Somalia deployments, and the Canadian Forces were spread out from Cambodia to Croatia, the head of NDHQ's operations centre had bigger things on his mind. Lacasse, a major real estate development company into which O'Brien had sunk loads of senior officers' savings, had gone belly up. DND mail and secretarial services at the operation centre were heavily tasked by the rotund infantry colonel as he tried to orchestrate a class-action lawsuit on behalf of his clients. At this juncture, his secretary issued a formal complaint up the chain of command, but it was disregarded. O'Brien was doing his best to get his bosses' money back and they weren't about to chastise him for it.

By 1993, with the Somalia scandal brewing up throughout DND, the military police requested additional secretarial support. By coincidence, O'Brien's secretary was seconded to help Major Vince Buonamici for a few weeks. Once she came to realize that Buonamici dared to fight up the chain of command, the secretary provided a catalogue of O'Brien's financial abuses.

There was enough evidence gathered to initiate a further investigation into O'Brien and/or lay charges. While the military police proceeded, the judge advocate general kept stalling the process. By December 1994, O'Brien had been under investigation for nearly a full year with no result. However, that same month, his prime benefactor, Bob Fowler, was demoted from DND to his new post as UN ambassador. Coincidentally, that same month O'Brien announced that he would retire early the following August.

As more documents were made public at the Somalia inquiry in May 1995, the pivotal role O'Brien had played throughout the cover-up began to surface. As director of operations, he had "hand delivered" all important message traffic to Fowler. Meanwhile, the original whistle blower, realizing no official action was being taken against O'Brien for his conduct, had approached *Esprit de Corps* with details. Access-to-information requests had been filed and questions put to public affairs officials.

On May 31, 1995, DND's legal officers finally decided to proceed with charges and a court martial against O'Brien. Despite the substantial press interest in this hasty trial (and repeated requests), no public information on the court martial was made available. Retired Colonel Michel Drapeau, working for *Esprit de Corps*, telephoned O'Brien directly at his farm for the date and details.

In that June 18, 1995, phone interview, O'Brien told Drapeau that the media would be wasting their time as his trial the next day was going to be a non-event. He predicted that DND would drop six charges, he would plead guilty to the other two, the judge might give him a $1,500 slap on the wrist and then they would all belly up to the officers' mess bar.

Not surprisingly, right down to the dollar figure of his fine, O'Brien was completely accurate in his prediction, and because of the plea-bargain arrangement, no evidence was submitted by either counsel. Therefore, there is no public record detailing O'Brien's activities—not even the ones he admitted to. The presiding officer noted that the stain on O'Brien's reputation at having been charged was a punishment far in excess of the $1,500 fine. O'Brien just smiled contentedly when the judge read that rather dubious statement.

Although the brass made it look as if justice had been done in O'Brien's case, the fact is, the Canadian military have long practised the art of dodging scandals through minimal public disclosure. This has been made possible in the past by officials' invoking their abundant security resources and independent judicial powers to keep even major international incidents "quiet internal affairs." Throughout the Second World War, unsavoury incidents of any sort were not publicized, as a matter of national security. While such wartime censorship should hardly have been considered appropriate during Canada's United Nations effort in Korea, the mostly wartime veteran officer corps still practised this same "report no evil" public relations philosophy. There were a couple of shocking incidents in which members of the Princess Patricia's Canadian Light Infantry raped and killed South Korean peasants, the details of which make Shidane Arone's death look humane by comparison.

On March 17, 1951, there was a regimental birthday celebration in the rest area of Second Battalion PPCLI in the Kyon Ki Province of Korea. Towards the end of the festivities, drunken soldiers of the 2 PPCLI left their area in search of women. In due course, they arrived at a farm house wherein were found, in addition to the owner and his wife, several Korean soldiers and two Korean girls. The 2 PPCLI soldiers entered the house and proceeded to terrorize the occupants. The women tried to protect themselves, but violent attempts were made to assault and rape them. Several rifle shots were fired, and in the excitement of the moment a grenade was thrown into one of the rooms, and the resulting explosion killed two Korean soldiers. Acting swiftly, the military justice system held four separate general courts martial in Seoul, Korea, with the following results:

- In August 1951, Private Gibson, on being found guilty of attempted rape, was sentenced to imprisonment for two years less a day;
- in December 1951, Private Sterling, on being found guilty of attempted murder, was sentenced to seven years' imprisonment;
- in August 1951, Private Blank, on being found guilty of manslaughter of Ke Chong Sung, an officer of the Army of the Republic of Korea, was sentenced to penal servitude for life;
- in September 1951, Private Davis, on being found guilty of attempted rape, was sentenced to eighteen months' detention.

In this instance, the soldiers involved were charged, court-martialled, convicted and incarcerated with no attendant press coverage. Even in the PPCLI regimental history books, there is barely a passing reference to these sordid affairs. However, despite the "invisibility" of the crimes, justice was served, the military discipline system itself remained intact, and the integrity of the regiment involved was preserved.

This was not the case in 1968, when a Canadian sergeant in Cyprus with the Queen's Own Rifles beat to death a Turkish-Cypriot policeman. Sergeant Johnny Carson had been drinking at his observation post when he decided to take a jeep and driver and head into the local village. Carson was in search of more alcohol and he began pounding on the garden-wall door of a local villa, believing it to be a café. It was late in the evening and a Turkish-Cypriot policeman making his rounds attempted to dissuade Carson from causing a disturbance.

The burly sergeant, by now quite inebriated, went berserk. The startled policeman just had time to free his nightstick before the Canadian soldier was upon him. In the ensuing struggle, Carson grasped the Turk's throat while the policeman pummelled the drunken soldier's head with the riot baton. Eventually, the Cypriot's eyes glazed over and his body went limp. Bleeding profusely himself, Carson ordered his driver—standing by in awe—to drive him and the seriously injured Turkish Cypriot to the hospital.

The policeman was in a coma on arrival at the medical facility, and Sergeant Carson required nearly 170 stitches to his face and head. Since the condition of the Turkish Cypriot was serious and worsening, the regimental authority acted quickly to charge Sergeant Carson in connection with the incident. As Carson recalls, two young officers—Captain Dick Cowling and Lieutenant Lewis MacKenzie (who later became the country's high-profile general of Sarajevo fame)—laid him on the hospital floor, as he was so heavily sedated that he was unable to stand. They charged and summarily tried Carson at the same time for having been drunk and disorderly. Found guilty, he was busted to the rank of private as punishment. Mere hours later Private Carson was on a transport aircraft back to Canada.

No charge of manslaughter was ever laid against Carson, and nowhere in the official documents concerning this case does it mention that the policeman later died. Johnny Carson sought redress, questioning the validity of the summary trial which had stripped him of his rank (he was largely unconscious throughout the proceedings). A year later, National Defence Headquarters upheld his appeal and reinstated Carson as a full sergeant, awarding him back pay as well.

Although justice was not ultimately served in the Carson case, the military judicial system had been deliberately subverted by the unit involved "to protect" one of their own soldiers. Nevertheless, a dangerous trend had begun, whereby the rationale of operational security could be used on all military exercises to keep matters "internal." This attitude insidiously crept into the highest offices of DND during Fowler and de Chastelain's ill-starred tenure, with devastating results.

On May 29, 1992, a twenty-eight-year-old Canadian corporal sexually assaulted a seventeen-year-old Croatian girl in the wartorn village of Sirac. Manuela Petran spoke no English and Corporal Jean Pierre Thériault knew no Serbo-Croat. The two had met before at a sportsfield and had communicated through broken German. After Thériault visited her home on May 29, Petran had agreed to go for a walk with the Canadian infantry soldier.

It was not fully dark when Thériault and Petran had intercourse in a

roadside ditch in the rain. She claimed to police it was rape, and the corporal's defence was that it had been consensual. Immediately following the
incident, Thériault had returned to camp and requested to see his company commander, Major Peter Devlin. Anyone familiar with the strict rank
structure in the military knows this would be a highly irregular occurrence, and certainly never done to discuss an episode of consensual sex.

When Petran launched her complaint with Croatian police, and subsequently with Canadian military police, it set off a shock wave felt right
back to NDHQ. Not only was Petran's brother in the local Croatian militia, but consensual sex before nineteen years of age is illegal in this Balkan
country. National Defence Headquarters informed External Affairs, and
top-level discussions took place with the Croatian judicial authorities.

In the meantime, the Canadian military police investigated the alleged
rape, and on July 15, 1992, Lieutenant-Colonel Michael Jones laid charges
of sexual assault against Thériault. Incredibly, no subsequent or secondary
service charges were laid against the Corporal. By his own admission, he
had fraternized with a local, against strict unit regulations; he had violated
the national laws of the country he was serving in; and he had had sex in
a public place (certainly grounds for the military standard "conduct unbe-
coming" charge). Lieutenant-Colonel Jones later admitted that pursuing a
single charge (and a very difficult one to prove beyond reasonable doubt)
was not his decision. "That was taken at a very high legal level and I had
no say in the matter."

Colonel Pierre Boutet himself headed the three-man legal team flown
into Croatia to conduct the court martial. They arrived just three weeks
after the charge against Thériault was laid. (A normal preparatory period
for a military trial of this sort runs between eight months to two years.) A
secluded hotel room was the setting for this hasty court martial, and after
only three days of testimony Thériault was acquitted.

Interestingly, the May 29 conversation Thériault had had with Major
Devlin was ruled as inadmissable testimony, since Devlin, the company
commander, had not advised Thériault of his right to counsel before hearing the Corporal's confessions. Less than a week later, Corporal Thériault
was flown home to Canada "for his own protection."

There had been only two small media mentions of the original rape
investigation in May 1992, a column in the *Toronto Sun* and a note in

Maclean's magazine. The source for both small items can be traced to jour-nalists' being in Yugoslavia at the time the investigation occurred, not a DND press release. No mention was ever made of this unusual court mar-tial, or of the verdict.

When *Esprit de Corps* magazine was first informed of the rape story in January 1995, public affairs officials at first denied all knowledge of the incident. "Lieutenant-Colonel Jones has no recollection of any such cir-cumstance." Three months later, when just two pieces of paper were released following an access-to-information request—Thériault's charge sheet and his posting message home—DND's story changed, but their efforts were still aimed at obfuscation. "There is no transcript of this trial yet [three years later] due to our heavy workload," a JAG spokesman told *Esprit de Corps*. Curiously, all Significant Incident Reports regarding this issue had long since been destroyed "as is DND's new policy of keeping such documents for only a six-month period."

When the court-martial transcripts were finally produced and released in January 1996, it was readily apparent that justice had not been the main aim of the Thériault case.

Manuela Petran and her family are still seeking to appeal the acquittal, Corporal Thériault's marriage did not survive the incident and the soldier is currently under long-term psychiatric care at a Canadian Forces hospi-tal. Colonel Pierre Boutet was promoted to brigadier, a promotion endorsed by Robert Fowler. Boutet is presently the judge advocate general.

In another case, officials conspired to hide the killing of a Canadian soldier serving in the Balkans. It was about noon on June 18, 1993, when Corporal Daniel Gunther was murdered by Muslim militiamen while on UN peacekeeping duty in the former Yugoslavia. Gunther was standing in the driver's hatch of his M113 Armoured Personnel Carrier (APC) when a deliberately aimed anti-tank rocket punctured his chest and exploded on the turret behind him. The ensuing blast flung apart the young Canadian soldier's torso and threw the remains of his shattered helmet thirty metres from the vehicle.

The tremendous explosion rocked the inside of the personnel carrier, and Sergeant Roberts was catapulted to the floor. Reacting instinctively, and knowing they'd been hit badly, Roberts yelled for Gunther to "get us the hell out of here." Looking up, the platoon sergeant saw the lower half of Daniel Gunther still in the driver's seat with the rest of his body "splattered like tomato soup all over the compartment." Fighting back his nausea, and still fearing another attack, the unqualified Roberts grabbed the tiller bars, fired up the carrier's engine and drove hell bent for leather to get behind some adequate cover.

Radio messages flashed back immediately to Battalion Headquarters said Gunther's death was the result of an anti-tank rocket. An immediate Significant Incident Report (SIR) was dispatched to NDHQ providing the same details of a "deliberate attack by an anti-tank rocket." This SIR arrived in Ottawa about 6:40 a.m. and was processed in time to be the main item on Fowler's daily executive meeting agenda. There are no records released under Access to Information detailing the return message to Lieutenant-Colonel Pierre Desjardins, Corporal Gunther's commanding officer in Bosnia. However, six hours later, a second message was sent back to Ottawa, this time claiming that Gunther had been hit "directly" by a mortar bomb.

Bob Gonzales, then head of DND Public Affairs, had been issued with both SIRs and had been in attendance at Fowler's meeting. However, when the press release was issued later that evening, the story had become a complete fabrication. "Corporal Gunther was killed when a mortar round landed near his APC while he was observing a bombardment." The incident was no longer a deliberate murder; it was now, according to the DND official statement, just a case of bad luck in a dangerous environment.

The death of Corporal Daniel Gunther received little coverage in the next day's papers, which were adorned by headlines of the Progressive Conservative party leadership convention. All that same week, Defence Minister Kim Campbell and the other Tory candidates jostled each other to replace Brian Mulroney as the next prime minister. One of our soldiers being murdered by Muslim troops would certainly have roused the Canadian public's ire in response to the dangers these troops faced while supposedly "peacekeeping" in the Balkans. Defence Minister Campbell would have come under fire at a very critical time in her quest for the job of party leader. The Somalia scandal had only just subsided temporarily with the initiation of the board of inquiry, and Fowler and his team of managers felt it was important to keep the Yugoslavian peacekeeping mission pristine. Hence, the public story about a mortar round was concocted, and it worked like a charm. There were no follow-up articles, and editorials in connection with the story focused on the unsuitability of our old armoured personnel carriers.

Documents released under Access to Information show Ken Calder, Assistant Deputy Minister of Policy and Communications, was in direct contact with Kim Campbell's campaign manager, Allan Gregg, that same week on a number of subjects. Nobody higher than the rank of major called Captain Peter Gunther to tell him his only son had been killed, and even that call came after Dominique Gunther had read about it in the morning paper.

Several soldiers from Daniel Gunther's unit, the Royal 22e Régiment, returned to Canada determined to get the truth out about the murder of their comrade. They contacted *Esprit de Corps* in November 1993 and told their incredible tale. Once Bob Gonzales realized the truth was soon to come out, he offered to allow the official board of inquiry report on Gunther to be viewed by an *Esprit de Corps* reporter. Despite his best efforts, Gonzales was unable to give a plausible explanation for the falsified mortar story. Nor could he explain why no clarification or correction had been issued to the media, even after the military board of inquiry concluded July 10, 1993, that it had been a deliberate murder.

Although Peter Worthington of the *Toronto Sun* reported the Gunther cover-up in November 1993, his story was never picked up by the national wire service or broadcast news. Ironically, it was pushed off the front pages by the revelation of another cover-up involving the mock execution of eleven Canadian soldiers being held hostage by Serbian troops. The story had appeared in the *New York Times*, but DND said they considered it so "routine" that they didn't bother with a press release. In the media uproar over this failure to disclose information about a mock shooting, the impact of Daniel Gunther's murder became lost.

Boozing and whoring soldiers is also an image that NDHQ tried keeping from the public. In January 1994, a detachment of soldiers from Lord Strathcona's Horse, an armoured regiment headquartered in Calgary, relieved the Royal 22e Régiment, a unit of the 12e Régiment blindé du Canada, of guard duties at a mental hospital in Bakovici, Bosnia. Just months earlier, the world's attention had been focused on Canadian soldiers bravely dispensing humanitarian aid to the Bakovici mental patients and a nearby children's hospital. Both of these facilities had been stranded in a no-man's-land between warring Muslim and Croat factions. The local employees could not risk going to work and, as a result, the inmates had been left to fend for themselves.

Many were starving and covered in their own filth when the UN protection force intervened. Mostly Canadian troops from the 12e Régiment blindé du Canada performed above and beyond the call of duty to clean up the mess and restore function to the hospital. The nurses and cooks were brought back to work in UN-escorted convoys and a small detachment of Canadians protected the hospital compounds from the two belligerent factions.

When the Lord Strathcona's Horse personnel arrived, things had pretty much settled into a routine at the Bakovici hospital and the outgoing 12e RBC had apparently made the most of their circumstances. A lot of the Canadian-delivered "essential" supplies, such as food and fuel, intended for the Bakovici hospital were in fact ending up on the black market. The nurses were also exchanging sexual favours for quantities of alcohol and foodstuffs, which the 12e RBC soldiers brought from the main camp in Visoko. There were strict rules at the Visoko headquarters that limited alcohol consumption to two beers per man, and only when off duty. There was to be no fraternization with the local populace (even married Canadian military couples were quartered in separate facilities throughout the six-month tour). At the Bakovici hospital, the seven-day guard duty was supposed to be alcohol free, as a high state of alert was to be maintained at all times.

When the incoming soldiers learned of the black-marketeering and prostitution the Vandoos had engaged in, the Lord Strathcona's Horse guard commanders notified the UN military police. In their initial report, it was further detailed that wild, drunken parties had occurred at Bakovici involving the nurses and Vandoos soldiers. On one such occasion, several patients broke into the Canadian soldiers' liquor cabinet and stole several bottles. Furious at the loss of their booze, several of the young infantrymen beat up a mental patient to retrieve the bottle he'd stolen.

With UN police involved in this affair, there were undoubtedly top-level discussions at the senior bureaucratic level and Army high command. Yet no public mention was made at the time of the serious allegations made by Canadian soldiers against Canadian soldiers.

In total, five military police investigations were subsequently conducted between January 1995 and January 1996. All of them were limited in their scope and all faced strong resistance from Major-General Armand Roy, commander of the Quebec region. Just after Fowler left in January 1995, the head of military police, Colonel Peter MacLaren, wrote a briefing note to Defence Minister David Collenette, which detailed the Bakovici allegations and hinted at top-level interference. Nothing changed, except that that summer Roy was promoted to lieutenant-general and, as deputy chief of the defence staff, became MacLaren's boss.

Acting on an insider's tip, *Esprit de Corps* magazine, in September 1995, requested under Access to Information the file on Bakovici. But it took a full six months for DND to release even the MacLaren briefing note. When reporters began to question DND about the subject, they were stonewalled by public affairs officers.

As the story broke, Brigadier-General Christian Couture called a press conference to angrily denounce the *Esprit de Corps* allegations of impropriety in Bakovici. Couture told the media that five military police investigations had been conducted and all of them had proven no misconduct had been perpetrated by the Vandoos. Naturally, military police don't make a habit of investigating non-crimes five times without closing the book, and Couture refused to hand over any of the actual reports to journalists. "They can be obtained under Access to Information," said the General.

Unfortunately for Couture's argument, those reports were never released. Thirty days later, when they were due to be released, DND announced that a sixth investigation had been launched because "new evidence had been brought forward." (Ironically, it was brought forward by the same guard commander who filed the original complaint with the UN police three years earlier.)

Six months later, on July 20, 1996, Army Commander Maurice Baril held a press conference to announce that the original allegations had been substantiated and that a full inquiry into the cover-up would take place. Baril's startling public confession was accompanied by a stern admonishment of the entire Army high command.

In August 1995, Lieutenant-Colonel Jacques Morneau told his soldiers that their tour in Yugoslavia would be cut short as a result of that summer's Croatian offensive. It had pushed the Serbs out of the Krajina region,

which Morneau's battalion patrolled. There were no longer two belligerents, only Croats, and hence no need to enforce a ceasefire. Although he
had no way of confirming the dates, Morneau told his men they were all
to be home by September 1. The Canadian Headquarters staff in Zagreb
were furious at his proclamation because they could not confirm an available airlift. By September 6, when there were still no confirmed flights
home, morale in the Royal 22e Régiment had begun to plummet. NDHQ
authorized a single airbus be sent to pick up one-third of Morneau's men
on September 10, and they specifically instructed the Lieutenant-Colonel
to be on this advance flight.

Naturally, the troops left behind in Croatia felt abandoned when their
commander flew home and they still had had no word on their own
departure date. By September 10, the mood was ugly and discipline was
breaking down. The soldiers openly violated the "two-beer" rule and
began emptying out the liquor stocks. A violent brawl erupted in which
several soldiers were badly injured and hospitalized. The duty officer and
some senior non-commissioned officers closed the bar and dispersed the
crowd, but they could do little to dispel the raging fury which still boiled
in their men.

The troops lost complete control at this stage, setting fire to two
portable buildings and looting the bar of all remaining alcohol. The damage to the camp would have been even more extensive if two combat engineers had not bravely bulldozed the blazing ATCO trailers away from the
rest of the sleeping quarters.

No official mention was made of this riot, other than a press release
saying a "small fire" had occurred on the Canadian base in Croatia—cause
was unknown and no one was injured in the fire.

The details of the fire were not revealed until January 1996, when soldiers volunteered the information to Esprit de Corps. Even then, DND
spokesman Lieutenant-Commander Jeff Agnew, while admitting the details,
refused to acknowledge a link, and he defended the misleading "small fire"
press release. "Sure there were injuries that night, alcohol was stolen and a
fire happened. Those are three small separate incidents," said Agnew.

In yet another case where liquor was involved, authorities tried to hide the
facts from the public. In March 1996, an instructor at the Armoured Battle
School in Gagetown, New Brunswick, phoned the office of Esprit de Corps.

He wanted to report that a vulgar hazing ritual had taken place in the barracks on the previous Sunday (seventy-two hours earlier) and that top officials, including the Minister of National Defence, had already been briefed.

The caller feared another cover-up was being orchestrated and thought the truth should be told before that happened. Fed by the *Esprit de Corps* tip, a number of journalists pressed Collenette on the subject. Caught unawares, Collenette admitted having knowledge of the hazing but declined to comment. The version detailed by *Esprit de Corps*'s caller said nineteen individuals were involved and that faeces had been involved in the incident.

DND Public Affairs officers were quick to denounce these claims as exaggerations based on hearsay. David Collenette likened the incident to a college prank involving no more than the comical "mooning" of a fellow recruit, which had been blown out of proportion by *Esprit de Corps* in an attempt to sensationalize the issue. (A military police report quietly issued one month later confirmed that nineteen individuals were involved and that an unwiped "wet arse" had been rubbed on a recruit's face while he was "lightly" held down by the other soldiers.)

Despite DND's quick, albeit inaccurate, damage control, the following day Colonel Michel Drapeau discovered that an even more violent ritual had occurred, unreported, at this same school one year earlier. This hazing involved officer cadets from the military college abusing a fellow classmate with electrical cords and excrement. While the media gave this cover-up and barbaric behaviour fairly wide coverage, the long delay in reporting it had saved David Collenette from a political disaster.

Ironically, the first Gagetown hazing occurred on March 4, 1995, the same weekend that the Airborne Regiment was formally disbanded at an extravagant ceremony in Petawawa, Ontario. Collenette, against the advice of General John de Chastelain, had ordered the Airborne disbanded following the public release of a hazing video in January 1995.

One would expect our Defence Department to inform Canadians if one of our soldiers goes "missing" while on overseas duty. Especially when the circumstances surrounding the disappearance are clearly suspect in nature. And, if that same soldier turns up dead in the bottom of a Belgian canal six months later, one could argue that the military has a moral obligation to advise the public of the event. Well, obviously DND senior brass felt differently about the subject, and hence the bizarre mystery of Master Corporal Owen Cabanaw's death has remained largely unreported.

In January 1995, Cabanaw and his wife, Janet, were stationed in Geilenkirchen, Germany, as part of the small Canadian Forces Support Unit. By trade, the young master corporal was a finance clerk, and when the Canadian office at NATO Headquarters needed a temporary replacement, Cabanaw was sent up to Brussels on a ten-day posting.

While his wife remained in Germany, he took a small hotel room in the town of Mons for the duration of his work at NATO HQ. As a quiet individual unknown to most of his new co-workers, Cabanaw made little impression on the small Canadian staff in Mons. They only really took note of the newcomer when he failed to show up for work on January 30. It was on this day that he was to have turned in the foreign currency he had signed for and to relinquish his temp duties.

By 11:30 a.m., the Canadian Forces reported Cabanaw as missing to the Belgian authorities and a search was initiated. He had not checked out of his hotel, and there police soon found his Canadian passport and various other personal effects.

It was soon noted that $13,500 in U.S. funds and 59,000 Belgian francs had gone missing from the Canadian NATO office at the same time as Cabanaw had. The military police reinspected the personal effects from the hotel and discovered the $13,500 in consecutive U.S. fifty-dollar bills tucked into the false bottom of a carry-all bag. The money was found in a military envelope addressed to Mrs. Cabanaw at their home in Germany. At this point, a Europe-wide APB was issued for the arrest of Master Corporal Owen Cabanaw—yet the Canadian military authorities released no information whatsoever and did not notify Canadian civil police agencies.

For six months, there was no progress made on the case; no word on Cabanaw's whereabouts and no sign of the remainder of the cash. (The 59,000 Belgian francs were never found.) Mrs. Cabanaw was sent back to CFB Trenton, where she subsisted on the pension contributions of her missing husband while waiting for news of his whereabouts.

On June 20, 1995, the police got a lucky break when the Belgian Waterway Authorities found an unidentified cadaver in a Canadian-licensed car at the bottom of a canal. It had been intended as a routine sonar search, but the Belgians had discovered no fewer than eighty wrecked vehicles in that single stretch of canal near the town of Baudor.

Once the mud-filled car had been pulled from the canal, the mystery surrounding the whole affair intensified. The body was severely decomposed, but dental records positively identified it as Owen Cabanaw. It was estimated by the Belgian coroner that the death had occurred at about the same time that the young Canadian serviceman had gone missing in January.

The car's automatic transmission was locked in the drive position, but the ignition switch had been turned off. A seatbelt, still buckled, held Cabanaw's body in place. In his wallet was another $500 in crisp U.S. fifties, a bank draft of 1,000 Deutschmarks and several thousand Belgian francs. A carry-all bag was also uncovered, containing his personal toiletries and several changes of clothes.

Incredibly, given the evidence available, the Belgian police concluded that Owen Cabanaw had committed suicide and decided to close the case. Canadian military police have no jurisdiction in Belgian civil matters and were unable to investigate the affair any further on their own, so this ruling was accepted without challenge.

Other than notifying Mrs. Cabanaw of her husband's death, the military still did not release any information to the press about the unusual incident. Thus, virtually unnoticed, the whole affair would have slipped blissfully into oblivion for all the bureaucrats involved were it not for two loose ends. First of all, the King's Crown Attorney in Belgium refused to accept the police verdict of suicide—and so did Cabanaw's family.

While the case has been kept open by the Belgian *gendarmerie*, little constructive progress has been made to date. Canadian military police fear that the whole affair "will die a natural death unless something is done to agitate [their Belgian counterparts]." Sergeant Serge Levesque, the MP attached to NATO HQ, now believes "it'll have to get to the ambassadorial level for anything to get done about it."

Of course, Canadian officials are unwilling to put any pressure on the Belgians, because they've already accepted the original assessment of suicide. As such, Mrs. Cabanaw is not entitled to receive the Sudden Death Benefit which all Canadian Forces spouses receive if their mate is killed while on active duty.

⌐

On August 5, 1992, there was another suicide which received very little attention, despite the fact that it involved a top-level defence executive who had been implicated in corrupt activities. At thirty-nine years of age, Denys Henrie was very young to hold the powerful position within NDHQ of director general of the Executive Secretariat. Henrie had previously spent three years working as the deputy minister's executive assistant. Upon Fowler's promotion to deputy minister in 1981, Henrie found himself catapulted into the deep end of the civilian executive pool at DND.

For months before his death, Henrie had been under extreme pressure, because his secretariat was full of brewing scandals and corrupt activity. Whistle blowers had forced Bob Fowler to commission the Lagueux Inquiry in order to keep the RCMP at bay. Pierre Lagueux had been hesitant in his probe, but even so, it was impossible to keep the trail of corruption from heading right to the top officers of DND.

Two of the key contracts examined by Lagueux were the excessive renovations to Bob Fowler's office and the purchase of the Louis St. Laurent Building. In Lagueux's March 1992 report, there was enough testimony gathered to indicate Fowler had intimate knowledge of both these files. Yet it was Denys Henrie and Micheline Clairoux who received stern letters of reprimand (from Fowler) as a result of the findings.

Publicly, seemingly nothing was done with Lagueux's report. The file itself was stamped "TOP SECRET" and only three copies of the document were ever produced. To his friends and co-workers, Henrie laughed off the whole thing by admitting to having been given a slap on the wrist. Colonel Michel Drapeau worked within Henrie's directorate at the time as a commissioned officer. The two men had a good working relationship and a personal friendship. Henrie felt Drapeau, by virtue of his principles, could help to clean up the problems he was facing, and he convinced Drapeau to retire from the Forces and accept a director's position in the Executive Secretariat.

August 5, 1992, was Michel Drapeau's first day on the job as director of corporate accounts, but his friend and boss was not available to welcome him aboard. Denys Henrie had called in sick that day. At 5:30 p.m. that same day, Henrie's fiancée arrived at their Gloucester, Ontario, home to find Henrie slumped across the steering-wheel of his car in the garage. He had been dead for several hours. In the kitchen was a half-eaten bowl of tomato soup and a hastily scribbled suicide note on the back of a dry-cleaning receipt.

The note was divided into two halves, one a personal farewell to his fiancée, the other a message to Colonel Drapeau. It read: "Michel, I leave to you my briefcase to help you continue your work. For my death, I hold responsible [Bob] Fowler, [John] McClure, [Ann] Larkin, [Rod] Gillespie and [Micheline] Clairoux."

Drapeau had been out to dinner that night and did not get the message of Henrie's death until 11:00 p.m. He immediately rushed to the Gloucester residence to find members of Henrie's family and the police still at the home. To the Gloucester police, the names on the suicide note meant nothing, and they had no idea that Denys was a top-level defence executive, recently investigated for corruption. They quickly listed the case as a "routine suicide."

The briefcase Henrie wanted him to have had been opened and Drapeau went through it with only casual interest. The file on top he recalls was marked "DM's renovations." After attempting to console the fiancée and recover from his own shock at this unexpected event, Drapeau returned home exhausted at 3:30 a.m. Four hours later, just his second day on the job, Drapeau found himself in Bob Fowler's office. The former colonel detailed the note Henrie had left behind and whom he had listed as "responsible." The Deputy Minister took note of the names, and then asked Drapeau to temporarily accept Henrie's responsibilities as director general. (It was quite a promotion, following just one day's work, but Drapeau understood it was in light of the other, more senior directors being under investigation.)

A Significant Incident Report was prepared on Henrie's suicide by the military police, and they began to circulate it to the top offices. "When Fowler saw this report, he went ballistic," recalled Drapeau. The only unofficial word that had passed through the thirteenth floor was that Henrie had "died of a heart attack."

About noon that same day, two Special Investigations Unit operatives appeared at Drapeau's office and asked him to turn in Henrie's briefcase as evidence in their investigation. In the interest of full co-operation, Drapeau complied.

There was no inquest and no autopsy in the case of Denys Henrie, and at the time the whole affair received no more than an obituary in the *Ottawa Citizen*.

When the whole issue surfaced in the media two years later, the Gloucester police immediately reopened the Denys Henrie file: they had not been aware of any of the extenuating circumstances. Unfortunately, the briefcase Henrie left to Drapeau had long since been destroyed, along with the secrets it contained.

None of the above cases ever came close to changing forever the public's perception of Canadian military justice. That dubious honour was left to the Somalia affair, where deception and lies generated by the brass brought disgrace and discredit to a once proud institution, the Canadian Forces.

CHAPTER NINE

The Lid Blows

When an authoritarian figure tries to assume total power over an organization as vast and complex as the Department of National Defence, the first step has to be control of all public disclosures. Bob Fowler realized this early on in his tenure as deputy minister, and he was quick to impose his will upon the public affairs branch. The strategic placement of trained individuals into the executive positions was all that was required, and Fowler went to great lengths to ensure that only his loyal followers had access to the truth, prior to the compilation of official response lines.

Ken Calder, as the assistant deputy minister for Policy and Communications, was Fowler's right-hand man in these endeavours, but Calder did not share his deputy minister's tireless work ethic. Therefore, the generals selected for the position of associate assistant deputy minister (policy and communication) tended to be hard-working, young, ambitious officers. Larry Murray and Jean Boyle each held this job during key crises, and both were rewarded by Fowler for their loyal service to him. (As of May 1996, they were the youngest VCDS and CDS ever appointed, at the age of forty-eight.)

Even though many of the issues these two generals tried to control blew up into national scandals, they had at the time done the bidding of DND's senior management. To their credit, they had been cunning and creative in their obfuscation and attempts to stave off media discoveries. For quite a long period, these talented generals had worked tirelessly to keep all of Bob Fowler's brewing scandals under wraps and away from prying eyes. Unfortunately, their misplaced loyalty to an incumbent (albeit a very powerful man) rather than to the "good of the service" eventually led to the discredit and destruction of the Canadian military's credibility.

What brought Fowler's empire crashing to its humbling conclusion in 1994 was the one pot which nobody could have kept the lid on—the Somalia scandal.

Most, if not all, Canadians have by now become aware of the basic facts related to the Canadian Airborne Regiment's ill-fated mission to Somalia, and the attempted cover-ups that followed. The most disturbing image to emerge from the widespread media coverage was certainly the photograph of a maniacal Master Corporal Clayton Matchee posing in a pit with a bloody and battered Somali boy, but by the time these trophy photographs were revealed to the media in October 1994, much of the circumstances surrounding the March 16, 1993, beating death of Shidane Arone had already been publicized.

From the various court-martial proceedings, it was reported that an order had been given by Airborne Commander Lieutenant-Colonel Carol Mathieu for his paratroopers to "shoot looters between the skirt and the flip flops." In response, Major Anthony Seward had told his men in 2 Commando that they should "abuse" prisoners instead. Seward's attempt to deter Somali thieves by having Canadian soldiers physically punish captives backfired with dire results.

While the hundred men of 2 Commando listened to his screams, sixteen-year-old Shidane Arone was tortured to death over a period of three hours on March 16. Master Corporal Clayton Matchee was arrested in connection with Arone's murder on March 18, and twenty-seven hours later he was found unconscious and hanging in his cell. The Canadian public was not officially informed about this brutal incident, or of Matchee's attempted suicide, until the story broke in a small-town newspaper, the *Pembroke Observer*, near Canadian Forces Base Petawawa, home of the Airborne Regiment.

On April 1, 1993, DND held a press conference to announce that the matter was under investigation, and four apparent suspects in Arone's death had been charged and were being repatriated to Canada to stand trial. At this announcement, the media fired questions of an attempted cover-up due to the two-week delay, and the fact that Minister of National Defence Kim Campbell was engaged in a race for the Progressive Conservative party leadership. DND strenuously denied the allegations.

On April 24, another story broke involving a shooting incident in which one Somali had been killed and another wounded by Canadian soldiers. The source was a letter military surgeon Major Barry Armstrong wrote home to his wife, Jennifer. In it, he indicated that the killing had in fact been a murder. Since this incident had occurred on March 4, almost two weeks before the Arone case, the media really cried foul over DND's lack of disclosure. The response from the military was to order another police investigation and a board of inquiry into all activities of the Airborne Regiment.

The results of that BOI and the testimony given at the various courts martial were fraught with massive gaps and illogical premises, raising more questions than they answered. As for the justice imposed by the military on those involved, a clear trend of punishing only the most junior in rank led to a public outcry over such blatant scapegoating.

When Barry Armstrong came forward to the media in November 1994 with allegations that he had been ordered to destroy incriminating evidence and photos, the Liberal government had no choice but to call for a public inquiry into the whole Somalia affair. As this independent probe got under way, other officers broke ranks to describe interference by top officers in police investigations and to say that senior officials had altered and destroyed vital documents related to the scandal.

Regardless of the evidence-tampering and faulty memories the public commission of inquiry must overcome in their investigation of the Canadian military's deployment to Somalia, their final report (expected no sooner than September 1997) will undoubtedly shed public light into even darker corners than that haunting pit in Belet Uen.

In an April 17, 1996, CBC Radio interview, Major-General Romeo Dallaire told host Michael Enright that, despite the extraordinary revelations that had been heard to date, "the possibility of there being a top-level military conspiracy [to protect individuals involved in Somalia] was inconceivable."

Ironically, it was Romeo Dallaire himself who set in motion the domino effect which culminated in the biggest setback suffered by the Canadian military since they were mowed down on the pebbled beaches of Dieppe in 1942. Dallaire's 1992 failure to enforce the law so as to protect a junior officer's career and, by extension, not jeopardize his own imminent promotion, was the spark which eventually ignited the Somalia powder keg.

On February 7, 1992, the citizens of Quebec City, thousands of tourists and most of the Canadian soldiers stationed in the vicinity were enjoying the sights and sounds of the winter carnival. It was a cold night, but the cobbled streets of old Quebec were filled with merriment and frivolity. Up above the revellers, the bleak stone ramparts of the historic Citadel, still home to the Second Battalion of the Royal 22e Régiment (the infamous Vandoos), was to be the site of a bizarre happening.

Unbeknownst to the throng below on that fateful night, terror and sadism were stalking the corridors of the majestic fort above them. Captain Michel Rainville was leading a patrol to "test the security" of the Citadel by attempting to break into the weapons locker. On guard duty were two young privates, Savage and Leduc. Although they were surrounded by weapons, they themselves were unarmed and had no access to ammunition. The only defence they had against a forced intrusion was a phone to call the Quebec City police.

Rainville led twelve men, all senior non-commissioned officers from 2 R22eR, and all clad in civilian clothing and balaclavas, through the empty corridors. These men were armed with civilian weapons such as Uzi sub-machine-guns, pistols and shotguns to complete their disguise as terrorists. This ferocious-looking mob burst into the arsenal, catching Savage and Leduc by complete surprise. There was no time for either soldier to sound the alarm.

Although terrified for their lives, to their credit both young privates courageously refused to provide Michel Rainville's men with access to the weapons. Rainville then allegedly beat the two in a brutal fashion. The "exercise" went on for more than two hours, and ended only when one of the young privates escaped his captors and scaled down the outer wall of the Citadel, clad only in his underwear. He alerted the city police to what he still believed to be an actual terrorist attack.

By the time the Quebec City Emergency Task Force arrived at the gates, Rainville had called off "Operation Bonhomme" and his men had taken off their ski masks. According to a Quebec police source, it was only lucky timing which prevented a bloodbath from occurring, because the emergency squad were prepared to shoot on sight.

Lieutenant-Colonel Pierre Daigle was in command of 2 R22eR at that time, and the commander's residence is located right inside the Citadel. With the arrival of the city police at the gates, he was awakened and forced to explain the circumstances. Daigle's original story was that it had been an authorized training raid, for which he was not responsible but would discipline internally.

There was very little press coverage at the time, and Daigle called on both Savage and Leduc to remain silent about the whole affair. He assured them that disciplinary action would be taken against Rainville and that he would be transferred out of the battalion. (He went to the Airborne Regiment.)

Rainville received no disciplinary action of any kind for his actions. As soon as he was in the clear on Operation Bonhomme, he wasted no time re-exerting his physical control over his men. In a March 1992 unarmed combat session, Rainville demonstrated to his platoon how to take out a sentry. In the ensuing attack, Rainville allegedly beat the defenceless recruit bloody and unconscious. The soldier was hospitalized and the incident reported to Daigle, but still no action was taken against this sadistic young captain.

Two months later, during an escape and evasion exercise in CFB Gagetown, Rainville apprehended one of his own men. To make his prisoner talk, he allegedly held the soldier's head underwater until he passed out. Medics had to revive the rifleman and, once again, Rainville's senseless brutality and abuse of rank were brought to the attention of Lieutenant-Colonel Pierre Daigle. Again no discipline was meted out.

In fact, it was not until September 25, 1992, three months after Rainville was transferred to the Airborne, that any official mention of these actions was recorded, and then only in the form of a letter to his new brigade commander, Ernie Beno. Following the annual officers' merit board meeting of the Royal 22e Régiment, it was decided that Rainville's brief career was too promising to sidetrack it with any form of reproof. On Lieutenant-Colonel Daigle's recommendation, it was decided that a verbal warning would suffice to curb young Rainville of his "enthusiasm."

Brigadier-General Ernie Beno was the commander of the Special Service Force in the autumn of 1992, and it was his job to ensure that the Airborne Regiment was operationally fit for duty in Somalia.

When Beno got wind of Captain Rainville's case, he immediately telephoned Brigadier-General Romeo Dallaire, saying, "Thank you very much for sending me this soldier. I would now like to send him back to you because I don't trust him." Dallaire replied to Beno that he [Dallaire] had personally reviewed all of the police reports and there was nothing in them that warranted further investigation. The Citadel incident was put down to the Quebec police's simply not understanding the "realism" under which soldiers must train. Rainville stayed in the Airborne and, despite Beno's concerns, he deployed to Somalia with the regiment's reconnaissance (recce) platoon on December 14, 1992.

The next day, on December 15, Brigadier-General Ray Crabbe forwarded another warning sign to Beno in the form of newsclips taken from a Montreal newspaper. In the article about the Canadian troops headed to East Africa, Rainville claimed that his men were trained in "kidnapping and assassination." He was pictured with three commando knives strapped to his body, and the caption claimed he could "kill a man in three seconds."

General Beno immediately fired off a warning to Lieutenant-Colonel Carol Mathieu to watch this officer closely, but the ingredients for disaster were already in place. Three generals had recognized a fault in Captain Rainville and had failed to take responsibility for "fear of inhibiting this young officer's career."

Admittedly, Brigadier Beno had a lot of other major concerns in readying the Airborne Regiment for its mission to Africa. Their role had been changed at the last minute from that of UN peacekeeping in Boosaaso, to being part of the U.S. Intervention Force destined for Belet Uen. This switch had come about due to de Chastelain's "not wishing to be left out of battle." The short (seven-day) notice of such a major change threw off the prepared logistics plans.

As a result, when the Airborne battle group did arrive in Somalia, their supporting supplies and equipment were in utter disarray. Rifles were shipped without breech blocks, vehicles arrived without oil or transmission fluids, and vital spare parts were packed underneath non-essential kit, making them virtually inaccessible.

To make matters worse for Beno during the planning phase, the Airborne Regiment still had a serious discipline problem in Major Seward's 2 Commando. There had been a number of serious incidents involving illegal use of military pyrotechnics, and a duty sergeant's car had been burned on the parade square by "rogue elements" of Seward's sub-unit. Several of these paratroops were even under continuous Special Investigations Unit surveillance for their suspected involvement in racist activities.

Lieutenant-Colonel Paul Morneault had tried unsuccessfully to deal with the rebel element and had, in fact, recommended to Beno that a replacement sub-unit be activated to be sent in 2 Commando's stead. Dutifully, Brigadier Beno informed his superior, Major-General Lewis MacKenzie, about the discipline situation, Morneault's recommendation to leave 2 Commando at home and his own doubts about Morneault's command style.

Beno recalls telling MacKenzie, "If I have to pull 2 Commando out of the Airborne and replace it with a company of [Royal Canadian Regiment], I am destroying two units. He [Morneault] is paid to resolve those issues, and if he can't resolve them at his level, then it would become a Brigade-level issue. In other words, I [Beno] would then have to step in and I'd be most displeased if that has to happen."

Since leaving 2 Commando out of the mission would also pose serious future logistical problems to an already over-stressed Canadian Army, the solution to remove Morneault from command was determined to be the easier choice. This momentous decision was taken by MacKenzie, Army Commander Jim Gervais, Deputy-Commander Gordon Reay and Army Chief of Staff Brian Vernon. The location where the order was drafted was in the back of a staff car at Fort Bragg, North Carolina. All four of these generals were down on an exchange visit, being wined and dined by their U.S. Army counterparts.

The best candidate to replace Paul Morneault was Lieutenant-Colonel Peter Kenward, but politically sensitive considerations dictated that only a francophone officer could be chosen. Beno objected to this convoluted process by maintaining that the best candidate should be chosen, and it should be his decision as brigadier-commander to appoint Morneault's successor. Unfortunately for the Airborne Regiment, Beno did not get his way. "As things developed, I was told who the replacement would be," recalled Beno. "It was insisted that a Francophone would replace a Francophone because there was a referendum going on at the time."

Although it was Lewis MacKenzie who passed onto Beno the Army high command's choice for Morneault's successor, later testimony indicates that this whole issue had attracted the personal involvement of none other than Bob Fowler. At his very first appearance before the public inquiry, Fowler admitted that not only was he aware of the discipline problems within 2 Commando, but he had conducted his own "inquiry" into the events surrounding Lieutenant-Colonel Morneault's being relieved of his command.

So it was presumably with Fowler's blessing that Lieutenant-Colonel Carol Mathieu was given command of this elite regiment on the eve of their operational deployment. Mathieu's chronic alcohol abuse had been kept off his personnel file by his superiors so as not to hamper his career. In the short work-up period prior to leaving for Somalia, Mathieu's faults remained undetected by his new brigade commander, General Ernie Beno.

The overall commander of the Somalia mission battle group, which included an armoured squadron and support elements in addition to the Airborne Regiment, was Colonel Serge Labbé. This young officer fitted the mould for rapid promotion in the Canadian Army and often boasted that his regiment, the R22eR, were grooming him to become the chief of the defence staff. Fluently bilingual, ruggedly handsome and politically astute, the Quebec-born Labbé possessed all the right attributes to achieve his lofty goal. The Somalia operation was to be his springboard to general rank, and he was determined to make it a successful operation, whatever the cost.

At the time he was selected to command the battle group in Somalia, Labbé was the deputy commander of the 1st Canadian Division. This Kingston, Ontario–based organization is a fully staffed headquarters with only notional troops assigned to it (real units with imagined wartime strengths on paper only). From his resources there, Labbé planned his unit's structure—from the top down. To ensure that he himself had plenty of qualified personnel on hand, he deployed a full division-sized headquarters unit for a force less than one-tenth of that strength.

Naturally, something at the bottom had to give way to make room for this bloated command contingent. "We left a lot behind," said Labbé. "We left entire functions behind, like a civil–military cooperation function, and the provost marshal [and his military police platoon]. We did so because we were down to the process of counting individual bodies and we just couldn't fit it all in." Rather than trim his own officer ranks, Labbé also decided to leave his cooks at home. The troops in Belet Uen would live on hard rations for six months, while the headquarters staff had access to hotels and U.S. Army canteen facilities.

So it transpired that the Canadian Airborne Regiment headed into Africa with all of the volatile elements necessary for its own self-destruction. An untested and undetected drunk as its commander, an incompetent major who had no control over his command, a sadistic platoon commander who thought he was above military law, and a rogue element of tough junior-ranking soldiers who were openly disloyal to formal authority. To fuel this mix, the overall commander had increased the physical deprivations these men would endure and eliminated all internal military control.

All of these warning signs had been noted by the Army high command and passed on to the senior management at NDHQ, but they had chosen to ignore rather than deal with them. The stage had been set.

Right from the outset of their deployment, things began to go terribly wrong for the Airborne Regiment, and their weaknesses came rapidly to the fore. Since the Somalia operation was no longer that of a peacekeeping mission but one of armed intervention, the planners in Ottawa and the officers on the ground overreacted to the potential threat. Two U.S. Special Forces "A" Teams, in four-man groups, were attached to the Airborne vanguard, 4 Platoon of the renegade 2 Commando. The soldiers of that sub-unit were surprised at the fact that these elite commandos were accompanying them, but what was more perplexing was that these Americans were issued Canadian combat uniforms. No one ever briefed the junior-ranking Airborne soldiers as to why this ruse was being used, but such a risky international practice could only have been approved by NDHQ. The message that the ill-disciplined troops of 4 Platoon got from this clandestine U.S. Forces' presence was that Somalia was war, and that anything goes.

En route to East Africa aboard U.S. transport aircraft, Colonel Serge Labbé openly boasted to his officers and men that he would provide "a case of champagne to the first soldier who killed a Somali." It was macho bravado probably intended more to assuage his own personal doubts than to bolster his men's courage, but once he'd spoken, his offer of a reward became widely circulated among the contingent.

On December 28, the men of 2 Commando first entered the town of Belet Uen. They were the first coalition troops to arrive in the area and there were still plenty of "technicals" (Somali soldiers) in the vicinity. To establish a secure environment, as per their mandate, the Airborne sent out foot patrols through the town both day and night. After 2 Commando established a compound near the airfield, this fledgling camp was immediately placed on a state of high alert at all times.

Three days later, just past midnight on New Year's Eve, Sergeant Mark Boland was leading a combat patrol through the blackened streets of Belet Uen. His men wore their heavy flak jackets and carried a full upload of ammunition and grenades. Despite the heat and their fatigue, they cautiously proceeded in tactical bounds, as per the Canadian military textbook street patrol. Boland's progress was interrupted when he observed two figures weaving their way down the main street. Both men were obviously drunk and one was brandishing his pistol, screaming at the top of his lungs, "Happy fucking New Year!"

Sergeant Boland quickly recognized that the pistol-toting drunk was his own commanding officer, Lieutenant-Colonel Carol Mathieu. The young NCO radioed the 2 Commando compound to dispatch a jeep and driver to take the pair back to base.

A two-vehicle armoured patrol had also witnessed Mathieu's New Year's Eve antics, and soon the word spread throughout the regiment that their commanding officer was a drunk. From that moment forward, no one bothered to respect the standing order, issued by Mathieu himself, that "no more than two beer per man per day" could be consumed.

As the first weeks in Somalia passed in a relatively uneventful fashion in terms of hostile action, the strict regulations and level of readiness were relaxed somewhat throughout the Canadian contingent. It was during this phase that alarm bells should have started going off back at NDHQ. There were links within the Airborne Regiment that were beginning to come apart.

On January 16, 1993, a record of reproof was issued to Major Anthony Seward by Lieutenant-Colonel Carol Mathieu. The reason for this official slap on the wrist was:

"Despite repeated direction by the Commanding Officer to reduce the level of aggressiveness exhibited by his command, while conducting patrol in Belet Uen, Major Seward continued to permit his commando to act aggressively toward the population. This was in complete contradiction to the policy being implemented by the unit."

In an entry in his diary, dated the same day he received Mathieu's reproof, Anthony Seward wrote, "If I hear any more [of Mathieu's] hearts and minds bullshit, I'm going to fucking barf."

Eleven days later, on January 27, it appears that Seward had chosen to disregard his formal warning. In a letter to his wife, he wrote, "Just now I am in the Command Post. Five Somali teenagers have been caught stealing from Service Commando. They have been passed to me for security and transfer to the Somali police. The troops are, however, taking advantage of the situation to put on a demonstration. They're pretending that their intentions are to cut off the hands of these kids with machetes. It sounds awful, but if you were sitting here, you'd be laughing too. Soldier's humour is infectious."

Although Major Seward had been considered unfit for Somalia service by Brigadier-General Beno, and reproofs are rarely issued (but always filed immediately with NDHQ), it remains inexplicable as to why he was not relieved of command at this juncture. Colonel Labbé could easily have replaced him in theatre, either from regimental headquarters or from his own bloated staff. But he did nothing to prevent a disaster. In fact, both Labbé and Mathieu were, instead, sending out mixed messages. After chastising Seward for showing aggression to the local populace on January 16, twelve days later Lieutenant-Colonel Mathieu altered the Rules of Engagement by which his soldiers operated. The seven pages of regulations given to the battle group by NDHQ had been approved by General John de Chastelain, with direct input from Bob Fowler. In fact, it was Fowler himself who insisted on the inclusion of a clause prohibiting the shooting of looters. Fowler told the public inquiry that he felt no Somali should be killed for just trying to feed himself.

Nevertheless, Mathieu took it upon himself to change this directive, in the presence of, and therefore with the full compliance of, Colonel Serge Labbé. The new order said any suspected looters could be shot "between the skirt and the flip flops." Neither Labbé nor Mathieu thought to inform NDHQ (officially) of this dramatic change.

By contrast, Captain Michel Rainville sent out very public warning signs of his continued instability when he gave an interview in early February 1993 to the *Toronto Star*. In that article, he defended the vigilance which his soldiers showed while patrolling the quiet streets of Belet Uen. Rainville cautioned the reporter not to be "taken in" by the smiling faces and waving of the local populace. "Often it's the people who smile the most as we go by that end up stoning us. You can see it in their faces. They're hypocrites. They'll give us a little smile, but if we turn our backs, we'll probably be stabbed right away."

Since all the senior managers at NDHQ receive these press clippings, it wouldn't have taken long to realize that Rainville's statements had no basis in fact. Looting at the camp had increased, but no Canadian soldier suffered a wound as a result, no weapons were ever stolen, no ammunition lost or fuel siphoned during the entire deployment. Most of the items stolen by thieves were soldiers' personal possessions such as Sony Walkmans or various foodstuffs. On one occasion, a Somali *looter* was arrested taking a late-night shower.

Given Rainville's previous sadistic behaviour and the fact that his quoted comments painted a picture which could only be attributed to his "enthusiastic imagination," he too should have been relegated to a rear-echelon post. Instead, he remained on as recce platoon commander, fighting a war that didn't exist.

The logistics problems created by poor planning and the last-minute switch of roles remained constant for the paratroopers. Message traffic obtained under Access to Information illustrates just how out of touch with the troops NDHQ had become.

The supply officer for the Airborne Regiment had made a request for a supplementary shipment of undershorts to be sent to Somalia on a rush basis. The substantiation for the order was: "Due to the excessive heat and lack of laundry facilities, they [Airborne Regiment] were experiencing an unexpected demand" for replacement briefs.

The message back from the operations centre in Ottawa denied the request and reminded the Airborne supply officer that he had a special fund for such contingencies. The recommendation from NDHQ was that the Airborne make good their shortfall of underwear through "local purchases." The exasperated response from Belet Uen was: "OK, but where the fuck are we going to find an underwear store in the middle of the Somali desert?"

The lack of comprehension in NDHQ as to the deprivations suffered by the soldiers in Somalia was certainly not a result of the Airborne's being "forgotten" by senior management. In fact, quite the reverse was true. Between January 1 and March 31, 1993, no fewer than twelve generals and senior officials made the effort to visit Colonel Labbé and his troops in East Africa.

Bob Fowler himself visited Somalia in mid-February clad in combat clothing and surrounded by top generals. There was the usual posing for the cameras and staged routine operations which convinced these travelling tourists that all was well in hand. All of these top executive-level officials went to Somalia to inspect a mission they knew to be plagued with problems, yet nobody spotted the trouble looming.

Included in Fowler's entourage was Brigadier Beno, Lieutenant-General Reay and Vice-Admiral Cairns. Photographs taken at the time of their visit show these gentlemen drinking Tusker beer in a relaxed setting with Lieutenant-Colonel Carol Mathieu at his local watering-hole in downtown Belet Uen. No doubt these unarmed senior managers would have recognized throughout their stay that Belet Uen was not a combat zone and that the threat to our soldiers' safety was minimal in that region.

Immediately following Fowler's departure from Somalia, things began to come to a boil for the Airborne. The U.S. Special Forces "A" Teams were still attached to Mathieu's regiment and, despite the mandate our contingent had been authorized to conduct, these commando troops began to play a larger role. In late February, it was decided by higher command to launch a joint U.S.–Canada counter-ambush on a Somali road-block. The Americans had obtained permission from Canadian authorities, presumably from Colonel Labbé, for Major Seward's 2 Commando to provide the assault force for this mission.

Captain Michael Sox was chosen to lead this unorthodox raid and Sergeant Boland was his second-in-command. The U.S. Special Forces had observed a gang of Somali thieves operating at a crossroads just outside a small village close to Belet Uen. These highway robbers would often kill the occupants of the cars they stopped and were seen as a threat to the stability of the region.

Captain Sox's plan was to rent a local van, complete with an interpreter. He would then disguise himself as a Somali, in black face and a cloth shirt, while Boland and Corporal Matt Mackay hid under a tarp in the back. (Sox had even inquired about obtaining an Afro wig from Canada, but had to make do with a cloth cap to complete the disguise.) Once they were stopped by the robbers, Sox, Boland and Mackay were to jump out and make an arrest. In support of Sox's van was a support fire group armed with machine guns and para-flares, which would be in position on a hilltop in case something went wrong.

As it turned out, everything went wrong on this little "hunting expedition." When their rented van pulled into the intersection, a Somali man indicated they should stop and then approached to converse with the driver. Captain Sox was too excited by the prospect of real combat to even wait for their translator to inform him of the stranger's request. According to Sergeant Boland, "Sox was so pumped that he just leapt out of the van and started shooting, blowing away the side mirror with his first shot. I don't know how he missed the guy at point-blank range, but [Sox] emptied his whole clip without scoring a hit." As soon as Sox opened fire, Corporal Mackay slid back the van door and attempted to exit the vehicle. In his rush, his leg became tangled in the tarp and he fell face first onto the roadway. Hanging helpless, Mackay started blasting away at every shadow with his pump-action shotgun. Boland radioed for the back-up team to pop para-flares, and they quickly complied. However, instead of their illuminating the crossroads ambush site as intended, their pyrotechnics lit up a dried riverbed nearly two kilometres away. The back-up team was on the wrong ridge.

Once Sox and his team stopped firing, there was nothing but silence. A thorough search of the area revealed no blood trails, only their own spent casings. No one had shot at them and in firing fifty to sixty rounds, they had scored no hits themselves.

The cluster of huts next to the roadway had been hastily vacated when the shooting erupted, and was devoid of inhabitants when Sox's men entered it. Originally, they were looking for the highway robbers, who were reportedly living in one of the huts; however, once it was determined that everyone had fled, the Canadian soldiers decided to amuse themselves. Sergeant Boland took Mackay's reloaded shotgun and blasted dishes and pottery while the other men helped themselves to street vendors' cigarettes. "It was crazy," said Boland, "but we were really pumped for action and this was a bit of a release."

Captain Sox radioed in to headquarters that the mission had failed, but his story did not reflect the facts. His report stated that only "two to three warning shots had been fired after an armed suspect refused to surrender." In total, more than one hundred rounds had been expended, but no one at headquarters questioned the discrepancy. The story of Sox's poor marksmanship rapidly made the rounds through the regiment's unofficial grapevine, and he was the laughing-stock of the Airborne. Their whispered insults visibly rankled him.

On March 2, Robert Deeks, an American sergeant with one of the two U.S. Special Forces "A" Teams, was killed when his vehicle struck a land-mine. This NCO had been a popular addition to Captain Michel Rainville's recce platoon and, although he'd been killed by a land-mine, many felt that the Somali technicals had deliberately targeted U.S. vehicles.

Two nights later, Captain Rainville led out a hand-picked patrol to "avenge" the U.S. sergeant's death. It was described by troops involved as a "hunting party," but it was set up as a classic ambush, complete with a cut-off fire position. To ensure that "looters" would enter the compound and qualify as targets under Lieutenant-Colonel Mathieu's new Rules of Engagement, Rainville had his men cut a gap in the fence. Just inside the wire was placed a tempting assortment of food and drinks—seemingly unattended. In reality, nine soldiers were staked out with automatic weapons, shotguns and night-vision goggles waiting to pounce on the first "looter" to go through the wire.

Two Somalis did finally appear at the perimeter fence, and their progress was tracked continuously by those with night-vision sights. For some unknown reason—perhaps they smelled a trap—these two men did not take the carefully arranged bait. Instead, they turned and headed out into the open desert. Rainville raced to the wire fence and began screaming instructions for his ambush teams to open fire. A rapid volley cut through the night, followed by whoops and cries of "I got one!"

The wounded Somali, Ahmed Heraho Aruush, lay where he'd been hit, but the second man, Abdi Hamdure Aruush, who was seemingly unhurt, bolted farther into the desert. Rainville's team had just reached the wounded Ahmed when the cut-off team caught the fleeing Abdi in a withering hail of gunfire. Again shouts rang out, "Hey, we got one too!"

Another two shots were then heard, back where Rainville had come upon the badly wounded Ahmed Aruush. According to Rainville's men, the Somali looter had tried to escape and had been shot dead when he resisted arrest. When Major Barry Armstrong examined the body, he clearly felt that the Somali had been the victim of an execution-style shot to the back of his head.

Rainville wasted no time in reporting his "successful" mission directly to Lieutenant-Colonel Carol Mathieu. As usual, the commanding officer was at his favourite watering-hole in Belet Uen, but on March 4 he was in the company of Serge Labbé and Colonel Mike O'Brien, the director of operations at NDHQ. (O'Brien visited East Africa from February 28 to March 7 in preparation for Admiral John Anderson's short visit on March 6.) While the Significant Incident Report (SIR), which was drafted and forwarded by Colonel Labbé, made no mention of the prepared ambush, it still contained enough details to set NDHQ—and Bob Fowler in particular—ablaze with panic.

The secret message had been forwarded from the Canadian Joint Headquarters in Mogadishu back to Ottawa in the early hours of March 5, and it was the first item of business at the daily executive meeting. Fowler chaired the meeting as usual, and the magnitude of the Somalia report did not escape his keen grasp. Even in the sketchy details the SIR provided, it was made clear that two unarmed men had been shot outside the Canadian perimeter while attempting to flee. This was clearly a violation of the strict Rules of Engagement the Airborne Regiment had been issued. To make matters worse, Major Barry Armstrong's assessment that the dead Somali had been murdered had been passed to Carol Mathieu and subsequently was verbally relayed to Ottawa. It was noted that the commanding officer, Mathieu, was to conduct an investigation into Armstrong's allegations.

Bob Fowler knew that they had a major crisis in the works, and he immediately gave instructions to set the damage control in motion. Vice-Admiral Larry Murray was to prepare a police team at NDHQ to deploy, if necessary, to investigate a possible homicide.

Major-General Jean Boyle was in attendance at the March 5 meeting as the associate assistant deputy minister for Policy and Communications. It was his job to control the department's public position on this issue. No mention was to be made of the irregularities of the shooting incident to the media. General Boyle was fully aware of the murder allegations and of the excessive use of force, but when he left the meeting and consulted with his public affairs officers, the March 4 action was described as "routine" and "fully above board."

Admiral Murray had a different role to play. He notified Major Vince

Buonamici (at approximately 12:00 noon on March 5) to prepare a stand-by police team to fly to Belet Uen on short notice. In that preliminary briefing, Buonamici was told by top officials of their serious concern that excessive, and possibly illegal, force had been used in the death of a Somali citizen. There was an immediate flurry of preparatory activities in the NDHQ police operations section.

On March 6, Chief of the Defence Staff Admiral Anderson arrived in Belet Uen to visit the troops and inspect the Airborne Regiment's operations. On hand to meet him were Colonel Labbé, Lieutenant-Colonel Mathieu and Colonel O'Brien. Anderson had been *en route* when the original Significant Incident Report was sent to Ottawa, so these three officers quickly brought him up to date, not only on the circumstances, but also on how NDHQ wanted the affair handled.

In a speech to the assembled troops later that day, Anderson specifically told them to be very careful in what they wrote home in letters about the "incidents" which the soldiers encountered. He also stressed the point that Kim Campbell's bid for the Progressive Conservative leadership would put DND under acute media scrutiny, and they should go to great lengths to ensure that there were no embarrassing disclosures.

This directive was taken to heart. Instructions were given to individuals, including Dr. Barry Armstrong, to destroy photographs and evidence pertaining to the March 4 shooting. Armstrong courageously refused the order, but he was immediately ostracized for his disobedience.

Back in Canada, due to their misleading reports, there had been only moderate press coverage of the Somalia shootings, but Fowler, Boyle and Murray were taking no chances. To head off any possible further probing, Admiral Murray telephoned Colonel Labbé and told him that they would arrange a CBC-Radio interview. In that broadcast, Labbé calmly told the announcer that the two Somalis had been "armed saboteurs," and that these "trained commandos" had been scouting out the Canadian airfield near the helicopter pads. To complete the story, Labbé said that the pair had compasses and maps on them which marked out all of the key installations on the Canadian camp. Colonel Serge Labbé knew, even as he spoke, that the only military gear found on these two "saboteurs" was a pair of Canadian-issue khaki undershorts, presumably stolen from the local laundry days earlier.

By March 8, Fowler pretty much had the genie back in the bottle. The media had gone back to sleep and the commanders in Somalia were fully on board with the cover-up. Lieutenant-Colonel Mathieu's official report said everything had been in accordance with regulations in the shooting— but that only put him and Labbé on the hook for changing the Rules of Engagement without authority. Captain Rainville once again knew he was in the clear, and Fowler knew he could trust Labbé and Mathieu to remain silent, given that all was in order. Buonamici was given the order to stand down his investigative team. That order was given about noon on March 8.

According to Fowler's daily diary, that same afternoon he met with Colonel Al Wells, the head of military police, and Lieutenant-Colonel Weatherspoon, assistant judge advocate general, to discuss "the destruction of a security document." Following that meeting, the Deputy Minister's office frantically prepared four rush packages for urgent delivery.

The unofficial "signed for" receipts kept by Gerry Hébert, Fowler's DND driver, are the only official record of this top-level correspondence. Hébert realized that he "had to, at all costs" get these deliveries out by the end of the working day, and he was told that all four recipients would have clerks waiting to receive them.

Since access-to-information requests failed to uncover any trace of these important documents, it is safe to assume that their handling instructions—as was the case with most of the Somalia documents—were "Secret—to be hand carried only, not to be posted to any file." The four addressees were Minister of Defence Kim Campbell, Chief Clerk of the Privy Council Glen Shortliffe, Minister of External Affairs Barbara McDougall and Prime Minister Brian Mulroney.

For the time being, Fowler had kept the lid on things, but he and the top generals who complied with the cover-up would have had no way of knowing that the Somalia scandal was just beginning to boil.

From March 4 onwards, the attitude of the Canadian paratroopers in Belet Uen became more aggressive, and the relations with the local population more hostile. The morale of the unit was being eroded by the sense of futility in the mission, the continued deprivations of their environment and the homesickness which affects all such six-month tours of duty.

To show how out of touch the high command was with the needs of the troops and the perilous state of the mission, Lieutenant-General Gordon Reay had 1,000 parachutes shipped to Somalia. The cost to taxpayers for this extravagance was more than $300,000, and the rationale given was that a paradrop would boost the Airborne's spirits. The occasion was the Royal Canadian Regiment's birthday on April 12, and all soldiers had the opportunity to jump from a helicopter.

The premise and cost of this exercise were questioned by various command levels back in Canada. Land Forces, Central Area wrote to General Reay stating, "This HQ is somewhat confused at the priorities being established given the current situation. Material difficulties are being experienced, there are manning shortfalls and we already have an over-extended [transport] system. . . . It is therefore requested that authority be sought to rescind any expenditure of funds and resources until these issues are resolved."

Instead of heeding his subordinate's advice, Reay and Admiral Murray processed the parachute scheme through the more costly commercial airfreight, and thereby circumvented the military transport system. As it turned out, Reay should have saved the taxpayers' money. As one paratrooper succinctly put it, "All we wanted was clean underwear and maybe a steak dinner, and instead the generals sent us a parachute."

The nuisance thefts from the 2 Commando compound had increased steadily, despite the fact that Rainville's patrol had shot two looters on March 4. Major Seward took it upon himself to seek support from the local police chief. The Belet Uen police force was a new one. It had only been established by 2 Commando upon their arrival. Nevertheless, Seward felt that they would best know how to deal with such problems. The Somali police quickly told Seward that he should kill at least three looters as a deterrent to the others. At that juncture, many thieves were being apprehended, held overnight by the Canadian troops and then turned in to the local cops the next morning. Often the very same individuals would be back under the compound wire the next night. There was no effective court system in place, and the Somali police station claimed it could not feed these detainees. (The wheat Canadian soldiers provided them for just such a purpose was openly sold on the black market, out the back door of the station-house—often while the paratroops were still unloading it through the front door!)

Although Lieutenant-Colonel Mathieu's new Rules of Engagement would have permitted him to follow the Somali's advice on shooting looters, Seward was not comfortable with that solution. Instead, on March 16, he held an "orders group" with his platoon commanders and instructed them to "abuse" any future thieves who were caught, before turning them over to the local police.

Captain Michael Sox decided to be sure his platoon had the distinction of capturing a prisoner and abusing him, as per Seward's new order. He had four paratroopers camouflaged in desert dust to conceal themselves in the debris of an adjacent compound. This area had previously housed an American Construction Battalion (Seebees) and, after they had pulled out, the U.S. stores left behind had proven to be a magnet for Somali thieves. The Canadians protected this perimeter as well as their own, even though the material left behind was abandoned surplus and scrap.

On the evening of March 16, Captain Sox had his men open up the main gate of this "Seebee" fence and they, like Rainville's patrol, put out tempting bait to lure Somalis inside. It was at approximately 2045 hours that sixteen-year-old Shidane Arone fell for the trap and was seized by the waiting paratroopers. They manhandled him to the fence which separated the 2 Commando lines from the "Seebee" camp, and threw him over the barbed wire into the waiting arms of Captain Michael Sox.

What happened over the next three hours was revealed in shocking detail throughout the courts martial of those charged in connection with Shidane Arone's beating death. Sox brought his prisoner to show Major Seward before turning him over to Sergeant Mark Boland at the holding bunker. Other soldiers, including Master Corporal Clayton Matchee, witnessed Sox striking Arone and roughly handling him during his interrogation at the command post by Abdi, the regimental translator. Arone claimed that "he'd only been looking for a lost child," but as this answer was translated, Sox became visibly angered. According to Sergeant Mark Boland, who witnessed the interrogation, Sox said, "You're going to die boy. Do you understand me? You're going to die tonight."

For the first half-hour of Arone's internment, he was guarded by Sergeant Boland without incident. Trooper Kyle Brown had the second shift, and Master Corporal Clayton Matchee, although off duty, joined him at the pit. At Matchee's insistence, Brown threw a couple of punches at Arone to comply with Seward's order of abuse. Clayton Matchee then got involved himself and began to physically assault the prisoner in Brown's presence. After a short spell of this, Matchee went to the tent lines to get some beer. Boland was still awake and was chatting with Corporal Matt Mackay (who had been bedridden with dysentery) when Matchee came in looking for beer. In a brief consultation, Matchee described to Boland how he wanted to "really beat" the prisoner. The sergeant mistakenly assumed that this was just more of Matchee's macho bragging and thought nothing of the remarks. "Use a phone book to cover any bruises and, whatever you do, just don't kill him," quipped Boland just before he headed off to bed.

Over the next three hours, Master Corporal Clayton Matchee ignored this advice and sadistically tortured young Shidane Arone to death in 2 Commando's holding bunker. By the end of Kyle Brown's shift, Matchee had broken Arone's nose, burned his feet with a lit cigar and, using a riot baton, pulverized a ration pack on the young Somali's head. At one point, Brown implored the senior-ranked Matchee to ease up "or you'll kill him." "That's OK," replied the abusive Master Corporal, "because Captain Sox told me to euchre [kill] this fucker!"

When Trooper David Brocklebank arrived to take over from Brown, Matchee sent both soldiers out on errands: Brown was to grab his camera and Brocklebank went to fetch his pistol. Matchee wanted to take some hero shots of himself and the bloodied prisoner.

Following his shift, Kyle Brown tried to alert Warrant Officer Murphy, his platoon's second-in-command, that he felt matters in the pit were getting out of hand. The next day was the regimental birthday for the Princess Patricia's Canadian Light Infantry, the parent regiment of 2 Commando. To celebrate the occasion, March 17 was to be a sports day, and an extra shipment of Tusker beer had been brought in from Kenya.

On the night of March 16, almost all of the off-duty senior NCOs, including Murphy, had gotten into the alcohol and, with the luxury of a non-work day on the morrow, had become intoxicated.

Trooper Brown then tried to solicit support from the duty sergeant, but when he entered the Command Post, Sergeant Perry Gresty was sound asleep. After failing to find support from anyone in authority, Kyle Brown went to bed. Throughout Brocklebank's shift, Matchee continued to pummel Arone so violently that, when Trooper Shawn Glass arrived for his guard duty, he was visibly shocked at the sight of the prisoner. Brocklebank went to bed and Shawn Glass left the bunker as well. Glass wanted nothing to do with what was transpiring, so he remained at the front gate. Once he was left alone with the prisoner, Matchee reportedly went to even greater depths of depravity. According to one of the medics who inspected Arone's corpse later that night, there were cigar burns on the young Somali's genitalia and it appeared that something (probably the riot baton) had been forcibly inserted into the prisoner's anus.

At approximately 0100 hours on March 17, Sergeant A.E. Skipton entered the holding pit and discovered that the prisoner was unconscious and bloody. He found no pulse, so he put the mirror from his compass beneath Arone's nose. When no breathing was evident, Skipton ran for the Command Post. There he encountered Sergeant Joseph Hillier, who had led the patrol that had originally captured Arone, and Captain Sox.

The body was then transported to the unit medical station, where it was inspected by Captain Neil Gibson and pronounced dead at approximately 0150 hours. Major Seward was awakened by Sox, and he quickly made his way to the regimental hospital. According to his diary, Seward said the condition of the young Somali's body was "appalling."

Realizing they had a serious crisis on their hands, Seward went to report the death to headquarters while Sox roused Matchee and Brown out of bed to immediately take the body downtown to the Somali morgue in Belet Uen.

Lieutenant-Colonel Carol Mathieu was on leave at the time, and acting in his stead as commanding officer was Major Rod Mackay. Seward explained to him that night's events and Mackay, in turn, notified Colonel Serge Labbé in Mogadishu. By 0300 hours, Labbé had forwarded a "secret" message back to NDHQ, reference this "death in custody." The urgent report concluded by saying "Photos of the body, the holding area and statements would be taken and forwarded to Ottawa immediately."

Lieutenant-Colonel J.V. Arbuckle received this sensitive message at NDHQ, and he immediately stamped it with "regular Significant Incident Report distribution list." These "routine" addressees would include the top twenty officers in Defence Headquarters, including the minister of national defence. This document was to be handled differently, however, as Fowler had instructed Colonel Mike O'Brien to oversee personally all of the Somalia messages. According to Lieutenant-Colonel Archibald, "O'Brien had to hand deliver all the traffic concerning this issue on a strict need-to-know basis only. Only Mike O'Brien knew exactly who knew what when, but definitely Kim Campbell's office was not on his delivery list." John Dixon, Campbell's policy adviser at the time, said that whatever bits of belated information they did get at the Minister's office came through Richard Burton, Fowler's executive assistant.

Although there has been no written message traffic released under Access to Information detailing the exact instructions NDHQ gave Colonel Labbé on how to handle this issue, the facts of what transpired speak for themselves.

After telling the top brass in Ottawa, in the middle of the night, that the Airborne Regiment would forward photos of the body and bunker "immediately," none was even taken. In fact, the only Polaroids Dr. Neil Gibson had taken of the Somali prisoner's body "were turned over to the Belet Uen police for body identification purposes." Major Seward would later claim that the body of Arone had not been kept at the Canadian base because the hospital morgue fridge was full of beer that night.

Since the evidence gathered on the March 4 shooting had proven so difficult to eliminate, it was deemed simpler to just not collect any incriminating material in the first place.

There was one military policeman attached to the Airborne Regiment, but Major Rod Mackay chose to detail his adjutant, Captain Paul Hope, to conduct the investigation into Arone's death. On March 17, the day following the murder, the only statements taken were from Dr. Neil Gibson, Major Seward, Captain Sox and two junior NCOs. None of these individuals had been in contact with the prisoner between the time he was captured and the time his body was brought in to the hospital. Both Seward and Gibson deliberately lied in their statements, claiming that Arone had only "two small bruises on his body" and that these injuries were consistent with a "rough apprehension."

That information was evidently passed directly on to NDHQ in very short order because the same details were included in a briefing note

Admiral Murray prepared that same day for Kim Campbell. Back at NDHQ, they added to the original fabrication by hinting at the "poor health" of the Somali at the time of his capture. It was also stated that an autopsy was to be conducted in order to determine the cause of death.

Once again General Jean Boyle, as the associate assistant deputy minister for Policy and Communication, was involved in DND's public position on this new crisis. No media in theatre were aware of the event, and no one in Canada had started asking questions. The decision was to remain "reactive"—Responses to Queries were produced in case the story was leaked, but no release was issued.

By the time a weary Bob Fowler headed home late from his office on March 17, he probably felt that he had this latest emergency well in hand.

Unfortunately for those trying to keep the lid on, the rank and file of 2 Commando were simply not prepared to accept the fact that nothing was happening. Everyone knew what Clayton Matchee had done, yet the sports day had gone on, with this murderer still taking an active part in the drinking and games. When word came that morning that Corporal P. Sprenger, a Native Canadian, had shot and killed a Somali in a firefight, Matchee, himself a Cree, began running around the sports field shouting "It's red men two, niggers nothing."

Kyle Brown did not take matters so lightly. He was deeply troubled by what he knew and he was afraid of retribution (from both Matchee and the military justice system) if he came forward. Throughout March 17, Brown spoke to several NCOs about what he'd seen, and they all shared his concern over what Matchee had done. None of them could figure out why there was no investigation. Sergeant Mark Boland said, "We were kept thinking that any minute the American Military Police would come pouring through the front gate to tear the place apart."

Kyle Brown watched as Captain Sox had the holding bunker cleaned of blood, and Major Seward held long discussions with Neil Gibson. That evening a medic approached Trooper Brown and told him to relax because "Seward and the medical officer have fixed everything." The one thing nobody counted on was Brown turning himself in, along with the photos he'd taken.

It was about noon on March 18, a full thirty-six hours after Arone had died, when several non-commissioned officers asked to see Major Seward. Among them was Sergeant Hillier. At first, Seward told these NCOs that the investigation was over: "Arone died as a result of a rough apprehension—case closed." To their collective credit, these sergeants refused to accept the cover-up. Hillier had been the sergeant who captured Arone, and he hadn't even been interviewed. "That prisoner was fine when I brought him in, sir." To clinch their point, they told Seward about Brown's roll of film and his intention to give a full statement.

Major Tony Seward had seen Arone's battered body, and he knew just what Brown's undeveloped roll of film would contain. The game was up and he knew it. Matchee was placed under arrest, and Captain Michael Sox began collecting some of the evidence which had been hidden.

At regimental headquarters, Seward informed Major Rod Mackay of this new development. The next step was to report the death in custody as a beating-death murder to Colonel Serge Labbé in Mogadishu. However, when Mackay relayed this shocking reversal in the story to Labbé, the response from the contingent commander was: "I already know."

The day before, on March 17, Master Corporal J. Alaire, an airman from 427 Helicopter Squadron, had returned to Mogadishu from Belet Uen with a troubling tale. He had asked to see his commanding officer, Lieutenant-Colonel Jim Sorfleet, and declared that he wished to make a statement.

Throughout the night on March 16–17, Alaire had been on guard duty at the airfield in Belet Uen when paratroopers had invited him to witness a brutal beating. Alaire did not know the soldiers, but he watched them kick a Somali prisoner repeatedly about the head and strike him with a metal pipe. The airman was frightened and sickened by the soldiers' actions, and he had told one of his supervisors in 427 Squadron. They, too, had visited the pit and observed a looter being beaten. While they did not stop the paratroopers, they vowed to report it through their own squadron's chain of command. This they dutifully did upon arrival back in Mogadishu. Lieutenant-Colonel Sorfleet immediately informed Colonel Labbé of what his men had witnessed.

While the scene the 427 airmen had observed appeared to match the circumstances of Shidane Arone's captivity, there are some troubling additional bits of evidence which point to a far darker conclusion. The log book at 2 Commando clearly indicates two Somali looters were captured on the night of March 16; in fact, both were seized within fifteen minutes of each other. "Call sign 23" (6 Platoon) radioed in at 2059 that they had chased two looters and captured one. This platoon was providing security at the airfield, where the 427 Squadron helicopters were parked. Shidane Arone had been captured at 2045 in the Seebee camp, and this was carefully logged in as well.

The direction radioed back from 2 Commando command post to 6 Platoon was for them to "retain looter for the night, bring to police station in the morning." One minute later, 6 Platoon reported "a medic was going to look at their captured Somali for any injuries."

The fact that two looters were being held in 2 Commando's captivity that night would mean little, were it not for the description Master Corporal Alaire gave of the two antagonists whom he'd seen beating the prisoner. In several passages, Alaire distinctly identified the paratroopers as being dark blond men, one over six feet tall, the other much taller. It is difficult to imagine him mistaking Kyle Brown (at five feet, six inches tall) and Matchee, both of Native Indian descent with jet black hair, as being blond.

In court-martial testimony, it was learned that an airman from 427 Squadron had been the one who provided Master Corporal Matchee with the riot baton, which he then used to explode the ration pack on Arone's head. This airman was just up from the airfield to make a phone call, when he stopped by the holding pit to observe Matchee and said, "Here try this," offering Matchee the metal pipe. Even more puzzling was what Commando Sergeant-Major Brad Mills told military police and testified to at the court martial of Major Seward. Mills claimed that the body he saw at the unit medical station March 16 was "not the same man that 4 Platoon had captured earlier that night in the Seebee camp."

Mysteriously, the only official record that could identify exactly what happened to the Somali looter captured March 16, 1993, by 6 Platoon at the airfield has disappeared, presumably forever. The March 1993 radio log from 6 Platoon, which was headquartered at the airfield, has never been found.

Whether it was one body or two mattered not back at NDHQ. The operations centre, despite the strict "need to know" secret classification of the Somalia messages, was abuzz with rumours on March 18. DND had released no Significant Incident Reports detailing the fact that Master Corporal Clayton Matchee had been arrested for murder that day. But there is no doubt that high-level telephone calls took place over the issue.

Major Brian Reid worked in the operations centre and, like Colonel Mike O'Brien, he lived in Kemptville, Ontario, sixty kilometres southwest of Ottawa. These two men, along with two other Canadian officers, car-pooled to work. On the way home on March 18, the Somalia issue was the subject of conversation and much speculation. O'Brien, in an uncharacter-istic breach of security, told his travel companions what he knew about the development of the whole affair. Reid recalls O'Brien describing it as being a torture death, and that trophy photos had been taken by the paratroops involved. He told them the perpetrator had been arrested and charged with homicide. Already stunned into silence by the impact of what they had just been told, O'Brien's companions were further shocked when O'Brien said, "The grown-ups [top brass] have decided the Canadian public can never know what took place. The public image of the Canadian Forces would never recover if the truth were known." Reid and the others objected to this strategy by stating the obvious: this was too big to cover up. O'Brien's response was that this wasn't his decision, he was just the messenger boy. Reid remembers O'Brien stating, "The gang of eight is running the whole thing from here on in." The director of operations was obviously referring to eight very senior officials, but Reid had never heard the phrase before and didn't know to whom O'Brien was referring.

In Belet Uen, no further evidence was being gathered, and photographs had still not been taken of the holding bunker. Master Corporal Clayton Matchee gave no statement and was offered no legal counsel following his arrest. No police team was being readied at NDHQ, even though they were aware of the homicide charge. In fact, for the next twenty-seven hours, vir-tually nothing seemed to be taking place.

At about noon on March 19, Matchee seemed to be enjoying his custody. His guard at that point was Master Corporal Mario Guay, a fellow biker and close social associate from 1 Commando. Matchee was held in a small bunker at the regimental headquarters compound (not the same pit where Arone was murdered). This "cell" was approximately five feet, six inches in height with open windows all the way around its six-by-ten-foot interior.

There was no door of any sort on this structure, Matchee still had his camera with him, and he shot the last three frames of film at this time. Two were taken by Guay of Matchee sitting on his bunk, drinking what appears to be beer out of a water-bottle. The third photo shows an empty cell and was presumably taken by Matchee himself standing outside the structure.

Following his shift, Guay took a letter from Matchee which he wanted sent to his wife, and brought it to Corporal Matt Mackay for him to post. Mackay read the letter; in it Matchee confessed what he had done, but he also talked about being able to see his daughter soon, as he was being flown home early to stand trial.

Four hours later, Clayton Matchee's six-foot-three-inch body was discovered by his guards hanging from the low ceiling of his cell by a bootlace. Their cries of alarm brought help from the nearest available soldiers—a U.S. Special Forces "A" Team, which just happened to be in the vicinity of Matchee's bunker. Major Barry Armstrong and medic Corporal Paul Adkins ran to the scene, as did a DND photographer. In the series of photographs shot of Armstrong reviving Matchee, the U.S. soldiers are clearly evident.

Matchee was battered and his face was gruesomely bloated, but he was not dead. Because of Armstrong's prompt treatment, he was to live, albeit with permanent brain damage. To make matters worse, a journalist from Canada visiting the Airborne Regiment in Somalia had spotted the commotion involving Matchee's attempted suicide and had begun asking questions. Colonel Labbé was advised of these developments, and he immediately sent another secret message to NDHQ. In bold type was the warning that "a journalist [had been] in the vicinity."

Had Matchee actually been found dead, the whole matter could still have been put quietly to rest. The Airborne would assume justice had been done. For the sake of both Matchee's widow and the regiment's reputation, they would have gladly closed the book on Arone's death. There are still many unanswered questions about Matchee's attempted suicide, and those soldiers who were close to him refuse to believe he tried to take his own life. Mario Guay and Matt Mackay both insist that Matchee had shown no remorse in his final hours, and he still believed that he would win his court martial because "Captain Sox had ordered him to kill Arone."

Incredibly, the two guards who had let Matchee fashion a noose from a bootlace he never should have had (and which did not come from the boots he was wearing), in broad daylight, in a doorless cell with windows on each wall, and hang himself to near death (approximately eight minutes) were never charged with negligent performance of duty.

On the morning of March 19, the top officers at NDHQ were in a total flap. There had been no reports in the Canadian press linking Matchee's attempted suicide with the death in custody of Shidane Arone, and no questions were being asked to indicate anything was even suspected by the press corps. However, the senior management were faced with a serious dilemma now that Matchee was expected to at least partially recover from his injuries. Vice-Admiral Larry Murray called an emergency meeting with his police operations staff, and it was then that Master Warrant Officer Paul Dowd was selected to conduct the investigation into the homicide/suicide in Belet Uen.

Although the new National Investigative Service was not officially authorized into existence until September 1993, Dowd was already commander. The fact that it was this clandestine covert police force that was chosen for this job indicates the top managers still had hopes of keeping everything under wraps.

In the briefing which he received on the morning of March 19, Paul Dowd already knew Matchee was the prime suspect in Arone's murder and that the Master Corporal had been incarcerated in connection with that crime at the time of his attempted suicide.

Admiral Murray did not even prepare a briefing note for Kim Campbell outlining this direct connection between the two incidents until March 26, one week later. That note was never delivered, according to John Nixon, Campbell's policy adviser. "We [Campbell's staff] first learned it was a homicide on 31 March, from Richard Burton [Fowler's executive assistant]."

Paul Dowd, Sergeant Mario Pierre Coté (also NIS) and Captain M.B. Phillipe, an assistant judge advocate general, were *en route* to Africa within eighteen hours and arrived in Belet Uen by March 23 after a short layover in Nairobi, Kenya. There they had met Sergeant Robert Martin, the Airborne Regiment's sole military policeman. Martin had been sent to develop Kyle Brown's roll of film. When he met with Dowd's team, he displayed the damning photos and the duty roster from the night Arone was killed. It was immediately determined by Dowd that he had four suspects and, since they had only one legal officer present, it was going to be impossible to provide them all with adequate defence counsel. This information was relayed to Admiral Murray, but the investigators were told to proceed regardless.

Once Dowd arrived at the Airborne Regiment's compound, he immediately let Major Rod Mackay know the accommodations allocated to his team were unsuitable: they were too close to the media tent, and this investigation was to be conducted away from "prying eyes." Dowd noted in his diary that same day that he had briefed Major Mackay on the "disclosure policy" which NDHQ expected on this case, namely, that everything was to go through Dowd back to Ottawa.

Major Seward was terrified at the prospect of being investigated by Dowd's NIS team. He wrote to his wife on March 23, 1993: "I have no energy. My thoughts are for my well-being while I dread the forthcoming investigations. It is my intention to openly and readily state that I did order Somali intruders to be abused during the conduct and apprehension of arrest. To what extent this order caused Master Corporal Matchee and Trooper Brown to beat to death a Somali intruder will be a matter for litigation. I may not be found criminally responsible but my military career is certainly finished."

Major Tony Seward did not intend to just roll over and take the fall for the whole scandal. On March 22, the day before Dowd arrived in camp, Lieutenant-Colonel Carol Mathieu called together his majors and the regimental sergeant-major to attempt some "damage control of his opening fire policy and the [4 March] recce platoon shooting." While these Airborne officers were quick to make the connection between the two incidents, they had no way of knowing that Paul Dowd wasn't even aware of Rainville's hunting party and had no mandate to investigate this action. Nevertheless, Seward and Mathieu clearly knew these two events were directly linked. Major Seward actually noted in his diary, "I think Mathieu understood my veiled threat that I will drag him to the stand of any court martial if he does not support me and my Commando."

From March 23 to March 30, Dowd and his partner conducted an almost leisurely investigation at the 2 Commando compound. The number of soldiers who had been willing to come forward with information had quickly diminished, as word soon spread through the ranks as to Paul Dowd's "unorthodox" and "bullying" style of questioning. "When the first four guys who went into Dowd's trailer to give evidence came out under arrest, the line of volunteers got shorter in a hurry," recalled Sergeant Boland, one of those who had been surprised to find himself charged in connection with Arone's death.

Despite Dowd's incompetence as an investigator, and the limitations his rank level and the military justice system imposed upon his independence of action, the amount of evidence to implicate Major Seward, Captain Sox and Captain Gibson in an attempted cover-up was overwhelming. There was also a staggering amount of testimony gathered that implicated Sox in the actual physical punishment of Shidane Arone, not the least of which came from Major Seward himself on March 30. Everyone in Belet Uen expected Captain Sox was to be charged by Dowd and that he would soon join Troopers Brown and Brocklebank and Sergeants Boland and Gresty in police custody.

The Regimental Adjutant, Captain Tim Reinholdt, had been the one to draft and send Paul Dowd's message about Sox's arrest back to NDHQ. Major Seward noted this turn of events in his diary on March 30: "Expectancy hangs in the air. I fear that Mike [Sox] has been implicated and my use of the word 'abuse' yet causes me severe regret. The Commando sergeant major is expecting Sox to be put into custody today. I find myself doubting myself; particularly because of the conversations I had with Mike [Sox] the morning he woke me to tell me the Somali had died. Yesterday, I was worried about salvaging my career, now I am fearing unemployment and possibly incarceration."

Although both Seward and Sox were eventually charged and found guilty (with Seward being jailed for ninety days on appeal in May 1996), at that time the NDHQ managers did not want to start unravelling the cover-up by implicating commissioned officers. Seward was relieved of command but was not charged until July 1993 (after it was already apparent Lieutenant-Colonel Mathieu would be standing trial as well). Incredibly, Captain Michael Sox was not arrested until September 1994, coincidentally following an article in *Saturday Night* magazine by Peter Worthington. This feature story drew heavily upon the original notes taken by Paul Dowd, which had been leaked to *Esprit de Corps* magazine. After detailing the facts obtained by Dowd in March 1993, Worthington asked why Sox was not charged. Two weeks later he was.

However, on March 30, 1993, Paul Dowd had more to worry about than what NDHQ was doing with his reports. He was still attempting to have Arone's body exhumed and an autopsy performed. The snag had been the family's demand for financial compensation for their murdered son. Legal officer Captain Phillipe had met with Arone's clan on March 30 and thought he'd resolved this impasse. The family agreed to accept the equivalent of one hundred camels ($15,000 U.S.) in return for allowing the body to be examined by a pathologist.

Paul Dowd sent back this information through the NDHQ operations centre, and immediately a major at the National Defence Medical Centre was given notice to leave for Belet Uen. An airline ticket on British Airways was purchased for the doctor and he was to depart in less than twenty-four hours. Before that could happen, events in Ottawa took a dramatic turn. The reporter from the *Pembroke Observer* had returned to Canada, and his tale of the suicide/homicide was beginning to gather wider interest. In his notes for March 30, Paul Dowd recorded that Captain Phillipe had just telephoned Admiral Larry Murray and everything was to change. "Heat coming from somewhere, Matchee's name known in Canada, pressure to prosecute quickly" was the verbatim entry in Dowd's log.

The next day, the story first broke in the Canadian Press, and Brocklebank, Brown, Boland and Gresty were flown home under arrest. The forensic specialist was told to "stand down," and no further attempts were made to conduct an autopsy.

At NDHQ Robert Fowler had yet to blink and was trying desperately to salvage the situation. His aide Richard Burton advised Richard Clair, executive assistant to Kim Campbell, of the "possibility" that a cover-up would be alleged, but Fowler's angle was that this had been a "communications breakdown"—something which was to be expected when dealing with operations in a Third World country, which was "a long way away."

In the meantime, Fowler called Brigadier-General Ernie Beno in Petawawa and told him he needed to meet with him on an urgent matter. That afternoon, in a one-on-one interview, Fowler told Beno for the first time about the torture death–suicide link, and he filled in the details about there being grisly trophy photos. Again Fowler used the "communication breakdown" line, and he advised Beno that the national media were just beginning to get wind of the story. He told Beno he wanted him to field the press conference the next day, because "after all, these were [Beno's] troops." Realizing he was being set up as a scapegoat for the affair, Beno refused Fowler's request and reminded him that a general's reporting chain of command was through the chief of the defence staff, not the deputy minister. Fowler was furious.

A visibly perturbed Lieutenant-General Gordon Reay swallowed his pride and faced the media on April 1. He gave a clipped statement about Arone's death, the ongoing investigation and the fact that four soldiers had been charged in connection with the murder. On his way out, the diminutive Reay booted a chair out of his way to avoid a media scrum.

The press corps was brutally cynical about the military's version of this incident, and the two-week delay in releasing the information led to the obvious cries of cover-up. Quite naturally, Kim Campbell became the immediate suspect of this attempted suppression. She was a candidate for the leadership of the Progressive Conservatives, and the logic ran that this ugly blemish on the Forces would somehow hurt her chances to succeed Brian Mulroney. Campbell's denials of prior knowledge were in fact legitimate, in her own case, and even once this story became public Fowler continued to keep her out of the information loop.

As a measure of Bob Fowler's influence in the Canadian public service and political circles, one need only read the letter he sent to Chief Clerk of the Privy Council Glen Shortliffe on April 1, 1993. In his correspondence, Fowler provided some sketchy details of the Arone incident, but then he advised the Chief Clerk to take heed of a "caution" which he (Fowler) had received from one of his assistant judge advocate generals. The attached letter was a carefully worded warning for outside agencies not to meddle in this DND internal affair. "Any statement which could be construed as urging a particular outcome, or even great rigour, in the application of appropriate sanctions might have the effect of tainting subsequent prosecutions. . . . We are not trying to be reclusive about this, but it is essential that the integrity of process be protected." Cleverly, though, Navy Captain Fred Blair, the AJAG who wrote the "caution" Fowler apparently endorsed, had included enough information to indicate the warning to "back off" had come from the Deputy Minister himself: "For the reasons we discussed yesterday, I urge you to caution public officials . . .," wrote Blair.

This hands-off approach to military justice ran in stark contrast to the "prosecute quickly" call made to Paul Dowd two days earlier.

While Fowler may have bought himself some precious time with these manoeuvres, he had no way of knowing that the second hovering shoe was about to drop. On April 14, Major Barry Armstrong was taking his leave in Kenya, but his primary purpose was to make contact with Paul Dowd and enlighten him as to the events of March 4. Paul Dowd and Lieutenant-Colonel Peter Tinsley, a DND prosecutor, were staying at the Safari Club Hotel in Nairobi, preparing their preliminary cases in the Arone murder. Both Tinsley and Dowd sat and listened intently to Armstrong's tale of murder and cover-up. Neither of these two men had been briefed on the controversial shooting death, and they naively assumed they were telling NDHQ something shockingly new when they called back to Ottawa later that night.

After some discussion, Vice-Admiral Murray advised Tinsley and Dowd that a board of inquiry (no criminal charges) would be the best way to proceed on the Armstrong allegations. What Murray did not fill them in on was the fact that Lieutenant-Colonel Carol Mathieu had already filed his report on the affair—clearing everyone of any wrongdoing. Nor was it mentioned that Colonel Serge Labbé had also filed his own detailed report on March 23. This second review had been requested just after the Arone/Matchee incident surfaced. Military Police Major Vince Buonamici recalled the March 4 file had been closed on March 8, but it was quietly reopened again, presumably by Admiral Murray on March 19. "The case was not 'active,' simply 'open' at this point," Buonamici claimed. The senior managers were hedging their bets in the hopes the Rainville murder would remain undetected.

On April 15, the morning after Tinsley called Murray and told him of Armstrong's testimony, Major Vince Buonamici was finally ordered to gather his team and proceed to Belet Uen to investigate the March 4 homicide and wounding. The game was now up, but Bob Fowler refused to admit his defeat. It was in his nature to continue managing the problem.

That dim hope was snuffed out on April 21, when Jennifer Armstrong gave Tim Harper of the *Toronto Star* the letter sent to her by her husband, Major Barry Armstrong. His correspondence outlined the theory that Ahmed Aruush had been killed with an execution-style shot to the head on March 4. With questions soon coming in from national media outlets, and the second Somali scandal beginning to grab headlines, Admiral Murray sent off a three-page letter to Colonel Serge Labbé on April 24. The purpose of this communiqué was to put on the official record the fact that the original Rules of Engagement should never have been altered without prior approval from NDHQ. This was something that should have been transmitted on the morning of March 5, when NDHQ first learned of the change and the excessive force used by Rainville's patrol. It was in essence a too-little-too-late attempt to limit the blame to Colonel Labbé's contingent.

The top managers in Headquarters had known in detail from the outset what was transpiring in Somalia, but now they had to distance themselves from their own implicit involvement. The best way to do this was by deliberately sacrificing the reputation of the Airborne Regiment rather than accepting command responsibility. On April 28, 1993, Defence Minister Kim Campbell announced a top-to-bottom board of inquiry into "systemic problems" in the Airborne. A Forces-wide gag order accompanied this board of inquiry, and DND could use the excuse of the inquiry's being in progress to deflect all probing media questions. The chapter on events in East Africa had essentially been closed, but the cover-up was still in its infancy. A very tangled web of deceit had been cleverly woven, but it would be some time before the Canadian military command's moral rot and ineptitude would be thoroughly laid bare to a shocked Canadian public.

In order to facilitate his control over this worsening situation, Bob Fowler knew that he had to have extremely loyal people at all of the key posts. The public record shows he wasted no time in doing just that. Admiral John Anderson was still a relative newcomer to NDHQ and had never established himself with any authority after his arrival as chief of the defence staff in January 1993. According to Anderson, he had sought advice on his new duties as CDS from the outgoing John de Chastelain. However, the hand-over briefing had been decidedly short. "Whenever you don't know something, just ask Bob [Fowler]" is what de Chastelain advised him. Anderson had thus placed his faith in the Deputy Minister's ability to run the department. The Somalia scandal was admittedly out of Anderson's capability to manage as he did not have an experienced Headquarters staff at his disposal. He was therefore out of the loop and Fowler had complete control at this stage, said Colonel Michel Drapeau, who was the director general of the corporate management structure at NDHQ until June 1993.

Although all message traffic sent from Somalia, even the critical SIRs were officially addressed to Drapeau, he never had access to them. He, too, was out of the loop at this stage, meaning that Fowler didn't even trust the head of his executive secretariat to handle this issue.

Between March 31 and June 15, there was a major shake-up of the three key offices Fowler needed to have onside in his attempt to manage the Somalia scandal. Commodore Peter Partner, the judge advocate general, retired in April 1993, and on May 3 Brigadier-General Pierre Boutet was appointed JAG. He was the military legal officer who conducted a potentially explosive rape trial in Croatia in August 1992 (as detailed earlier, in chapter eight).

Colonel Al Wells, head of military police at the time Fowler terminated the March 4 homicide investigation, did not have such an easy exit. The big Newfoundlander had made much of his military career and gone farther in rank than most would have expected. The initial impression he gave was one of a simple man, a rather slow thinker. But those who worked closely with him said this image was misleading as Wells was actually a perceptive, deep thinker with a solid conscience.

It was his inherent honesty that ate him up both physically and mentally at the end of his tenure as top military cop. Colonel Drapeau recalls that a troubled Al Wells was visibly nervous about the potential repercussions of his actions with regard to Somalia. "I have a lot of respect for Al [Wells]," Major Vince Buonamici told *Esprit de Corps*. "But for his last few months on the job in 1993, we were all more than a little concerned for him. You might say we put him on suicide watch."

To replace Colonel Al Wells, Fowler brought in a man he knew to have the nerves required to handle a worsening situation at a critical juncture. Peter MacLaren, the former SIU commander, fit the Deputy Minister's prerequisite character criteria to a tee. His covert operatives, and Paul Dowd in particular, were already deeply involved in the Somalia affair, and MacLaren's track record was well established as that of a willing rule-bender.

Brigadier-General Michel Matte, as the director general for Public Affairs, was the last top officer to allow himself to be shuffled by Fowler as this whole mess began to hit the media fan. Matte is not a brilliant soldier, but he was known by his peers as being straightforward and honest in his approach to public affairs. On April 2, Major Brian Reid had met up with Matte, a former staff college classmate, and he had a brief chat with him. The general seemed distracted and was quick to clear his conscience when pressed by Reid. "They've decided they need a scapegoat for this mess [Somalia], and guess who they chose," stated Matte, pointing at himself. The news of Arone/Matchee had just broken in the media, and DND's response to the cover-up charge was to claim "full details were published at the time [on a noticeboard in Mogadishu]." DND's stated reason that this news hadn't been released in Canada was a "judgement failure" on the part of the public affairs staff.

At this stage, Matte accepted the public ridicule for incompetence of which he was not guilty. Without prior warning, he was relieved of his post in early June 1993. His replacement, Roberto Gonzales, had just shown up at Matte's door with his personal desk items and said, "I thought you'd be gone by now." Furious to be fired from his post without so much as an official notice, the enraged Matte stormed up to the thirteenth floor and burst into the office of the diminutive Admiral Larry Murray.

The Vice-Admiral was caught off guard by Matte's verbal attack, but he was quickly able to regain his composure and placate the former DGPA. A one-year posting to RMC in Kingston, unaccompanied by his family, followed by a guaranteed return tour of NDHQ, was agreed upon. Brigadier Matte's brother had suffered for years with a debilitating illness and needed constant hospital care. For this reason, Michel Matte needed to remain close to Ottawa. He had emotional and financial baggage which prevented him from breaking ranks and following his conscience. This factor was well known to most of those at the senior-management level, and they unscrupulously exploited it to their own advantage.

Matte's sudden successor, Roberto Gonzales, was a former infantry officer who had turned in his uniform for an executive post at DND Parliamentary Affairs. Following a staff college course on which he befriended Bonnie Brownlee, Mila Mulroney's former personal assistant, Gonzales began cultivating close Tory connections. Bob Fowler liked Gonzales's style.

True to form, Gonzales's first move was to have Bob Fowler bring Bonnie Brownlee into the DGPA directorate as an executive in charge of DND's strategic public relations policy. At this stage, Roberto Gonzales fancied himself as a political "player," and he hitched his ambitious aspirations to Bob Fowler's powerful star—whatever the cost.

The original board of inquiry called by Kim Campbell on April 28 to review the systemic problems within the Airborne Regiment was chaired by Major-General Tom De Faye. This probe was restricted in its scope by the fact that there were two ongoing police investigations into the two "separate" murders. In fact, due to the overlap of key witnesses and potentially damaging testimony, Chief of the Defence Staff Admiral Anderson had to split the De Faye inquiry into two phases. The ever-increasing media clamour for a complete explanation as to events in Somalia led to a decision to release De Faye's "Phase One Report" on August 31, 1993.

The botched press conference at which Admiral Anderson appeared to be poorly prepared, and at which Roberto Gonzales tried to thwart any educated media questions by not releasing copies of the De Faye report until after the briefing, failed to achieve its stated aim. Rather than a full disclosure of circumstances and events in Somalia, what was issued to the press was a heavily censored report which answered few, if any, public concerns about what had gone wrong. The rationale that the judge advocate general had made the numerous edits to protect the legal rights of those involved in ongoing courts martial made no sense, since it had been clearly stated in the terms of reference for De Faye that his committee was to steer clear of the two incidents.

The main item of news which emerged from the August 1993 release of the De Faye report was that there had been a number of suspected racists in the ranks of the Airborne. Gonzales did his level best to make sure journalists didn't miss those passages. In fact, in the copy he brought to *Esprit de Corps* magazine, he had already highlighted the words "nigger" and "gimme" along with references to the Confederate flag symbol. The DND press angle on this was based on the "few bad apples" theory, in which the Airborne was portrayed as a rogue regiment.

When the uncut version of the De Faye inquiry report was finally made available to the public inquiry in June 1995, it looked as though edits had been made in 1993 to protect senior officials. Material such as details concerning Captain Rainville's 1992 incident in the Citadel and Colonel Labbé's offer of a case of champagne to the first paratroopers who killed a Somali appeared to have been clipped out in such a way as to make a pattern of top-level incompetence impossible to ascertain with any degree of certainty.

What was more startling to discover was that, despite the evidence pointing to senior management's micro-managing of all aspects of the mission, of the seventy-nine witnesses who gave testimony, no top generals or bureaucrats were even called to testify at the De Faye inquiry, with the exception of Brigadier-General Beno and Commodore Dave Cogden. In his testimony at the board of inquiry, Colonel Serge Labbé told the panel that, for the sake of continuity, all communications from Somalia to Ottawa went through one man only. This officer was Colonel Mike O'Brien. Incredibly, given that he was the only individual who knew exactly what was told to whom and when at NDHQ, O'Brien was never called before the board.

Immediately following the debacle of the Anderson/Gonzales press conference, Fowler began to shorten his bench and take an even more active role in the damage-control activities. Major-General Jean Boyle was assigned, in addition to his role as associate assistant deputy minister for policy and communications, to control a new team known as the Somalia Working Group. Because Boyle himself had been directly involved in the non-disclosure policy at the critical daily executive meeting on March 5, this ambitious general had a vested interest in keeping DND senior management's direct involvement from being discovered. Admiral Anderson was shuffled aside, playing a relatively impotent role until his relief from command in December 1993. With John de Chastelain brought back in as chief of the defence staff on Fowler's recommendation, the Deputy Minister easily retained his full sphere of influence over all aspects of the Defence Department.

At DGPA, Roberto Gonzales was proving to be something of a liability. Since the Liberals had swept into power in November 1993, Gonzales's inside political clout had disappeared along with the Tory party, and Fowler quickly recognized his limitations. The courts martial were about to commence, and Fowler knew this would be a crucial phase. The details that would be revealed in testimony at the trials would undoubtedly cast a shadow over the Armed Forces, so it was imperative that the top bureaucrats keep a good working relationship with the government of Canada.

For this reason, Bob Fowler had Ken Calder recruit Ruth Cardinal to replace Gonzales. Cardinal was a career government spokesperson with strong Liberal connections and, more important, a long-time personal friend of Fowler. In fact, when Ruth Cardinal managed the communications strategy at CIDA, her executive assistant was none other than Mary Fowler, Bob's wife.

The one drawback in hiring Cardinal as a major-general equivalent to run DND's press office was that she had no experience whatsoever with the military. As a former Trudeau aide and elitist bureaucrat, she had a jaundiced view of the army's rank and file, and no love for the military institution.

The actual courts martial were probably even more tightly controlled by senior DND management than De Faye's inquiry had been. Even the order in which the accused were tried was designed with justice as the last possible consideration, and keeping the lid on public disclosure first and foremost on the agenda.

By the time Trooper Kyle Brown was court-martialled in March 1994, both his company commander, Major Seward, and his regimental commander, Lieutenant-Colonel Carol Mathieu, were also facing charges for the orders they had issued. Under normal circumstances, those who issued an order would have to be tried first to determine the legality of the directive and the criminal culpability, if any, of the officer responsible. Of course, it was realized that the first court martial would reveal the bulk of the unsavoury details, garner the largest headlines and stir the greatest public backlash. The senior management at DND played every card they had in their hand to ensure that Trooper Kyle Brown would bear the brunt of whatever blood-letting was demanded by an outraged Canadian public. No Combat Arms officers sat on Brown's court-martial panel; in fact, the only infantry officer selected was removed by the prosecutor for a possible conflict of interest. (He was from the same parent regiment, PPCLI, as Brown.) Instead of being tried by his peers, or even those who understood the unique soldiers' code and the responsibility of a command, Trooper Brown was judged by a potpourri of unqualified commissioned officers, all from non-combat trades—a musician, a dentist, a supply officer and a shore-based naval commander. The prosecuting attorney, Lieutenant-Colonel Peter Tinsley, deliberately hyped the media and this panel with the false claim that Brown's action had besmirched an otherwise unblemished forty-year Canadian record of peacekeeping. As a JAG officer, Tinsley should have known better than most that Arone's death was, in fact, only one of many that Canadian soldiers have perpetrated on active service in the last four decades, and he should also have been aware that the Somalia operation was not a peacekeeping mission.

As the courts martial proceeded, it became increasingly obvious (too obvious) that this whole process was rigged. The higher the rank charged, the less chance of a guilty verdict or a stiff sentence. One of the reasons for this was the careful manner in which the actual charges had been laid. In the case of Lieutenant-Colonel Carol Mathieu, his trial came down to the single question, Did a commander in the field have "the right" to alter the Rules of Engagement he'd been issued? Given the overwhelming evidence linking Mathieu's "skirt and flip-flop" order to both murders, such a narrow premise for his trial was ludicrous. Mathieu knew this and was so confident of his acquittal that he called only one witness in his own defence, Major-General Chuck Gauthier, an officer who had never even visited Somalia.

In the case of Captain Michel Rainville, he was charged only in connection with the wounding of Ahmed Aruush and not with the death of Abdi Aruush. Since Mathieu's order was not "illegal," and the Somali had indeed been shot in the legs, his acquittal was pre-ordained. There was no mention of Abdi Aruush being killed that same night, nor of Dr. Barry Armstrong's allegations that he had been murdered.

Journalists, editors and the general public were quick to see through this attempted whitewash. As the verdicts of not guilty for officers began to contrast with Kyle Brown's five-year jail sentence, a groundswell of support grew for the young paratrooper who was now seen increasingly as the scapegoat for his superiors. In an attempt to stem this tide of suspicion and scrutiny, and to put the focus back on the lower ranks, the decision was made to release Matchee's trophy photos for media publication. Technically, the photographs were the personal property of Kyle Brown, which he had voluntarily submitted as evidence in a homicide. As a property of the court, it was DND's decision to lift the publication ban on these photos. Although largely unquestioned at the time, the rationale for doing so was based on DND brass's desire to have people redirect their attention to the sordid events that had taken place in the bloody pit. The media bought this deliberate bait (in some cases literally) and gave the graphic photographs front-page, top-of-the-news coverage.

Virtually every violent crime tried in civilian court, including homicides, is documented by photographic evidence of the victim's injuries (or the body), yet the photos are never released for publication. For DND, of all agencies, to suddenly and uncharacteristically have been so forthright with this material should not have gone unquestioned. That it did testified to the talents of Fowler's hand-picked team.

The media, in fact, were almost lulled back to sleep following the explosive public outburst generated by the release of Brown's photos. The *Ottawa Sun* actually ran an editorial saying, now that the courts martial are concluded and we've seen the gory details, we can finally close the book on the Somalia scandal. Unfortunately for Fowler and his top officials, this single comment sparked Major Barry Armstrong to write a letter to the editor, outlining how he had been ordered to destroy photos and evidence by a senior officer, and that the tale of the cover-up had yet to be unveiled. Editor Rick Gibbons read the letter with disbelief, then contacted Armstrong directly. The cover-up story ran front page and was followed by all of the networks and wire services. Over the next three days, public pressure mounted.

True to form, Jean Boyle and Ruth Cardinal immediately attempted to discredit Armstrong with a poorly planned whirlwind campaign. Against the stern direction of Major Vince Buonamici, General Boyle released to the media an autopsy report, conducted six weeks after the shooting on a souplike corpse, that differed with Armstrong's initial findings. Although Armstrong had said Aruush was shot four times, the coroner believed it was only three, with one bullet making two separate holes. It wasn't much of a discrepancy and it didn't address the issue of "orders to destroy evidence," but public affairs officers held this up as "proof" that Armstrong was "wrong." The media saw right through this counter-attack, and it backfired terribly on Boyle and Cardinal. If anything, the discredit attempt added tremendous weight to Armstrong's allegations.

Quickly dissuaded by the editorial rebuffs, Cardinal and Boyle met to discuss a more indirect strategy of dealing with the military surgeon in the media's eyes. The tactic chosen was to insert an article in the political satire magazine *Frank*, entitled "Whistle Blower Sucks Wind." To make the Armstrong article appear arm's length from DND, John Thompson, the Mackenzie Institute's executive director, authored and forwarded the damaging gossip to his contact at *Frank*.

Again, it was a case of too little, too late and too obvious. Armstrong's evidence was too overwhelming to be shut down by unattributed hearsay. In the end, Defence Minister David Collenette was forced to announce a public inquiry into the whole affair. At this point, Robert Fowler realized that he was no longer playing the game to win; he was fighting for his own survival.

CHAPTER TEN

Out of the Ashes

In June 1993, Robert Ramsay Fowler conducted a senior management symposium at the Westin Hotel in Ottawa. In attendance were approximately two hundred of the top civilian and military officials in the Department of National Defence. Earlier that year, Fowler had authorized an independent managerial audit to be conducted at NDHQ by CROP Inc., a firm that specializes in such studies.

The scale used by CROP to measure effectiveness and good managerial principles is based on a perfect score of ten. However, unlike a school exam, where 50 per cent represents a passing grade, the expectation of executive competence is far more stringent. A major Japanese corporation held an immediate crisis-in-leadership meeting when their rating dropped from 9.7 to 9.2. Any score below a nine indicates a company in serious trouble, and less than an eight would reflect a company already in receivership.

The DND management team's score earned in the CROP report was a pitiful 7.2. As the senior department manager, Fowler realized this was as much a condemnation of his own inefficiencies as it was a reflection of the incompetence and corruption of his senior people. So instead of making the CROP report the focal point of the management symposium, Fowler had the damaging results verbally communicated in French only, with no accompanying paperwork to clarify the data presented. Thus the majority of these executives, nursing hangovers from the previous night's revelry, remained blissfully unaware of their own recorded incompetence.

In September 1995, when the equally damning Phillips Employee Feedback Survey internal poll results were returned to General Jean Boyle, he too tried to bury the report rather than respond to it. When 83 per cent of serving members said that they had no faith in senior DND managers to bring the department through this crisis period, Boyle told his top officers to "not keep any notes" on the subject: his fear was that even these hand-written notes would be acquired by the media under Access to Information, and his generals would only be somehow further embarrassed.

The simple fact is, the top-level brain trust at DND is bankrupt, and they themselves have known this for years but have chosen to simply ignore the problem rather than address it. Only the absolute, top-down authority which is inherent to the military system has allowed them to remain in control and to thwart outside intervention. This costly charade must stop, and the only way to achieve this is for the Canadian government to, in effect, place DND into receivership. A trustee must be named to take over the management of the department while it undergoes the massive structural changes that are necessary to put the Canadian military back on a sound footing and to put in place systemic controls which will ensure that the current problems would be unable to recur.

Major reforms to any institution must be implemented quickly, and they cannot be effectively introduced by those who created and ran the old system. What the Armed Forces need right now is a quick shot in the arm, and even just the symbolism of a new broom being appointed as an interim trustee would give them cause for hope. It would serve as an acknowledgment not only that they (the rank and file) matter, but that they are being listened to and supported.

It would not be necessary for the trustee to have any military experience. In fact, given the root cause of the present situation, a strong argument could be made for a qualified executive to be brought in directly from the private sector. However, the chosen individual should have no connection to either the recent Regular Force general officer corps or the current DND bureaucracy. To fill the niche, there is an abundant talent pool of dedicated patriots and successful businessmen to be found within the ranks of the honorary regimental colonels, and given their proven dual competencies, there are many who would make ideal candidates for just such a post.

The first objective of the new trustee would have to be the division of National Defence Headquarters back into two distinct entities: a strictly military Canadian Forces Headquarters and a departmental bureaucracy to support its needs. The National Defence Act makes it imperative that the minister and cabinet receive unadulterated military advice, directly from the chief of the defence staff. At present, the advice of the CDS is blended with that of the civilian deputy minister and the assistant deputy ministers.

The blurring of functions and loyalties between civilian and military officers at NDHQ has become entrenched in the attitudes and expectations of the current crop of senior officers, who have experienced no other system than this thirty-year-old peacetime experiment. As a result, accountable channels, normally very defined in a military system, have become vague and confused. This has eroded the confidence the troops have in their officers and led to an erosion of our military ethos. As quickly as possible, this middle ground or greying of purpose and principles must be reversed in order for the renewal process to begin.

As soon as these two organizations had been ripped apart, the appointed trustee would have to address each in turn to correct the fundamental and systemic deficiencies. By its very training and nature, a vigilant military must be responsive to rapid change and unexpected attrition. Battlefield drills since the days of Caesar's legions have been based on the command "close ranks and press on," with junior officers stepping up as automatons to replace their fallen commanders. Therefore, a sudden depletion of the top-ranking officers should be easily overcome, especially given the fact that this reduction would be imposed during the relative luxury of a peacetime environment.

A new chief of the defence staff would have to be appointed, and his rank should be reduced to that of a three-star general to better reflect the actual size of our armed forces. To select this individual, the trustee could either recommend going down several rungs to promote a major-general or brigadier with a reputation for honesty and integrity, or choose a complete outsider. This could be a Canadian reservist, or even a foreign general with exemplary credentials. While the idea of a foreigner commanding our armed forces may sound repugnant to Canadian patriots, it should be remembered that our troops often serve in hostile peacekeeping environments under the UN command of foreign generals. As well, it should be noted that John de Chastelain always maintained his British passport and dual citizenship, even while he was Canada's top general and ambassador to the United States.

Appointing a new three-star general as the top rank would immediately eliminate sixteen positions from the present paid strength of ninety-six generals. However, this in itself would not solve the problems of our over-ranked and over-officered forces. An increase in overall total force strength by some 4,000 regulars and 40,000 reservists could be achieved by reducing the total number of generals to forty positions and returning to a (still-bloated) pre-unification officer proportion of 16.7 per cent (down from the present level, the world's highest at 22.2 per cent).

To reach this level quickly without affecting operational effectiveness would not be that difficult. There are twenty-one generals stationed abroad as attachés with our allies, yet only one country, Britain, maintains even a brigadier position in Ottawa. France, with its standing army of 500,000 troops, keeps only a colonel in our national capital, yet Canada, with only 60,000 troops, keeps a brigadier-general (in a $2-million apartment) at the embassy in Paris. Why? The whole attaché function has lost its original purpose of maintaining interoperability with our allies, and instead it has become a cushy retirement gift for generals, complete with lavish expense accounts. This entire process would need to be revamped, first addressing the continued necessity of each posting, and second effecting a large reduction in the rank of the incumbents. In most cases, a young lieutenant-colonel with a promising future still ahead of him or her would make a far more suitable liaison than a retiring general.

Entire functions should be eliminated from the command structure, thereby eliminating other non-command general slots (complete with their attendant rank pyramid) from the Forces roster. Until recently, DND had two padre brigadier-generals, one Catholic and one Protestant. The head of the tiny dental branch is also a brigadier-general, as is the top officer in the mechanical engineering trade.

Tradesmen, medical professionals and the clergy all play an essential role in the Canadian Forces; however, their very necessity dictates the priority to which they would receive logistical/command support. Dentists and padres need only serve in operational units at the rank of captain, and, even then, this function could be performed by a reservist (temporary manpower-pool call-ups could then be invoked for UN deployments).

As for the mechanical engineers, again this trade need be represented only up to the operational level (i.e., a major at brigade level, and one lieutenant-colonel in Army headquarters to provide advice on procurement and maintenance of vehicles and equipment).

In May 1996, Major-General Lewis MacKenzie wrote an editorial in the *Globe and Mail* claiming the reason Canada had to have so many generals was to enable DND "to compete with other government departments in terms of priorities and budget allotment." Unfortunately for MacKenzie and those who share this ill-founded belief, it runs akin to the philosophy of simply printing more money to pay the national debt: all you accomplish is a devaluation of the currency.

The proliferation of generals and their civilian counterparts over the past three decades has accomplished just that, and the once-cherished and respected rank means little to those inside and outside the Forces. As for the political clout of DND, as the government department with the largest discretionary budget, some $2.7 billion annually, whoever heads the institution, regardless of the title, is sure to command the same level of political clout.

One of the major findings of the 1995 Phillips survey showed that the soldiers regarded senior officers as "self-interested careerists." To correct this trend, it would be imperative to initiate a system of evaluation whereby the enlisted men would have an opportunity to evaluate their officers' performance on an annual basis. The results of these reports would have to be confidential and passed at least one rung up the rank ladder to ensure confidentiality and encourage frank responses. Universities conduct such course evaluations of their professors on a regular basis and, in fact, even some military courses have issued such "instructor ratings" surveys.

To make the system work, it would have to constitute a significant portion of the officers' career criteria. In this simple way, you would structurally ensure that the flow of loyalty return to that of "top down–bottom up"—officers would continue to ignore their men to please their boss only at their own promotion peril.

A long-dead French colonel once wrote: "An army which no longer practises vigilance is sick, only until the enemy proves it to be dead." The Canadian Armed Forces are not dead, but their senior command has long since forgotten their primary function is to prepare for war. Everything in Canadian training doctrine and practice is based on the lowest-level tactical units. In the Army this would be a battalion, in the Navy and Air Force it's a squadron. This is the highest stage at which any Canadian officer is tested on his tactical abilities and command responses. While large brigade exercises are occasionally conducted (when money and troops permit), these are "scripted" scenarios prepared by the brigade commander's staff and monitored from his own headquarters. There is no score given, or pass/fail rating which would contribute to the general's suitability for promotion.

Brigadier-General Kip Kirby has long advocated a common-sense solution to this problem of "lost purpose"; that is, to have general officers spend 20 per cent of their time (one a day a week) engaged in commanding a tactical exercise commensurate with their rank and appointment. With the present state of technology, there would be no need for actual troops to be deployed, as the whole war game could be easily computerized and conducted from mock operations centres. In addition to the computer ratings, the generals involved would be scored and critiqued by their own staff officers. These scores and the general's tactical ability would then constitute a large percentage of the officer's annual evaluation report.

In this way the troops, their officers and the generals themselves would have increased confidence in their own soldiering skills and the retention of a focused ideal which puts the profession of arms first and foremost. To keep the general officer corps in touch with their officers, one of the first moves that the new chief of the defence staff should make would be the elimination of their separate "messing" facility. After-hours social encounters remain an important unofficial means by which a senior officer can test morale and judge the impact of his commands. As for sending a message to the enlisted men that this new "regime" was interested in their welfare, the first order of business would be to eliminate the commander's grants and to establish an all-ranks elected committee to monitor the Central Fund. Major funding projects would be voted on by secret ballot so that rank would be irrelevant, and the panel members would constitute a representational cross-section of enlisted men and commissioned officers.

Rent subsidies for commanders' residences would need to be repealed and a standard formula introduced to ensure equity in the costs for government lodgings. The new rates for generals need not be punitive; even if the costs were merely in line for the accommodations, the troops would see the change as a commitment to integrity.

Obviously, when the rank and file see their generals retiring from the Forces and showing up as high-rolling lobbyists, double-dipping consultants for DND, or top executives with defence firms, the perception of "self-interest" is bound to undermine the integrity of the entire high command. Since senior officers already take a new oath of allegiance (to the CDS) when they are promoted to general rank, it would be in the interest of the military institution if they also took a vow not to seek post-employment in the private defence sector.

Priests take a vow of poverty and celibacy to demonstrate their willingness to serve a higher calling; a general's $70,000 pension at age fifty-five could hardly be considered a similar sacrifice. Nevertheless, the image of retired generals would improve immeasurably in the eyes of the troops and the Canadian public. The defence lobbying game would not be immediately sanitized, but it would be on the road to recovery. As for double-dipping, since the military pay and benefits are already equated to public services, the simple solution is to extend this equity to any continued employment within the civil service. For example, if an officer retires at age fifty-five, he could still collect his military pension; however, if he becomes re-employed (by the government of Canada) this would then be seen as a transfer. Simply put, you can't retire from the employer you're still working for.

Removing the opportunity to cash in on a lucrative post-career government executive job would make generals more likely to remain focused on their profession and the welfare of the troops.

The scope and scale of current media revelations regarding the Defence Department's top officers' inability to deal with issues in a fair and just manner indicates a serious systemic deficiency. There is no independent ombudsman to handle grievances or complaints. If the senior command is somehow involved, there is no check or balance to keep them accountable for their actions. Both the Canadian public and service members themselves have looked upon the military system with growing cynicism. Therefore, steps must be taken immediately to restore the confidence of Canadians in the military organization. Our soldiers, sailors and aviators must once again trust that the "system" will address their grievances squarely and fairly. Canada should follow the example of many of our allies' armed forces and appoint an inspector general (a civilian) whose overriding qualifications for the position would be absolute integrity and good judgement. Soldiers of all ranks could approach this inspector general directly, and with complete confidentiality assured. Through this channel, officers' abuses of authority, travel claim fraud, etc., could be safely reported by the troops with a guarantee that corrective action would be taken.

The Canadian military police still have an excellent reputation with respect to their main activities during hostilities: traffic control and the processing of prisoners of war. However, their systemic limitations with regard to the investigation of top-level abuses have been clearly demonstrated in the fall-out from the Somalia scandal.

In his external audit of the military police services in 1994, Judge René Marin concluded that "it is perhaps time to examine the total military police role . . . there is an increasing reluctance on the part of civil police authorities, because of budget constraints, to undertake investigations on military property, private married quarters, or other properties under the control of DND. As a consequence the military police are becoming, *de facto*, a civil police force." Marin also noted that civil police agencies are held accountable to the public they serve, not only by the courts, but also by external overseeing committees and commissions. By contrast, the military police respond primarily to their own internal command structure. Such an arrangement cannot help but bring into question the objectivity of the military police when they are investigating those who fall within their jurisdiction.

The simple solution to this problem is to eliminate the entire conflict by having those who police the military report through a separate chain of command. One young military policeman suggested that he and his colleagues should become a specialized branch of the RCMP, answering directly to the solicitor general. The administration, logistics and training of the military police would remain within the purview of DND, but they would be tasked and monitored by the Mounties. This concept could easily be made workable at all levels of military police enforcement by utilizing the existing manpower, equipment and facilities. Simply by having their uniforms and their reporting chain changed, the military police would become an extremely effective force. They would be completely familiar with their constituency's structure, but they would no longer be restricted by its internal authority.

In René Marin's original report on the Special Investigations Unit, he

244 ⌐ Tarnished Brass

strongly recommended removing their criminal-investigation mandate, and he suggested this covert force be relegated to conducting security clearances. DND responded to Marin's report by creating the National Investigative Service and further empowering the SIU. In the conclusions of his 1994 audit on the situation, Marin stated he was "not entirely comfortable with the concept behind DND having established the NIS," and he reiterated his intent that the SIU be limited to security duties only.

The National Investigative Service should be immediately disbanded, with its role of "high-profile" military investigations turned over to the new military branch of the RCMP. As for the SIU, this secret police force must be stripped of its sweeping powers and high-tech surveillance equipment. Even the security clearance responsibility could be controlled by the "military Mounties" and, therefore, such covert resources would not be available to either senior bureaucrats or top military officers.

Having an honest police force would restore the Canadian Forces' faith in the law enforcement process, and the removal of the NIS/SIU fear factor would be a tremendous boost to their collective morale.

At the tactical level, the wartime role of handling POWs and traffic control could be assumed by reservists. Minor service crimes (such as being absent without leave) would continue to be policed by the units themselves.

The military justice system is in serious trouble and, once again, the Somalia affair has highlighted its serious deficiencies. It is lacking in objectivity and credibility and, worse still, it is infected by habits and values which are characteristic of the worst traits presently ailing the Canadian officer corps.

One of the major lessons to be learned from the Somalia scandal is that the exercise of power, without the moderating influence of any ethical structure, public accountability and continuous media scrutiny, cannot help but lead to a corruption of the basic principles of justice. Under the present regime at DND, this philosophy of absolute power has become a deeply entrenched religion, and it must be dismantled quickly.

The easiest way to begin the necessary recovery would be to civilianize the position of the judge advocate general. At present, the JAG is a military officer charged with the administration of the Canadian Forces justice system. This task is in direct conflict with his day-to-day occupation of providing legal counsel to the minister, the deputy minister and the chief of the defence staff. To eliminate this conflict, the justice minister, not the chief of the defence staff, should select the individual to act as the military's judge advocate general.

Unlike the current JAG, the new incumbent should have previous judiciary (bench) experience, and he must retain full judicial independence from the military chain of command. Previous experience with the Canadian Forces would not necessarily be a prerequisite, or even an asset, in the judge selected to fill this appointment. This civilian JAG's day-to-day reporting would remain through the chief of the defence staff and the minister of national defence, but he himself would not attend daily executive meetings or be the personal counsel to the top defence officials. Ultimately, however, the JAG would answer to the justice minister.

In this way, the minister of national defence would have judicial responsibilities stripped from his office, thereby eliminating the glaring conflict of interest that has become all too apparent throughout the Somalia crisis and subsequent events at the public inquiry.

Recent decisions by the court-martial appeal court (overturning the original verdicts), evidence presented at the Somalia inquiry (regarding judicial interference) and documents released under Access to Information (detailing DND's inappropriate application of their legal resources), all serve to illustrate a system in crisis: the present senior management at DND have been singularly unable and unwilling to apply justice fairly across the Canadian Forces rank structure.

Under the two-tier system now in place, a court martial is used to deal with serious offences, and a summary trial is invoked to handle minor infractions.

The anachronistic system of summary trials is particularly susceptible to the influence of command bias. As the system now exists, Canadian Forces personnel are denied both the fundamental right to counsel and a meaningful participation in the proceedings, despite the fact that the accused is often facing a significant punishment, including up to a ninety-day incarceration in the military prison.

The time has come to examine and redefine the scale of peacetime summary trials. Commanding officers in combat units normally have only a rudimentary knowledge of the National Defence Act and little experience with criminal procedures, yet they are currently empowered with broad jurisdiction and significant powers of punishment.

The successful experiences of some of our NATO allies should provide the necessary role model to help the Canadian military redefine its justice system. Certainly, for instance, it should rely on civilian courts to punish soldiers for all but the most minor service offences (for example, disobedience and tardiness). German commanding officers can impose only a maximum sentence of twenty-one days' incarceration on their soldiers, yet the modern Bundeswehr remains highly regarded as a professional fighting force.

Given the state of the Canadian economy, coupled with the national deficit and crippling debt, it is safe to assume that defence policy in this country will remain driven by fiscal restraint. More cuts to the budget can be expected in future years, but with a properly managed military, the overall capability need not be diminished. Setting aside the question of the recent procurement projects and their attendant waste of massive cash resources, the personnel world of our National Defence Department is equally in need of restructuring.

Conventional thinking had been to steadily "shave the ice cube" every time another reduction in defence spending was announced by offering large cash buy-outs to an ever-dwindling number of increasingly aged soldiers. Recruiting has all but dried up as a result of trying to reduce manpower through retirement attrition. The training system has, therefore, become relatively rusty, and the pressing demand for peacekeeping troops has all but stripped it of personnel and resources. This is not a healthy situation in any army, and with the current crisis in leadership within the Canadian Forces, this problem has been steadily exacerbated.

Reducing the number of officers to the 16.7 per cent (pre-unification) level would create an additional 4,000 combat arms positions, and still save nearly $300 million in the salary differential. If these additional troops were to be recruited on a two-year short-term contract, which would include a six-month tour of peacekeeping duty, Canada could easily maintain a steady commitment of 3,000 troops to the United Nations. The veteran troops presently serving in the Army would provide not only the instructors necessary to train these recruits, but also the experienced non-commissioned officers to ensure a high professional standard within the battalions.

At the end of their two-year service, only the top 10 per cent of these soldiers would be offered a continuation contract to the Regular Force. This elite group would immediately go on to take a junior leadership course. By the time the next wave of new recruits had passed their basic training, these soldiers would be promoted to master corporal and would be section commanders preparing for their second tour of UN duty.

As for the 90 per cent of the soldiers who were not retained in the Regular Force, these experienced troops could still be contracted to serve in the militia for an additional three years, and they would be given an immediate promotion to the rank of corporal. (Two years' active experience with the Regular Force, including an operational tour, would be equal to at least nine years in the Reserves.)

The $300 million saved in salaries resulting from a reduction of the officer corps would be transferred to the militia budget, with the projected purpose of achieving a seven-year increase in personnel up to the 40,000 mark. Since the bulk of this manpower would be provided in the form of the trained veteran "two-year" regulars, the entire militia would be quickly revitalized into an effective force. The present skeletal infrastructure of undermanned and over-officered militia regiments would be a perfect framework (already in place) upon which to apply these additional resources.

With fresh blood being pumped into the Army at regular intervals, and a fully staffed training system in operation, the present complacency which many of our troops exhibit would quickly vanish. There is an old saying: "The best way to learn something is to teach it." With the rapid expansion, steady rotation and operational demands this policy would entail, Canadian soldiers would be steadily challenged at all rank levels.

A side benefit to such a rapid force build-up would be the immediate increase in public support it would generate. The more sons and daughters who don a Canadian uniform and serve their country, especially on dangerous UN missions, the more understood and publicly embraced the military will become.

At the moment, the Canadian Forces have a dismal record of public relations, and as a government department they have the worst record for public disclosure. The credibility of DND spokespersons was first stretched by their attempts to justify the excessive expenditures of senior officers, and eventually it was shattered at the Somalia inquiry. It was made known during this independent probe that DND public affairs officers conspired to alter and destroy damaging documents before releasing them to the media.

The problems of these designated spokespersons parallel those the chain of command imposes upon the military policy force. Junior officers are ordered, sometimes at the threat of being fired, to read false statements to a disbelieving media. Lieutenant-Commander Jeff Agnew was the public affairs officer designated to deal with the media the day General Jean Boyle ordered everyone in the Forces to cease work (for one whole day) to locate missing Somalia files. The media had ridiculed this wasteful exercise as being a PR sham and had mockingly dubbed the event "The Great Easter Egg Hunt." General Boyle, against the advice of Jeff Agnew ("This is bull-shit!"), had made a video statement telling his troops where to look for the missing files. Boyle had added a Nixonian "I'm not a crook" plea at the end of his message, and the video footage had received widespread coverage on the national news. With all of the media hype surrounding the morning of the hunt, Boyle demanded to see Commander Barry Frewer, Jeff Agnew's boss. In that meeting, an infuriated Boyle told Frewer "to get [him] out of this mess, or he'd fire every public affairs officer and hire someone that could protect him."

The answer to this problem is to eliminate the entire public affairs branch, thereby removing the temptation to have others (more junior in rank) face the media fire. Commanders have come to rely too heavily on the one hundred plus officers in this branch to front the Canadian Forces to the public. This is one of the responsibilities which accompanies command, and the sooner officers are faced with having to represent themselves, the quicker the department's credibility will be restored.

Soldiers, by their training and nature, are direct in their communications, and even junior NCOs are taught how to conduct briefings. Journalists love the rough and gruff demeanour of combat soldiers, and any possible miscues would be more than offset by the increased trust and confidence that would result. No reporter wants to talk to a professional spin doctor if he or she can speak directly with the source. The $8.5-million annual budget currently set aside for the public affairs branch could be diverted into training seminars, which would be offered to all officers and senior NCOs.

All operational units would still have a designated captain to deal with the media, but their primary function would remain that of a combat soldier. Internal communications within the military should not be relegated to newsletters or brochures, such as the ones currently produced within the public affairs directorate. This flow of information is the responsibility of the chain of command, and removing these ineffective communication crutches would put the emphasis back on solid leadership.

As for departmental public affairs, this function would be established in the separate bureaucratic headquarters. It could easily be performed by a tiny cadre (of no more than five personnel) who would prepare media backgrounders and seminars on such issues as procurement and policy.

In order for the Department of National Defence to support the Canadian Forces effectively, it is imperative that Canada determine a long-term defence policy and make that blueprint impervious to short-term political pressures. Obviously, certain military capabilities that are now being maintained only in a shell capacity, but at great expense, would have to be either resurrected or discontinued. Three thirty-year-old diesel-electric submarines (of which only one can be at sea at any given time) is hardly an effective means of patrolling the sub-surface ocean on three coasts. If we can't afford to replace them with at least a six-boat, two-ocean modern fleet, then it's time for Canada to get out of the submarine business.

The cost to operate and maintain just sixty fighter aircraft is budgeted at $700 million (more than we spent on all peacekeeping operations), yet this entire air-superiority capability would find itself outnumbered by the aircraft complement of a single modern aircraft carrier.

In 1994, Defence Minister David Collenette had a defence policy review conducted, and this was, in theory, based on input from a wide variety of national sources. In reality, the results of this study were preordained and drafted by none other than Bob Fowler and Ken Calder. Virtually everything that was already in the works (for example, the option to "lease" the four British Upholder submarines) was written into the review as a recommendation (taken from Fowler and Calder's submission to the committee). Not surprisingly, the '94 White Paper which Calder and Fowler drafted based on the "review" "accepted the recommendation that the lease of British submarines be pursued." It was a sham.

Rather than repeat the lengthy exercise of having public input into a defence policy, the interim trustee at DND and the Canadian Forces would be better served if a small team of educated, interested, but not already involved professionals was assembled to create a whole new doctrine. It would be advantageous at this point to have input from our NATO allies as to what role they expect our armed forces to support or specialize in. Regardless of the policy determined, the definition of the projected Forces structure would have to have clearly stated milestone objectives so that the bureaucrats responsible could easily be held accountable for any shortcomings which become evident.

Under the present system, there is no correlation between an executive's performance and his evaluations. The 1996 Auditor General's Report cited that Canadian troops in the former Yugoslavia had only 70 per cent of the equipment and weaponry of a similar-sized British formation. Of the supplies the Canadians did have, nearly 25 per cent were found to be defective. Considering that our troops on UN tours get "first pick of the litter" in terms of available stores, the Auditor General's Report should have led to the immediate removal of the chief of supply. Instead, less than two weeks after the damning assessment was tabled, the supply executive, Pierre Lagueux, was promoted to senior assistant deputy minister for materiel. The man who couldn't ensure that our peacekeepers were properly outfitted is now the top buyer for all of DND.

A new deputy minister would have to be appointed by the interim trustee, and it would be this person's responsibility to breathe new life and efficiency into the corrupt and incompetent ranks of the senior bureaucrats. As with the general officer ranks, a paring down of top executive positions would be the first priority of the new DM. Any close association to the previous "regime" would have to be seen as a disadvantage when the selection of new assistant deputy ministers took place. A restructuring back down to just three assistant deputy ministers (policy, personnel, procurement) would immediately eliminate much of the overwhelming redundancy under the present system (with seven assistant deputy minister empires).

An all-encompassing managerial audit at DND should be quickly conducted by an independent private firm. The results of this assessment would then be used to make drastic reductions in complete functions and redundant personnel. When former U.S. Joint Chief of Staff General Colin Powell was asked how he would go about trimming the waste at the Pentagon, he said that he "would start by closing down the entire top floor of the complex [comparable to NDHQ's executive thirteenth floor] for an entire week." Those offices whose reporting departments screamed loudly in protest would be recognized as essential, those offices that garnished a whimper from their underlings would be trimmed. Any function whose absence failed to be noted would be eliminated. The process would then be repeated at each successive lower level, until it was determined by practice just what amount of supervision was required for each specific directorate.

While this might seem a somewhat drastic approach, it is the basic philosophy that must be ruthlessly employed by an outsider (the trustee) in order to quickly restore a sense of purpose and mission to the Defence Department.

The defence procurement world would ultimately pose the largest challenge to the trustee. As its sheer dollar value creates political appeal and the temptation for abuse, the solution to this problem would, in part, be solved by the adherence to a defined defence policy. This would allow for the closure of numerous project offices, which have provided an abundance of career opportunities, often despite the fact that the military items being studied rarely end up being purchased. (Canada has maintained a fully staffed submarine replacement office for the past fifteen years.)

However, to cut through the deeply entrenched layers of unethical, immoral and illegal practices which currently constitute the world of defence procurement, it would be important to recognize that this corruption exists and, admittedly, will continue to exist, given the huge sums of money involved. To correct this, or to at least address the situation, an independent commission against corruption should be established for the sole purpose of providing a watchdog for DND buyers.

Complete with a well-respected and trusted commissioner and a team of trained investigators, this standing commission would have the sweeping power of audit, seizure and surveillance. (Perhaps they could even hire the disbanded NIS/SIU operatives.)

Any abuses detected by the commission would be prosecuted under the Criminal Code of Canada in civilian courts. The commissioner, like the inspector general, would answer through the chief of the defence staff or the minister of national defence, but ultimately he would report to and be appointed by the solicitor general.

This independent commission would publicize its progress and findings in an annual report and through interim press releases. In order to justify their continued existence and employment, this team would need to be both diligent and successful in exposing corruption.

Within a period of two years, once these checks and balances were in place and the Forces restructuring was complete (if not finely tuned), the trustee would be in a position to let a revitalized military proceed under its own direction. Only then will the darkest chapter in Canadian military history finally be closed.

Postscript

In some ways it was almost a blessing that Captain Jim DeCoste was killed on operational duty before the military institution he loved so dearly came to be exposed for the corrupted entity it has become. Admittedly, it would have been difficult for him to come to grips with the fact that the martial virtues of integrity, courage and duty, which he had not only learned but embodied, no longer exist within the senior ranks. These honourable values had been replaced with greed, careerism and cowardice.

It would have broken his heart to know that the only solution to these problems would be to bring in "outsiders" to control the abuses of the Army high command. DeCoste had no time for civvies and he detested both politicians and bureaucrats. However, as a loyal soldier, he had the ultimate respect for the chain of command and would have initially resented his generals being pilloried in the national media. I have no doubt that, for a time, he would have resented my participation in those revelations, and our friendship would have been severely strained.

However, Jim DeCoste expected near perfection in his leaders, scorned those who were soft and chastised those who were incompetent. Once all the facts were in, I know he would have understood "the mission was paramount."

Scott Taylor
Summer 1996

Index